REFERENCE

D1136366

Also by Peter McCarey

Verse:

The Syllabary (www.thesyllabary.com and www.knot.ch)

Collected Contraptions (Manchester, Carcanet, 2011)

Prose:

Slasher Two-Step (Geneva, Punastic Press, 2012)

Hugh MacDiarmid and the Russians (Edinburgh, Scottish
Academic Press, 1987)

Voices:

Cleikit (www.cleikit.com and www.scran.ch)

Find an Angel and Pick a Fight

Peter McCarey

Molecular Press

Published by
Molecular Press
Geneva
Printed and bound by Lightning Source
ISBN 978-2-9700376-0-6

Chapters of this book have previously appeared in *Edinburgh Review, PN Review, Slavonic and East European Review, Parnassus, British Library Centre for the Book, International Journal of Scottish Literature, New Writing Scotland, Southfields, Gairfish, ZeD20, About Edwin Morgan, A Gathering for Gael Turnbull, The Wider Europe: Essays on Slavonic Languages and Cultures, Without Day, Libraries of Thought and Imagination* and *Contraflow on the Super Highway*. The author thanks the editors.

Special thanks to Mariarosaria Cardines and to Desmond Avery.

Picture credits:
Stromness, Orkney, photograph © Charles Tait
Lower Manhattan from Staten Island Ferry, photograph © Jeff Prant
Maria João Pires photograph (detail) © Patrick de Mervelec from the sleeve of *Schubert: Fantasie D.940 Marches Militaires D.733 Rondos D.608 & 951*, played by Maria Joao Pires and Hüseyin Sermet
Ritratto di fanciulla (Saffo?) © Museo Archeologico Nazionale, Naples
Konrad Witz: St George, St Martin, both © Kunstmuseum Basel
Kazimir Malevich: An Englishman in Moscow © Centre Pompidou, Paris
Black Square © Tretyakov Gallery, Moscow
Black Cross © Russian Museum, St Petersburg
Arafat and entourage, photograph © El País, 30 September 2002
Hieronymus Bosch, Carrying the Cross © Museum of Fine Arts, Ghent
Cover design by mc^2

c (7, 11. 13)

Contents

Introduction

This is a book on reckless writing and careful reading, on invention and recognition. It's about how people find meaning and how we pass it on or lose it. The political expectations that drive it are inherited from religion; it tracks the chiliastic, digital divide between quality and quantity in the decades between the fall of the Berlin Wall and the receivership of democracy, venturing well beyond the author's stamping ground in poetry and translation, into philosophy, into linguistic and arithmetical pattern recognition, and into the merits and pitfalls of machine code as an aid to conversation. Mathematics and physics are admired from a distance, over the wall of algebra.

In 'Poetry as Political Philosophy'[1] Alasdair MacIntyre sets up a light, sturdy framework in which to show how Yeats drew on – and distorted – Burke, how the latter had used images in arguments, and how Yeats's heroic politics could not deal with modern bureaucratic statehood. In doing this, MacIntyre treats poetry *not* as decoration but as structured argument. This book tries to pull the blanket back, reading philosophy less as argument than as a wayward branch of poetry whose formal strictures include (or did) the law of non-contradiction and a horror of ambiguity.

---

[1] 'Poetry and Political Philosophy: Notes on Burke and Yeats', in Alasdair MacIntyre, *Ethics and Politics, Selected Essays, Volume 2* (Cambridge UP, 2006), pp.159-171.

Although the reader will find a bias towards philosophical poetry and lyrical or narrative philosophy, space is given to far from poetic thinkers such as John Broome and to antirational poets such as J.H. Prynne. Plus an anti-cogitational philosopher and the odd prosaic bard. Names such as Eliot, Brodsky and OULIPO recur for extrinsic more than intrinsic properties, while some of the usual suspects, close confederates or exemplars, have not been rounded up because they now are part of my understanding, the tacit component of identity as conveyed by language.

There are four parts. One reviews attempts at bringing order out of chaos through narrative, logic, pathetic fallacy, economics, symmetry and rhyme. Part II considers the international reach of a small country, for good and ill. In the third part, the work of several poets is sized up, not for its canonical value, but as a possible way forward. Part IV, like the first, pulls away from literature, not into abstract thought but into practicalities and silences of language and what is human about it. In brief: machines can write parodies; they will not write satires. The conclusion attempts, in a non-mathematical way, to find the border between language and number, identity and expression; it then considers some of the shapes in which these two halves of thought have combined in poetry, and what might happen next.

Part I

Fear of Chaos

This is about the function of ideas in Hugh MacDiarmid's poetry – ideas that came from Russia – and how they have been assimilated in Scotland. Considering the place of existentialism in MacDiarmid's poetry, a reviewer from the *Times Literary Supplement* (perhaps confusing him with Seamus Heaney) once remarked: 'I very much doubt that MacDiarmid understood any of these hard matters. Or, in his truest poems, needed to. He was not, in any sense that counts, a philosophic poet. His narrative gift was lyrical and descriptive.'[1]

Some years earlier in the same publication, the Scottish poet Douglas Dunn complained that Scottish poetry in general and MacDiarmid's in particular, almost always had some ideological axe to grind, and fought shy of the simple lyricism we find in English poetry. 'The lyric of leaf and bloom', says Dunn, 'is an extreme distance away from MacDiarmid's geological poetry, and the purposes to which he put it. MacDiarmid struggled with exercises of will in an attempt to answer the question, how to be "ourselves without interruption, /Adamantine and inexorable?"'

The Scottish philosopher George Davie sees the same difference between Scottish and English tendencies in verse, but he prefers the Scottish approach: of *A Drunk Man Looks at the Thistle*, he says that (like Anderson), MacDiarmid contrasts Scottish scepticism or pessimism, and Anglican Pelagianism with its optimism about things. He criticizes utilitarianism and the happiness-seeking philosophy from the Calvinist point of view.[2]

---

[1] *Times Literary Supplement*, 28 October 1988.
[2] George Davie, *The Crisis of the Democratic Intellect* (Edinburgh, 1986), pp. 121-23.

He won't take tradition for granted, but tries to return to first principles.

For better or worse, MacDiarmid's poetry can't get clear of ideas. The Anderson mentioned by George Davie was another Scottish philosopher, a contemporary of MacDiarmid's. Yet there is no evidence that MacDiarmid was aware of his work. Strange: in his *Contemporary Scottish Studies* (London, 1926) MacDiarmid makes a fairly systematic review of Scottish poetry, fiction, painting, sculpture, theatre and music – but not of philosophy. Why not? The short answer is that David Hume, known as the greatest Scottish philosopher, had 'consistently discarded everything distinctively Scottish in matters of intellectual attitude and belief'. Furthermore, as Alasdair MacIntyre puts it, for Hume:

> The rights of property are absolute. There is and can be no standard external to them in the light of which some particular distribution of property could be evaluated as just or unjust (III,ii,6). Justice on this view serves the ends of property and not vice versa... What Hume presents as human nature as such, turns out to be 18th-century English human nature, and indeed only one variant of that, even if the dominant one.[1]

MacDiarmid never had much in the way of property himself, and he had no respect whatever for property of the intellectual sort. MacDiarmid could conceivably have turned to Hume's rivals in Scotland, Thomas Reid and the Common Sense school, and indeed George Davie argues that, whether he was aware of it or not, in *A Drunk Man Looks at the Thistle* he did employ procedures favoured by Thomas Reid, particularly common sense as interpersonal knowledge, that knowledge of others and of the self – that can be gained only through human intercourse, evoked in the poem in the drunk man's relationship with his wife. That is true, but not the whole truth. It must also be said that the very mention of common sense sent MacDiarmid running in the opposite direction – to Dostoevsky in fact. Since I have discussed his debt

---

[1] Alasdair MacIntyre, *Whose Justice? Which Rationality?* (London, 1988), p. 295.

6

to Dostoevsky elsewhere,[1] I will just make one point, about Dostoevsky's influence on the form of *A Drunk Man*, which is both an attempted national epic and a Menippean satire on such pretensions. Like Virgil in Dante's Divine Comedy, Dostoevsky is both a formal influence and a character in the poem, helping the drunk man look for the sense of life in the depths of the psyche. The formal influence shows in the very structure of the poem, which has much in common with Menippean satire, as described by Mikhail Bakhtin in his book on Dostoevsky:

> Fantastic episodes and adventures whose sole purpose is the testing of philosophical ideas (often incorporated in the image of a wise man). It combines fantasy, symbolism and mystical or religious elements with coarse and primitive naturalism; often set in bars, brothels, highways etc. Academic philosophy is dropped and only the ultimate questions of ethics and practicality remain. Menippean satire shows the earliest examples of moral and psychological experimentation: the depiction of abnormal moral and psychic states, in dreams and madness, disrupting the epic and tragic integrity of man and his fate.[2]

This definition reveals a generic link between this poem and the Menippean elements in Dostoevsky: the 'Dream of a Ridiculous Man', 'Bobok', Raskolnikov's dreams, and the 'Pro and Contra' section of *The Brothers Karamazov*.

MacDiarmid had hoped that Dostoevsky's ruthless scrutiny of motivation afforded an insight into the purpose of the individual and the destiny of the nation; but as it turns out, the Dostoevsky-Virgil analogy holds good here, too: Dostoevsky was the best guide through splintered psychology, but he could not carry through to a vision of universal purpose; his own hopes for Russia derived from the conservative utopia of the Slavophiles, which became increasingly reactionary in the last quarter of the 19th century. MacDiarmid would not follow that line.

---

[1] Peter McCarey, *Hugh MacDiarmid and the Russians* (Edinburgh, 1987).
[2] See Mikhail Bakhtin, *Problemy poetiki Dostoevskogo*, 4th edition (Moscow, 1979), pp. 129-36.

He couldn't follow David Hume, and since he had no time for vulgar common sense he was not attracted to the philosophy of Thomas Reid; yet one thing that emerges from his recourse to Dostoevsky is that he decidedly follows the Scottish habit of going for first principles. There had been no such impressive attempt on the root of things since Hume's *Treatise on Human Nature*. Also, in its Menippean way of stripping away technicalities, the long poem opened essential questions to the non-specialist, and this is a feature of Thomas Reid's approach that has regained him an audience today.

Up to this point it is possible to discuss MacDiarmid's poems as if they were verse philosophy; it makes sense to talk of tradition, positions abandoned and ideas reconciled. *A Drunk Man Looks at the Thistle* and *To Circumjack Cencrastus* are long poems, and they are also philosophical investigations. The poetry of the 1930s, however, comes in smaller sections – whether or not they were originally intended to form part of an enormous whole – and attempts to read coherent philosophical positions from them run into insurmountable contradictions. Part of the problem is that throughout the 1930s MacDiarmid committed himself to mutually exclusive world views, the main ones being the metaphysics of Lev Shestov and the politics of Lenin. By the time he wrote *In Job's Balances*, which was the book MacDiarmid used most heavily, Shestov had come to see politics as a waste of time, while Lenin regarded metaphysicians as a waste of space. One vehemently denied the perfectibility of mankind and the other ruthlessly pursued it. There was no reconciling them, but MacDiarmid was not prepared to let either of them go. Nor can it be said that there was some misunderstanding on MacDiarmid's part, or that he was namedropping again.

One of the reasons the TLS takes such a dim view of MacDiarmid is that he was a terrible thief: his longest poem, *In Memoriam James Joyce*, consists almost entirely of quotation from other work, and much of that work was stolen by MacDiarmid from the pages of the TLS. This explains the fairly common tendency to dismiss awkward ideas in his poems as things he didn't really know much about anyway. Yet there is, it seems to me, a reasonably sure way of telling whether MacDiarmid really values a writer as much as he claims to: if the poetry he writes contains not only references and quotations but also structural influence, then MacDiarmid is serious. Using this acid test we see that Dostoevsky had a profound influence on MacDiarmid, and that Solovyov was a good sparring partner. The Scottish poet was serious about Lenin, and completely imbrued in Shestov's metaphysics.

Staying in Leningrad in 1980 I tried to find a translator for MacDiarmid's poems, but no one would read him because he wrote hymns to Lenin and no one would publish him because of what the Hymns to Lenin said. To be quite accurate, a handful of translations have been published in the Soviet Union, the first in the 1930s, when D.S. Mirsky published the 'Third Hymn to Lenin' in *Novaia Angliiskaia Poezija* – which was where Brodsky came across Auden – although offending lines were sanitized in translation: MacDiarmid wrote 'thought is reality and thought alone' (arrant idealism, as one Scottish Marxist complains), and that becomes 'thought is all-powerful'. Now that there exists a fine critical edition of *A Drunk Man* it should be possible to have a translation made.[1]

In the 'Second Hymn to Lenin' MacDiarmid repeats his commitment to Marxism, but points out that politics is merely 'a pool in the sands' in the tide of poetry. Since poetry is 'Unremittin', relentless / Organized to the last degree'[2] it is a much more serious business than politics. But first things first: give people the basics, then on to metaphysics. Thus MacDiarmid (helping himself to John Buchan's *The Gap in the Curtain* (1932)) fulminates against

> ... those who mistake blind eyes for balanced minds,
> Who practise, in Disraeli's words,
> 'The blunders of their predecessors'.

---

[1] Hugh MacDiarmid, *A Drunk Man Looks at the Thistle*, edited by Kenneth Buthlay (Edinburgh, 1987).
[2] *The Collected Poems of Hugh MacDiarmid* (henceforth referred to as *CP*) 2 vols (London, 1978), p. 328. A new edition of the collected poems, edited by Michael Grieve, was published by Carcanet in 1993 and 1994.

People to whom experience means nothing,
Whose souls exist in a state of sacred torpidity,
Prostrated before cold altars and departed gods,
Whose appeal to commonsense is only an appeal
To the spiritual sluggishness which is man's besetting sin,
And in the present unexampled crisis our deadliest peril.[1]

In *Whose Justice? Which Rationality?* Alasdair MacIntyre attempts to bring some coherence to the ethical debate, concerned as he is by:

> ...the type of self which has too many half-convictions and too few settled coherent convictions, too many partly formulated alternatives and too few opportunities to evaluate them systematically, so that it brings to its encounters with the claims of rival traditions a fundamental incoherence which is too disturbing to be admitted to self-conscious awareness except on the rarest of occasions.[2]

This is clearly a perception of the same fear from another side. MacDiarmid's view of the sufferers is much less sympathetic:

> Anywhere you go in Britain today
> You can hear the people
> Economizing consciousness,
> Struggling to think and feel as little as possible,
> Just as you can hear a countryside in winter
> Crepitating in the grip of an increasing frost.[3]

Both MacIntyre and MacDiarmid attempt ambitious solutions to the problem: MacIntyre by proposing a framework in which people can begin to recognize and resolve their problems, and MacDiarmid by the incendiary method: destroying the makeshift ideologies people shelter in – beginning with his own.

MacDiarmid repeatedly referred to Lev Shestov as his master. According to the acid test, he was not joking. MacDiarmid first

---

[1] *CP* 824.
[2] p. 397.
[3] *The Battle Continues, CP* 938.

refers to him in 1922; he was still quoting him in 1962, in his pamphlet on David Hume.

There is a wonderful moment in the Treatise when Hume quietly dismantles causality. Kant wrote that Hume had awakened him from dogmatic slumber, prompting him to write, 'That my will moves my arm is to me no more comprehensible than if someone should say that it could hold back the moon itself'. But then, Shestov complains, 'Kant exiled the wonders, in order not to be forced to see them, into the field of the "thing in itself", and bequeathed to mankind the "synthetic a priori judgments", transcendental philosophy, and his three miserable "postulates"'.[1]

This is the moment MacDiarmid refers to in his poem 'Thalamus':

> The truths that all great thinkers have seen
> At the height of their genius – and then
> Spent most of their days denying
> Or trying to scale down to mere reason's ken ...
>
> O misguided science pursuing
> All tasks but the greatest of all
> While away beyond this life's scant scope
> In a glorious unseen waterfall
> Pours all but all of life's best
> We turn our poor mills with the rest.
>
> These mills of Satan; these hellish hives
> In which men sink to the status of slaves,
> Treadmills of rationalizing . . .[2]

Far from censuring Hume's scepticism, as the Common Sense philosophers did, Shestov and MacDiarmid criticized Hume for not carrying it through. Why?

For Shestov, the fruit of the tree of knowledge was fear of liberty: man had to have to do things, we need necessity, causality, law, ethics, universal truth, because otherwise we wouldn't know what

---

[1] Lev Shestov, *In Job's Balances*, translated by Camilla Coventry and C.A. Macartney (London, 1932), pp. xxvi-xxvii.
[2] *CP* 413.

to do, and we need to know, and what we all know has to be the same for everybody, otherwise it wouldn't be right, would it? This is the way we build ideological prisons for ourselves, accommodating even God; this is common consciousness, omnitude, as Dostoevsky's *vsemstvo* is translated.

With his critique of causality Hume had blown a hole in it, which Kant quickly repaired. MacIntyre notes, 'Even the law of noncontradiction as formulated by Aristotle has encountered thinkers both sufficiently ingenious and sufficiently wrongheaded to deny it.'[1] If you want to build an ethical structure, you need to believe that actions cause consequences, and that a thing cannot be both A and not A at the same time. Unfortunately, these tenets do seem to be a matter of convention, and there will always be awkward philosophers like Shestov to point that out. Of course there is another group of practitioners who regularly refuse to call a thistle a thistle, and who feel free to call it a Russian novelist, or a nervous system, or a volcano or a map. Because the law of metaphor is as fundamental to poets as the law of non-contradiction is to philosophers. MacIntyre the moral philosopher and MacDiarmid the poet both discern a crippling fear of chaos in humanity; MacIntyre tries to subjugate the chaos, MacDiarmid to overcome the fear.

It was in the 30s, in *Stony Limits and Other Poems*, that MacDiarmid was most taken up with Shestov, and the attendant dangers are to be seen in the 'Ode to All Rebels', where a magnificent call to rebellion rises to an impossible pitch, calling for the removal of every stricture of opinion, finance, reason, sanity, law, science and even language – which would make victory an empty word, as the rebellious voice acknowledges.

If the 'Ode to All Rebels' relinquishes reason and pursues human emotion to extremes, 'On a Raised Beach' takes the opposite tack, and has reason pursue emotion to extinction. But Shestov is still there:

---

[1] MacIntyre, *op.cit.,* p. 251.

> Truth is not crushed;
> It crushes, gorgonizes all else into itself.[1]

The intuition that dead, universal Truth is inimical to human desires is as central to Shestov's philosophy as it is to this poem. And Shestov is quoted:

> ... These stones are one with the stars.
> It makes no difference to them whether they are high or low,
> Mountain peak or ocean floor, palace or pigsty. [2]

I know there is no weight in infinite space,
No impermeability in infinite time, ...[3]

Compare that to Shestov:

> Before the face of Eternal God all our foundations break together and all ground crumbles beneath us, even as objects – this we know – lose their weight in endless space, and – this we shall probably learn one day – will lose their impermeability in infinite time. Not so long ago weight seemed to man an inseparable attribute of things, even as impermeability.[4]

In that part of the book, Shestov observes that the anthropomorphic thinking implicit in ascribing a purpose to nature (that of preserving the organism, for example) is inconsistent with science's pretensions to objectivity. In 'On a Raised Beach' MacDiarmid tries to eradicate that anthropomorphism, to feel the world the way a lump of rock does. Well, if the 'Hymns to Lenin' were full of arrant idealism, 'On a Raised Beach' is rather too thoroughly materialistic. Lenin, putting the materialist case, describes 'sensation, thought, consciousness as the supreme product of matter organized in a certain way'.[5] Shestov shows that

---

[1] *CP* 430.
[2] *CP* 425, Compare Shestov, *op.cit.,* p. 189.
[3] *CP* 432.
[4] Shestov, *op.cit.,* p. 218.
[5] See McCarey, *op.cit.,* p. 190.

that adjective 'supreme' is anthropomorphic idealism; from a strictly materialist point of view, one configuration of matter is no better than another.

Not that Shestov would have recognized his own ideas in MacDiarmid's poetry: when Shestov attacked the legacy of the Greeks, he drew on Jewish tradition; his disciple Benjamin Fondane did the same, so that the line he took is comparable. However, when Shestov's methods are applied by a French ex-Catholic like Georges Bataille, or a Scottish ex-Calvinist like Hugh MacDiarmid, the results are quite different. MacDiarmid seemed to use antirationalism to get him above humanity, away from any vestigial common sense.

Something was happening to him. He had a severe breakdown around that time. His autobiography finds him, as he says, 'with my back to the wall, pleading quietly for power "to stay in no retreat and not to die" acknowledging chaos with a candour which cannot evade fear, but seeking refuge neither in an irrecoverable way of life nor in oblivion'. He quotes a testimonial to himself by other writers then rounds on them as a bunch of hypocrites, and he judges himself as follows: 'Faustus-like, I have tried to encompass all experience, and find myself at last happy enough marooned on this little island of Whalsay and only very slightly, I think, in any relevant respect, a failure'.[1]

The TLS reviewer I quoted at the outset found this book 'self-serving rather than self-revealing'; to me, all the ritual boasting it contains bespeaks shattering self-doubt, a condition that was compounded by total neglect.

Shestov clearly did have the desired liberating effect on MacDiarmid's imagination:

> And everywhere without fear of Chestov's 'suddenly',
> Never afraid to leap, and with the unanticipatedly

---

[1] Hugh MacDiarmid, *Lucky Poet: A Self-Study in Literature and Political Ideas* (London, 1941), pp. xxviii, 45. A new edition, edited by Alan Riach, was published by Carcanet in 1994.

Limber florescence of fireworks as they expand
Into trees or bouquets with the abandon of unbroken horses,
Or like a Beethovian semitonal modulation to a wildly remote key,
As in the Allegretto where that happens with a jump of seven sharps,
And feels like the sunrise gilding the peak of the Dent Blanche
While the Arolla valley is still in cloud.[1]

He overcame the fear, but not the chaos. The poetic persona retreats among.the quotations, dwindling at times to a grammatical ghost. The quotations and ideas are no longer assimilated or taken on by a central persona. Shestov's ideas, instead of providing direction and unity as the Dostoevskian search had done, allowed MacDiarmid to disengage from consequences, logical, social or linguistic. Ideas succeed one another in an exhilarating, exasperating and exhausting series of highs. As MacDiarmid himself put it in *In Memoriam James Joyce*,

> As a poet I'm interested in religious ideas –
> Even Scottish ones, Wee Free ones even – as a matter of fact
> Just as an alcoholic can-take snake venom
> With no worse effects than a warming of the digestive tract.[2]

He is like a stock market trader who has turned from shares in tin to treating money as a commodity. It can be done, but it is a practice that must slacken one's grip on the real world. Foreign texts and other facts were the commodities MacDiarmid was dealing in. In his late, agglomerative poems these texts are linked analogically: logical sequences tend to be within quotations, and he was quite happy to leave contradictions inside and consequences outside his poems for the readers to worry about. The present reader has long since stopped worrying about the contradictions, but there are consequences that bother me, such as the poem 'To a Friend and Fellow-Poet':

---

[1] *CP* 1020.
[2] *CP* 798.

It is with the poet as with a guinea worm
Who, to accommodate her teeming progeny
Sacrifices nearly every organ of her body, and becomes
(Her vagina obliterated in her all-else-consuming
Process of uterine expansion, and she still faced
With a grave obstetrical dilemma calling for
Most marvellous contrivance to deposit her prodigious swarm
Where they may find the food they need and have a chance in
life)
Almost wholly given over to her motherly task,
Little more than one long tube close-packed with young;
Until from the ruptured bulla, the little circular sore,
You see her dauntless head protrude, and presently, slowly,
A beautiful, delicate, and pellucid tube
Is projected from her mouth, tenses and suddenly spills
Her countless brood in response to a stimulus applied
Not directly to the worm herself, but the skin of her host
With whom she has no organised connection (and that stimulus
O Poets! but cold water!) ... The worm's whole
musculocutaneous coat
Thus finally functions as a uterus, forcing the uterine tube
With its contents through her mouth. And when the prolapsed
uterus ruptures
The protruded and now collapsed portion shrivels to a thread
(Alexander Blok's utter emptiness after creating a poem!)
The rapid drying of which effectually and firmly
Closes the wound for the time being... till later, the stimulus
being reapplied,
A fresh portion of the uterine tube protrudes, ruptures, and
collapses,
Once more ejaculating another seething mass of embryos,
And so the process continues until inch by inch
The entire uterus is expelled and parturition concluded.
Is it not precisely thus we poets deliver our store,
Our whole being the instrument of our suicidal art,
And by the skin of our teeth flype ourselves into fame?[1]

The juxtaposition of the Guinea worm with Blok's writing habits is
striking, but more striking yet is use of the Guinea worm as some
kind of ideal. Mention it to most people and they will tell you it is

---

[1] *CP* 1057-58.

one of the more noisome plagues of humanity: the larvae enter the human body in infected drinking water, and make their way to the mesentery. After mating and about a year's gestation, the female, about a yard long by this stage, burrows down towards the feet and a blister forms on contact with water, from which the larvae, and then the worm, emerge. The process is accompanied by much pain, nausea and vomiting (on the part of the human host). You wouldn't know from MacDiarmid's poem; a very anthropocentric complaint, you may say. Yes indeed, but then I am an anthropos. It seems to me that MacDiarmid's contempt for common consciousness brought him close to contempt for common humanity. His political poems show the same tendency.

Scottish writers since have tackled the problems he raised. Alasdair Gray in his novel *1982, Janine* goes directly to *A Drunk Man Looks at the Thistle* and Dostoevsky's *Notes from Underground*, and the picture of the Scot he paints is one that few would want to recognize. Yet when it comes to fear of chaos, his choice, like MacDiarmid's, is to kill the fear. The central character at the end is ready to face himself, whatever the result. If the result is *Something Leather*, then Gray, like MacDiarmid, is showing us that genius and immense courage are not enough to get us on the right road. The novelist James Kelman follows George Davie in advocating a return to common sense philosophy, attempting to subjugate chaos to human control.[1] But then, as Alasdair MacIntyre points out, what discredited Thomas Reid's philosophy in the United States immediately before the Civil War was its inability to account for radical moral disagreement within a single cultural and social order.[2] If the fearless individual can't win clear of chaos and common sense can't resolve it, then where is the answer? That is the question.

---

[1] James Kelman, 'A Reading from Noam Chomsky and the Scottish Tradition in the Philosophy of Common Sense', *Edinburgh Review*, LXIV, pp. 46-76.
[2] MacIntyre, *op.cit.*, p. 332.

'We believe what eases our minds'
John Anderson's Logic

I sent a draft of 'Fear of Chaos' to the philosopher George Elder Davie, who sent me his copy of John Anderson's essays in response. Anderson was a Scottish philosopher who spent most of his academic life in Sydney. Having tested a poet for ideas, let's check a philosopher for poetic justice.

A four-year-old was grappling with the problem of why the fourth wee craw he wisny there at aa.[1] Her seven-year-old sister told her he just wasn't. 'How do you know?' she was asked. She answered, 'I don't know *how* I know, but I know *that* I know'.

This is the common sense John Anderson appeals to in his logic – not the perhaps punning aspects stressed by George Davie of sense shared by the community or perception conveyed by the senses, but that autarchic sense which back-translates from Russian as 'healthy thinking' – where I know a spurious problem when I see one, and won't waste time analysing it. It reminds me irresistibly, though perhaps irrelevantly, of William Soutar's 'Fate':

> There wis a man fae Lunnon Links
> Wham Fate wrocht unco sair:
> Scarce richtit fae a dingin doun
> Or he was doun aince mair.
> Syne ae day he met Fate himsel

---

[1] 'Three Wee Craws' is a Scottish music hall song; a summary: Three wee craws sat upon a waa on a cold and frosty morning. The first wee craw couldny flee at aa, the second fell and broke its jaw, the third went greetin for its maw. The fourth wisnae therr at aa.

A bittock yont Anstruther
And spierd him why he warkd mair fell
Wi him nor ony other.
'Am I a dominie?' said Fate,
'Tae reel ye aff a rowt?
Aa that I ken's I dae it', he said,
Syne cluft him sic a clowt.

That may be the ultimate answer. But for those who cannot accept it, there is Anderson's logic, checking facts for inconsistency by means of syllogism. He tells us how propositions work:

> Rejecting (…) the distinction between necessary and other truths, empiricism takes up the position that in discussion or inquiry any proposition can be treated as (a) a conclusion to be proved from premises accepted, (b) a premise accepted to be used in proving some conclusion, (c) a hypothesis to be tested by the observation of the truth or falsity of the conclusions drawn from it, or (d) an observation to be used in determining the truth or falsity of conclusions drawn from a hypothesis.[1]

In his comments on *cogito ergo sum* we see the method working a treat. It's a very entertaining passage that couldn't have been done other than logically.[2] Sometimes the method doesn't work so well. Twice, for example, he maintains that externality is a symmetrical relation,[3] which it isn't (consider two concentric circles: the fact that one is external to the other does not imply the converse). At another point he maintains that 'either' means 'not neither', which it doesn't. (Present a seven-year-old with two pieces of cake; tell her she may take either piece and she will take one. Tell her she may not take neither piece; after a short pause she will take both.) In those instances, his own method can be used to correct the errors.

---

[1] John Anderson, 'Empiricism', based on a paper read at the Annual Congress of the A.A.P.P., Sydney, 1927; *Studies in Empirical Philosophy* (Sydney, Angus & Robertson, 1962, reprint of 1963), 3-14, p. 6. All quotations from Anderson are drawn from this book and all page numbers are from the same.

[2] 'The *Cogito* of Descartes' (1936), 101-114.

[3] 'The *Cogito* of Descartes', p. 108, and 'Empiricism and Logic (new paper)', 162-188, p. 168.

He declares boldly that philosophy should rule science.[1] He copes well enough with Marx and Freud,[2] so I had high hopes that this physics graduate would help me with Einstein and even Feynman. He rails at probability with such confidence that I expected to find some fundamental, syllogistic critique of quantum theory somewhere - but there isn't any.[3] As Feynman observed, you can philosophise on it as much as you like, but don't forget that it works. Shouting at it doesn't make it go away. On Einstein, Anderson seems to conflate Berkleyan relativism with relativity theory.[4] Oh well. Philosophy has to keep trying to govern science, but it's hard to see Anderson's single-minded logic keeping up with it.

Anderson describes logic as 'what is'.[5] He says philosophy should be systematic, not a comprehensive set of solutions, but a single logic. For him, it's as though all logic aspired to the condition of Switzerland, where everything that is not forbidden is compulsory. But even Switzerland isn't like that. John Broome seems to indicate that logic has to renounce some of those aspirations, at least for now, but that's for a later chapter.

Anderson approves of Hegel maintaining 'that this logic should be historical, if we take this to mean that it is the theory of things as historical; but it should not itself be considered as advancing, however the study of it may do so.'[6] Otherwise, he says, we fall into scepticism. And we don't want trouble, do we? Sad, though, that one who admired Heraclitus for his 'no granting of a privileged position in reality to gods, men or molecules, with conflict everywhere and nothing above the battle'[7] should put logic in a tabernacle. But then again, what if he is right? If logic is an

---

[1] 'Empiricism and Logic (new paper)', p. 185.
[2] 'Freudianism and Society' (1940), 340-358, p. 348.
[3] 'Realism and Some of its Critics' (1930), 41-59, p. 54; 'The Problem of Causality'(1938), 126-136, p. 128.
[4] 'Empiricism', p. 10; 'The Knower and the Known' (1927), 27-40, pp. 33-34.
[5] 'Causality and Logic' (1936), 122-125, p. 122.
[6] 'The Place of Hegel...', p. 80.
[7] 'Classicism' (1960), 189-202, p. 194.

ultimate good rather than just one way of organizing thoughts and feelings, then poetry that ignores or opposes it can't be worth much.

Anderson says he is a classicist, but logic is the only part of the trivium that interests him, just as geometry is the only part of the quadrivium. He makes a virtue of sticking to logic, though since he can't say what a virtue is, he resorts to rough rhetoric as grouting. He believes that 'we cannot travel away from logic, however distant a system we go to'.[1]

Anderson seems to regard logic and truth as innocent of time: 'how long it will take people to find out something, or how many other things they will not then have found out, does not affect the fact that what they do find out is something that is absolutely the case'.[2] On the other hand, 'Truths, we say, can be discovered but they can also be forgotten'.[3]

Is a forgotten truth still absolutely the case?

> Any of the elements in culture – Science, Art, Industry itself – no doubt operates through persons, but its 'needs', in the sense of conditions necessary for its continuance, its 'ends', as the effects its continuance will produce on its surroundings, its interactions generally with other things so that it does or does not 'survive', are not dependent on anyone's knowledge of them - any more than, as Marx points out (Preface to *Critique of Political Economy*), a man's own history is dependent on what he thinks of himself.[4]

If it is fair to interpret that as a 'yes', then Anderson seems to be taking his aversion to Berkeleyan relativism too far. Trees, I'll admit with some reluctance, might not depend on someone seeing them, but truths depend on someone believing them. If, on the other hand, the question is unanswerable - since a 'no' would indeed be absurd - then it doesn't seem that difficult to travel away

---

[1] 'Design' (1935), 88-100, p. 100.
[2] 'Marxist Philosophy' (1935), 292-313, p. 296.
[3] 'The Place of Hegel in the History of Philosophy' (1932), 79-87, p. 81.
[4] 'Marxist Ethics' (1937), 314-327, p. 324.

from logic, to escape its emprise. And indeed, by attributing 'needs', 'ends' and 'survival' to elements in culture, Anderson curiously anticipates the pathetic fallacy of the far from logical 'memes' that Richard Dawkins deployed in the 1980s (see next chapter).

Insisting on 'what is', Anderson maintains against Ryle and the multitude that 'We know things while we continue to exercise our minds on them, while we continue to grapple with the questions they raise' it being understood that when we are not doing so, we do not know them. 'Of course', he goes on, 'there is a quite widespread assumption of the storehouse view of knowledge (of any piece of knowledge as being tucked away in some mental compartment) and language is used so as to support that view; but it is one of philosophy's tasks to correct common assumptions and usages, not to follow them.'[1] This implies that when I'm using a Russian double imperfective verb I (more or less) know it, but don't know it when I'm not using it. Where is it in the interim: in the tabernacle with logic? In my unconscious? Or is it called into being (replete with mistakes, in my case) by my awareness of it? Bishop Berkeley might have liked that. Wouldn't it be easier to leave learning and knowing separate, and put the act of learning in the past? But Anderson has no time for the past.

Or for the future: 'doctrines like utilitarianism and progressivism whose special concern is the future are not merely anti-classical but are opposed to study, since the past is a field of study which can be constantly opened up, while the future is a field of conjecture or phantasy.'[2] Anderson, grounded in the present, is equally anti-classical: the past is not a field of study; it is what has been and gone, for the most part irrevocably. The field of study that can constantly be opened up is present awareness of the past or of anything else. In that it can be revised, it is as much exposed to conjecture and phantasy as is the future.

He is aware, nonetheless, of the limits to logic, and indeed says it is ultimately based on beliefs, which are 'what eases our minds'.

---

[1] 'Empiricism and Logic', p. 173n.
[2] 'Classicism' (1960), p. 197.

Anderson starts out from common sense, but his logic over-rules it time and again. What community of sense would do away with ideas,[1] the self, right and happiness,[2] conscience[3] and the distinction between inner and outer?[4] This is a view of the world that might equally have been arrived at by Rimbaud, through his 'long, immense et raisonné dérèglement de tous les sens', except that Anderson's version is not liberating but terribly prescriptive.

There is no need, then, for a poet to take Anderson's logic as anything more than an unitemized set of conventions. This is not to rule out immaterial entities that are independent of human volition: the poet – an intelligent seven-year-old in philosophic terms – will show more respect for prime numbers, say, than for the law of non-contradiction, for two reasons: the first is that poetry is often a joyous trashing of non-contradiction; the second is that primes can't be trashed. Even though there is no firm reason to believe that numbers are anything other than an arbitrary zoning of the continuum of existence, once numbers *are* introduced, the primes turn up uninvited, and they don't go away (more on this in part four).

If, then, we take logic not as a deep structure but as a more or less prescriptive grammar, how can we put it to creative use?

Arguing for determinism Anderson writes:

> ... selection of mind as a bearer of freedom is not due to any special interest in mind. Those who are interested in mind's workings will naturally take up a determinist position. The indeterminists are those with an axe to grind, with certain 'values' to defend, with the view that certain things ought to be or are to be done. Theoretical concern with what is the case is, it seems to me, coextensive with determinism.[5]

---

[1] 'Empiricism and Logic (new paper)', p. 168.
[2] 'The Place of Hegel...', p. 84.
[3] 'Determinism and Ethics' (1928), 214-226, pp. 217,219.
[4] 'Empiricism and Logic (new paper)', p. 169.
[5] 'Causality and Logic', p. 125.

That we can change nothing and that we can act freely are two powerful intuitions that meet in the centre of our being (a third intuition). The proponent of either extreme is in trouble. Anderson's solution is to deny the freedom of the individual and indeed the existence of the individual. Naturally enough: if past and future, knowing and striving, are deactivated, leaving only passive feeling, then the I is exposed to the weather and decomposed before death: 'We believe (or, as I should say, the motive believes)';[1] 'Nevertheless, none but subjectivist objections have ever been urged to the view that it is certain brain processes that think';[2] 'emotions (or feelings) know, emotions strive and, in general, interact with other things';[3] '... it is not so clearly understood that there is no faculty of "reason" which can guide the passions, but that thinking is an activity of the passions themselves';[4] 'The rejection of the conception of the "unitary person" went with the rejection of the "conscious self"';[5] 'In my article I took for granted the plurality of mental entities (sentiments, passions or whatever they may be called) for which I have argued elsewhere – the existence of a society of "motives", having distinct characters and a certain capacity for independent action.'[6] All assertion and no argument. And lest it be thought that Anderson has turned the despotic self into a democracy with a 'society of motives', you should note that he defines society as 'that false solidarity of group interests'.[7] Me? my name is Legion. I is the survivor of my component parts.

This animist view of the individual, with its motives that believe, thoughts that think and emotions that feel, is very strange. It reminds me of a slightly crazy hard man in the school I attended, who called his feet Albert and Ceecil; 'You'd better watch it', he'd say, 'or I'll set Albert and Ceecil onto you'.

[1] 'Determinism and Ethics' (1928), p. 218.
[2] 'The *Cogito* of Descartes', p. 111.
[3] 'Mind as Feeling', p. 73.
[4] 'Utilitarianism' (1932), 227-237, p. 236.
[5] 'Psychological Moralism' (1953), 363-374, p. 369.
[6] 'The Nature of Ethics' (1943), 268-278, p. 275.
[7] 'The One Good' (1945), 288-291, p. 290.

'Thus if we can rule out the supposition of a peculiarly critical faculty, we shall have disposed of both "conscience" and the "whole self" as candidates for that office.'[1] – leaving operations to Albert and Ceecil? I'd rather not.

Once again: that we can change nothing and that we can act freely are two intuitions that meet in the centre of our being (a third intuition). The proponent of either extreme is in trouble. Ambiguity, in this area, is not sloppiness but mediation. It is simply untrue that 'The principle of verbal communication is that the set of words used in making a given statement should have only one meaning'.[2] Tell that to the diplomats and poets.

We could avoid the unnecessary strain of keeping faith with either extreme by admitting we are implicated at every level in a process we won't escape alive. That would leave interstitial spaces for hope. But how does Anderson proceed, if he doesn't believe either in his self or in his freedom? Watch.

'…a classical period – a period in which disinterestedness stands out from the wrangle of special interests as it does not in culturally lower times'.[3]

Disinterestedness? Yes, that's it: 'The classicist recognizes the natural opposition between disinterestedness and interestedness, between concern with the ways of working of things themselves and concern with what we can get out of them.'[4]

'…should be obvious to all those who admit that such a thing as disinterestedness exists'.[5]

'Developing the "values" of initiative, emulation, care for exactitude and rejection of the notion of "reward", the factory

---

[1] 'Determinism and Ethics', p. 217.
[2] 'The Truth of Propositions' (1926), 20-26, p. 22.
[3] 'Classicism', p. 194.
[4] 'Classicism', p. 199.
[5] 'The One Good', p. 291.

worker becomes assimilated to the scientist, the artist, the warrior - types of disinterested activity.'[1]

'The common ethical notions of disinterestedness and of things which are "for their own sake"'.[2]

Disinterestedness is just one of those things: Anderson never tries to tell us how it can cohabit with determinism, and the nearest he gets to defining it involves the word 'values', which he puts in perverted commas because values, as he says in his discussion of determinism, are metaphysical nonsense. Why does he want it so much? Surely disinterestedness entails both a self whose interests are to be disengaged and freedom for that self to disengage them? For Anderson, however, I is allowed to open parliament, or to write a paper in the long vac., but not to interfere with realpolitik or the workings of the world, which it can only describe. Just the job for a professor, don't you think? 'What is done, whether it is good or not, will be determined by the forces that exist.'[3] Leave foreign policy to Albert and Ceecil.

Anderson claims that his 'pluralistic logic of events' offers the only logical answer to 'scepticism – theology, defeatism, leaving things in the hands of higher powers'[4] – but he does this by leaving them in the hands of lower powers. He seems to despise the 'tendency to seek safety and certainty',[5] yet subjects his mind to the laws of nature[6] and logic, and dismisses anything risky as unimportant or negligible:

'... in general, choice plays little part in human life'.[7] 'Although in our active lives we sometimes discover moral truths, we also

---

[1] 'Marxist Ethics', p. 325.
[2] *ibid.*, p. 327.
[3] 'Realism versus Relativism in Ethics' (1933), 238-247, p. 242.
[4] 'The Place of Hegel...', p. 87.
[5] 'Determinism and Ethics', p. 219.
[6] 'Empiricism and Logic', p. 167.
[7] 'The Nature of Ethics', p. 278.

discover other truths, in which, for the most part, we are much more interested.'[1]

'People in general do not think very much about the goodness of their activities'.[2] '...it is equally absurd to say that there is any such question as "What am I to do?"'.[3]

In general ... we ... people in general ... absurd. Where have all the syllogisms gone?

A man with a moral code was walking through the desert. After a series of camel jokes he met John Anderson, who said, 'To call it a norm or an ideal is merely an excuse for leaving it indefinite'.[4]

'You're none too precise in defining *goods* yourself', said the man: 'I mean look at "The Meaning of Good", especially page 263'.

Anderson replied, 'The fact that a good once established both communicates itself and assists other goods is not merely a reason for the continuance of the struggle against evils; it is itself the continuance of the struggle'.[5]

The man said, 'Seems fair enough; replace *good* with *Old Etonian* or *adventitious infection* and it would be just as logical. The question then would be what you meant by evils, and I smell a circular argument.'

'The task of the ethical theorist', said Anderson, 'will be to find goods and consider their ways of working, and in this connection he may well find how they are promoted and how prevented. His study will thus be a thoroughly deterministic one'.[6]

'How are you going to find them', said the man, 'if you can't bring yourself to define them? Why ask how they can be promoted if

---

[1] 'Determinism and Ethics', p. 218.
[2] *ibid.*, p. 226.
[3] 'Realism versusu Relativism in Ethics', p. 241.
[4] 'Determinism and Ethics', p. 218.
[5] *ibid.*, p. 224.
[6] 'Realism versus Relativism in Ethics', p. 241.

you don't have any criterion for judging them good? And how can you promote them if (a) you are as determinate as they are and (b) you don't exist?'

'The metaphysical conception of human freedom', said Anderson, 'is rooted in mythology and has played havoc with all the anthropological sciences'.[1]

'Here I am walking through the desert', said the man; 'I've lost my camel, I might be dead before it gets dark, I'd swap my putative freedom for a drink of water, but I don't give two hoots about anthropological sciences, and I don't think you do either. What's more, you're a counterpuncher when it comes to ethics. But you're a tub-thumper in economics. Look at this (he produced a copy of *Studies in Empirical Philosophy* from his saddle bag): *If moral forces exist in society at all, they must (as they obviously do) affect economic exchanges and the whole system of production, and any economic theory which puts them out of consideration will be defective on that account.*[2] You see? No room for morals in your ethical theory, but no way round them in economic theory. You know what you are? ...'

'The realistic angel', said Anderson, 'would, in fact, repudiate knowing by being; he would maintain that if we could only be ourselves, then we could not know ourselves at all'[3] - he smiled, and disappeared.

Some time later our man was still walking, pondering these things in his heart, as one does, when he met someone carrying two small headstones.
- What's that you've got?
- The Tablets of the Law.
- What does that one say?
- Thou Shalt Not Kill
- Oh yes. But you've done that, haven't you?
- Fifth commandment, fifth amendment:

---

[1] *loc.cit.*.

[2] 'The Servile State' (1943), 328-339, p. 330.

[3] 'The Non-Existence of Consciousness' (1929), 60-67, p. 64.

I refuse to answer on the grounds that I might
incriminate myself.
- Well, see Exodus II, 11-12? Enough said.
- It wasn't the Law then. And anyway,
it's Who Will Be I believe in, not the Law.
Look (SMASH!)
There: I've broken all of them
but they're all still there.
Because He made them,
like He made me. Tell me though,
what's that you've got?
- Oh, it's my moral code.
- Very nice. What does it do?
- For a start, it stops me killing people.
- Oh yes? How?
- Partly by appeal to tradition
such as your own decalogue,
partly through the argument
of enlightened self-interest:
that if I don't kill you, for example,
then you won't kill me.
- Surely you mean that if I *do* kill you
you won't kill me?
Or do you hope your own shining example will
make me like you or act like you?
You want a world full of yourselves?
It's not a moral code you want, pal,
it's a genetic engineer. Here –
(takes the moral code and rips it up)
that's better.

The Selfish Gene and the Pathetic Fallacy

There is something appealing in Richard Dawkins's conception of humans as throwaway survival machines for genes. It deflates self-importance. It accounts for the way parents come to see their children as more important than themselves: this isn't altruism but extended self-interest, looking after the genes. Still, if genetic survival is the reason for existence, then why am I not content to devote all my time to watching the children? It doesn't feel like my raison d'être. But, Dawkins would say, there are the memes too. There are two flaws in the notion of the selfish gene: one is selfishness, the other is the gene.

In order to convey new concepts we have to coin new words or use existing ones in different senses: 'World' in 'The world is all that is the case' is a little eccentric, but acceptable; replace 'world' with 'elephant' and you have a wilful absurdity. Dawkins, however, tells us that 'we can define a word how we like for our own purposes, provided we do so clearly and unambiguously'. Of course, one can do what one wants. Alasdair MacIntyre calls his habitual actions leading to virtues 'practices'; he would have been at liberty to call them 'perversions', but however careful his definition of the term, his readers would then have continued to associate them with vice, not virtue.

Dawkins acknowledges that genes have no self-awareness, no intentions; why does he call them selfish? His answer seems to be 'trust me, I'm a scientist'. Well, he knows his onions, and produces a fine array of information on flora and fauna, but his application of game theory to zoology has two flaws. First, it can explain anything at all, true or untrue; it can explain why an elephant has a trunk; it could also explain why an elephant had wings. Secondly, it explains in terms of bluff and double bluff – it psychologises zoology, compounding the intentional fallacy introduced with the notion of selfishness. Why?

Memes, the mental equivalent of genes, are 'propagated not in sperms or eggs, but in newsprint, images or airwaves. Again, bodies and brains are the temporary vehicles, pressed into service by potentially immortal replicators'.[1] This is culture as mad cow disease.

> ... memes should be regarded as living structures, not just metaphorically but technically. When you plant a fertile meme in my mind you literally parasitize my brain, turning it into a vehicle for the meme's propagation in just the way that a virus may parasitize the genetic mechanism of a host cell. And this isn't just a way of talking – the meme for, say, 'belief in life after death' is actually realized physically, millions of times over, as a structure in the nervous system of individual men the world over.[2]

At one level this is paranoid fantasy – an Invasion of the Body Snatchers. As metaphor, though, it has its merits, because ideas (a perfectly acceptable word; no need for this 'meme' business) or their expressions, do indeed mutate, get passed on; the meaning or function of the word changes, they get truncated and extended just like genes. But which is the reality here, and which the metaphor? The gene is an intellectual construct. Dawkins's great discovery or definition is that intellectual constructs are like genes. The gene is related metaphorically to the idea, and not by any organic pathway Dawkins has found. So why does he push an ordinary simile to book length?

Look at it from the zoologist's point of view. How does the cuckoo survive? And the honeyguide? Now how does an idea survive? – because it is a matter of survival, not of truth or falsehood: if you can propagate your idea then it becomes true. So you rubbish everything prior to Darwin and other than zoology and dismiss anyone who disagrees. 'The true reason for our existence is now

---

[1] Dawkins's review of his own book, *The Observer,* 15 October 1989.
[2] *The Selfish Gene*, 1st ed., p. 206

beyond educated dispute' (same review). Why does he psychologise genes? In other words, why does he come up with this combination of zoology and utilitarianism? Symbiosis: the zoology gives a scientific air to his views on the meaning of life, which in turn make the science more approachable, more popular.

And lest it all seem too bleak, with spurious human consciousness transpiring as nothing more than interference between grasping genes and ruthless ideas, Dawkins brings in 'altruism', his word for what utilitarians called 'enlightened self-interest', which was blown out of the water by Dostoevsky. Dawkins's theory, like Thatcherism, is a totalitarian process that excludes human failures, and tries to disguise the fact by appealing to virtues denied by the theory itself: charity in Thatcherism, altruism in Dawkins's zoological Thatcherism. It's Anderson's 'disinterest' all over again. And the naïve or faux-naif use of metaphor in science recurs, as we shall see in part IV, in Pinker's advocacy of Chomsky's generative grammar.

Weighing In

To the outsider it can appear that professional philosophers are happy to dispute everything except the assumptions their arguments are based on; perhaps those tacit agreements have better anthropological than philosophic explanations. They play by the rules. So what happens when the philosophers set themselves the task of establishing and justifying real rules? John Broome provides an interesting example in *Weighing Lives* (Oxford UP, 2004), where he seeks philosophical consensus (partly by ruling out arguments on the nature of the good, in order to restrict the scope for dissent), with a view to securing political support for his set of real rules. Let's consider the form and its conventions, as we will with verse in part III: whether Broome's argument succeeds in its own terms, whether those terms are divulged and, in the light of that, the meteness or ineptitude of its trajectory in the world.

> Betterness – comparative goodness – is all that matters in this book; we need not concern ourselves with any other aspect of goodness. We need not worry whether some distributions are absolutely good or bad in any sense. Nor need we worry about the amount by which one distribution is better or worse than another. (p. 20)

Cut out good and the weighing of lives comes down to intuition regulated by algebra. This calls for a clear apprehension of one's intuitions and a good grasp of the maths. On the face of it, the expulsion of good should make it easier to secure consensus: if we can't agree on an absolute, we might at least agree on specific relative merits, 'betterness'. However, since our intuitions probably draw on primal instincts as to good, I don't think that's likely. And although that might not matter in the book, it matters in practice, since *Weighing Lives*, with its relativity of merits, could

33

easily be suborned by politicians who want us to debate the distribution of what's on offer, rather than the justice or generosity of the initial allocation, and what has been withheld.

And on second thoughts it does matter in the book. Take my own disagreement with one of the intuitions espoused by the author, one he holds so dear that he asserts it eight times in three pages (pp. 108-110).

'It is surely true that our intuition normally rates continued life better than replacement.' 'One possible response to this objection is simply to deny it. This is a hard-headed, intuitively implausible response, but it is possible...'

Broome follows up by labelling those who object to his view 'complete utilitarians'. 'A complete utilitarian does not care in any way about how wellbeing is distributed. For one thing, she does not care how it is packaged into individual lives. All that matters is wellbeing; who gets wellbeing is irrelevant.' Now, I don't know what standing complete utilitarians have in the philosophical community these days, but I suspect it's not high.

In contradicting Broome I might simply resort to his own method on this issue: bald assertion. But the edifice he has founded on his intuitions gives him the benefit of the doubt. There is something fiducial about technical prowess, whereas I might simply be out to cause trouble. So I had better try to account for my own, contrary intuition, which has nothing utilitarian about it.

Broome prefers one long life to two short ones; it's not that I regard the matter with indifference, but rather that I think two short lives, very often, are better than one long one. I have known people whose biological life far outran their taste for it. I have worked in places where people don't last long at all. With the integration of the world economy, the doddering rich are stealing years from the poor. This is not leading up to a crude dollar argument. After all, a recent happiness survey found Bangladeshis to be the happiest nation on earth. My point is this: humans are rarely alive. Many people, given good health, are dulled by routine and eroded by anxiety at the prospect of it ending. Many more are struggling to reach that level of wellbeing. Once in a while, in moments of unbearable happiness or when pain jerks us out of the rut, we are alive, and that is good. Indeed, nothing else is worth a bean.

I don't believe that extending life will increase the number of those moments, but there is a better than even chance that adding a life will add an opportunity to be alive. This is not to suggest replacing birth control with euthanasia. Indeed, I don't want my intuition integrated in any theory that weighs lives. More on that later. Is this enough to establish that I seriously maintain the conclusion Broome holds to be intuitively implausible? For those who agree with me, it will be; it might give the others pause.

In the subsection on large numbers, Broome notes:

> Temkin finds curing a single person of AIDS intuitively so important that it is better than curing any number of short, mild headaches … I believe there is some number (which is very large) such that curing that number of people of a short, mild headache is better than curing one person of AIDS. I have no inclination to believe the opposite.
>
> However, Temkin and Rachels do believe the opposite. Rachels tells us that the opposite view 'is supported by the strong preference of competent judges'. Temkin lists a number of famous philosophers who think like him. The view of these competent judges and famous philosophers deserves a response.
>
> Their view is founded on their intuitions. But we are dealing with very large numbers of people, and we have no reason to trust anyone's intuitions about very large numbers, however excellent their philosophy. Even the best philosophers cannot get an intuitive grasp of, say, tens of billions of people. That is no criticism; these numbers are beyond intuition. But these philosophers ought not to think their intuition can tell them the truth about such large numbers of people. (pp. 56-7)

Attentive or flippant readers may have noticed Stalin in the background sniggering about tragedy and statistics. By dismissing the notion of good, Broome is able to turn a deaf ear to that. Many – philosophers and others – would agree that their intuition can't tell them the truth about such large numbers of people (though tens of billions is a bit much). But intuition can tell them the truth about individuals. The relevant intuition is that it is not good to kill someone or let them die for a trivial reason, or for any number of trivial reasons.

But I do kill people for trivial reasons. I am killing all the time in what I eat and how I travel. I can always kill less, but I can't stop completely. The physical causes of death are clear, and the reasons for it: we die because we kill. The contradiction gets resolved not in theory but in death, for most of us, I guess. But there are cases – children killed before they can hurt a fly – where there is a cause but no reason. This is the realm of tragedy, where there is good and its opposite, but no scales in which to weigh them.

On the other hand, Broome's is a practical book, is it not? So I shouldn't stray into areas it doesn't claim to cover. But how practical is it to consider at great length whether it is better to cure one person from AIDS or many thousands from a mild headache? In what society would this zero-sum dilemma arise? What health system manager in what manner of totalitarian régime would ever have the power to ponder this and put his decision into effect? Not even a British Primary Care Trust has such power, since those who are refused treatment for AIDS or a headache can still (if they can garner the cash) look for a solution outside the equation. And it is never a matter of patients' competing interests alone, because industry will exert pressure on one side or the other, and patients' support groups won't stand idly by. In his book on climate change, considered below, Broome clearly states that such problems cannot now be resolved by moral philosophy but need democratic debate. Religious beliefs too will come into the picture, aptly enough, since the philosopher's careful weighing of things he will never see has its precedent in subtle theology. And on philosophical method – which will still feature in that debate – it is worth quoting Morton Feldman on musical composition:

> One of the problems about functional harmony is that it hears for us, see. We no longer have to hear. We are the found object, you see, where it's listening for us. Harmony is like going to a public accountant to do certain work. Or it hears for us, it's fantastic,

it's marvelous, we don't have to hear anymore. But we have to be smart. We have to be smart, like Mozart, to make sure that it's the best kind of harmony that's working for him.[1]

There is indeed a fiducial quality in technique (a matter that will recur in the chapter on Tom Leonard). The other side of that coin is that technique can become a substitute for being smart, as Feldman puts it. Broome continues:

> For very large numbers, we have to rely on theory, not intuition. When people first built bridges, they managed without much theory. They could judge a log by eye, relying on their intuition. Their intuitions were reliable, being built on long experience with handling wood and stone. But when people started spanning broad rivers with steel and concrete, their intuition failed them, and they had to resort to engineering theory and careful calculations. The cables that support suspension bridges are unintuitively slender. (p. 57)

Stalin again: the engineers of human souls. In philosophy, as in music, if you rely on theory to the exclusion of intuition you won't even know when you are wreaking havoc. A formula for weighing lives is not a bridge. It's not those who trust to its strength whose lives are at risk, but those on whom the formula is used, and they have no say in the matter.

Weighing Lives is part of the drive to automation that goes from the Jacquard loom to computers, from Taylorism to Microsoft Project, from Kircher to Google Translate. At the crude and impersonal level on which a government ministry works, this book ought to improve the consistency and clarity of distribution. It's a good thing. Still, the automation of human functions is a demonstration of Zeno's paradox: the arrow never will reach its target. We're incurable.

We are incurable, and the ground rules of the discipline are undemonstrable. The entire edifice would seem to rest on conventions that are less firmly grounded in reality than forms of

---

[1] 'The Future of Local Music' (1984), XVIII, in *Give my Regards to Eighth Street* (Cambridge, 2000).

verse, whose prosody at least is linked to the action of heart, lungs and feet. Is philosophy anything more than a rather enervated epic form? If not, does it matter? Similar questions can be asked closer in: is humanity the result of anything other than random selection? If not, does that matter? It matters in both cases if genealogy confers not only dignity and status, but also meaning. But I can't see pedigree as that important, and meaning is conferred by something rather simpler.

'We are a finite species with a finite nature. Nothing that happens to us can be infinitely bad.'

This is one of those phrases which, like John Anderson's 'We believe what eases our minds', soars into poetry from a strictly non-lyrical line of thought. It is the kind of elegiac surprise that – to anticipate the third section of this book – can emerge in great simplicity from the routines and subroutines of avant garde poetic composition; examples are Jackson Mac Low's 'Odes for Iris', Jacques Roubaud's *Quelque chose noir* and Tom Raworth's 'Shoes', each of which might look fairly conventional but was arrived at across the tundra of experimental trial and error, and is all the more poignant for that.

The phrase in question comes from John Broome's *Climate Matters: Ethics in a Warming World* (2012), and it provides momentary solace of a kind, through the rhetorical *quid pro quo* in its appeal to the first person plural. For we, gentle reader, are not a species, but specimens. And something infinite and, we may fear, infinitely bad, does happen to us: we die.

Climate Matters is a book for the general reader that this general reader, on firmer ground now, recommends for its calm separation of the powers of science, economics, moral philosophy and politics. Once again its author is reassuringly clear as to the limits of his own arguments in particular. It is mentioned here not because of any link I wish to make between climate change and poetry readings (though I don't believe that any amount of carbon off-setting can assuage the harm done by some of us), but to bring out a difference in approach between this exemplary rational procedure and the examples of poetic thought that will be considered later. Poetry is very much about pattern recognition; Broome's philosophy aims to put decision-making on a computational basis. The Turing machine cannot encode the ending of its own programme, perhaps because pattern recognition is that which a Turing machine cannot do. The reason it can't is that machines do not die. Bluntly: meaning is a function of mortality, and pattern recognition in humans is honed constantly on that awareness. We are always watching out for the end, and looking for some justice or – however spurious – consolation in its advent. We therefore sense when different lines of force, various ostensibly unrelated circumstances, are converging on us. The arts rehearse the end for us in various ways, and we take great pleasure in seeing it coming, and in living to tell the tale. Any duo of buskers knows that the most important moment in a piece is the last half-second, because if both end on the same beat, all that precedes it seems as though it was intended, just as a simple tune, in the last note, states its key. The people applaud and shell out. At the other end of the scale, as it were, great musicians who improvise, and the people who listen to them, can feel an argument develop, and are waiting for its contradiction, resolution or collapse. A great part of the pleasure is in anticipating how the players are going to extract themselves from the corner they are assiduously painting themselves into. At the end of John Broome's book – it isn't the kind of ending that is spoiled by being divulged in advance – he writes:

> But the ethical theory of population is in a state of flux; moral philosophers are very unsure how population should correctly be valued. In particular, we are unsure how to value a collapse of population or extinction. Our uncertainty is not like the empirical uncertainty that expected value theory is equipped to deal with. Expected value theory depends on a given notion of value, but our uncertainty is about value itself. Chapter 10 concludes with the view that democratic public debate is at present the only means we have of coping with this sort of uncertainty.

This is astounding. Moral philosophy bows to democratic politics while politicians, in their turn, transfer power to the banks, which privatize profit and nationalize debt. Not all bankers are in it for the bonus, but to place our hopes for survival in the pin-striped equivalent of a philosopher king or warrior poet would be extremely rash. We must diversify. Even poetry should get a hearing in political and other conversations. It could be that even, or perhaps especially, the kind of poetry that avoids advancing any argument at all, while managing a great load of hopes and fears, hones our perception of pattern in a way that is not only pleasing but salutary, and guides us towards our various ends, rather in the way that clearing the mind of everything else and contemplating a subject, without necessarily drawing any conclusions on it much less writing about it, will also have its effect on all the unreckonable choices we confront.

Find an Angel and Pick a Fight

Animal, vegetable or mineral

A bird was footering about on the gravel of the roof below, and I
was trying to make out what it was. Charcoal head shading to mid-
grey body, white flashes on the wings, russet rump. Much of the
time it was only visible in movement, when the parallel white lines
showed up. And I wondered, knowing that the best method of
camouflage breaks up the lines of the structure, why every bird and
beast from the most ostentatious to the most sleekit has bilateral
symmetry. And plants extend round a line, and minerals round a
point. Mineral, vegetable, animal, growing from point, line, plane.
Fixed, flexible, mobile: the stricter the symmetry, the freer the
creature. Is there an order of symmetry above bilateral? or below
spherical? And humans, with our moral codes and formality in art,
are we looking for freedom in a higher symmetry? Could it be
formulated for verse? That's my real question, because as usual I'm
interested in theory only as raw material.

To be more precise, minerals in this world aren't spherical, unless
you count the oblate spheroid itself. But there's the stars, and the
planets. Other mineral states derive from them. Gravity, collusions
and collisions make the fractures and structures of rocks and
crystals here.

For the radial symmetry of plants I'm thinking of trees and their
roots, of thistles, roses, clumps of gorse and grass. I know they can
start with punctate seeds and end with superficial leaves, but the
governing axis of symmetry is the line. Animals have symmetry
about a plane, which is only pliant, into the reflex dimension, and
when the muscles relax they straighten up (watch how fish swim);
the line, though, can twist and loop into another two dimensions,

so that even when they are bilateral, plants are never so straightforward: a leaf is mapped onto its mirror image, the pair rotates up a tendril helically, boughs bend and twigs twist out to the light. Ach I should be writing this in winter. Theories work better then. As it is, spiricles are unfurling from under crumbs of earth, shaking out into crossed pairs of smooth and serrated leaves. There are hundreds of different options: spiral fern shoots, sycamore hands, and maple, where leaves are certainly bilateral but also, like side aisles, echoes of the centre, diminishing fractally into their own serrations. Corinthian sprouts from doric severity. As to animal symmetry, I'll take Tom Leonard's heuristic: if it's wee enough to stamp on it doesn't count – although creatures that would be *too* wee to stamp on are interesting also. By the time it has six cells, the *C. elegans* embryo has distinguished up from down and back from front, and is figuring out the left/right bias.

> One school of thought argues that asymmetry is phylogenetically and ontogenetically derived from a bilaterally symmetric ground state that is modified by superimposed signaling events (…). An alternative view postulates that bilaterality is imposed onto an evolutionary ancient, nonbilateral body plan and that asymmetries within a bilateral body plan represent a remnant of the ancient asymmetry.[1]

For aesthetic not scientific considerations I'm glad the authors plump for the latter.

Sea anemones may plant themselves on rocks, and starfish revert from bilateral to apparent radial symmetry, but they're not the only creatures that don't know what they're about. It's curious that animals, which are not particularly symmetrical inside, are quite symmetrical outside: animal limbs are congruent, and the colouring, to return to the start (it was a black redstart), is just about absolutely symmetrical. Why? There are compelling functional explanations of the symmetry of bodies that want to follow their nose – such as avoidance of walking in circles. But

---

[1] Richard J. Poole and Oliver Hobert, 'Early Embryonic Programming of Neuronal Left/Right Asymmetry in *C. elegans*', *Current Biology* 16, 2279–2292, December 5, 2006.

why bilateral symmetry of decoration? Pierre Aubry, after some head-scratching, came up with a counter example. The sole, which is born a flat, vertical fish, develops into a horizontal flatfish. One of its eyes migrates round the corner so it can have a better view of the ocean squashing it some more. This means that one of its sides has two eyes, the other none; one side is one colour, the other another. I checked this up at the fishmonger's, and in a way he's right: the sole's mouth is along one edge, like the zip on a toilet bag. Nevertheless, it's more than half-way towards achieving a new axis of symmetry of the traditional sort, along a line that runs at right angles to the shortest route between its eyes. Why?

Another species of flat fish: imagine a dozen nacreous hatchets with the features of Tam Dalziel (sorry, Tam). If you can't, then get to Basel Zoo and look at the creatures tacking round over the label *Selene vomer*. They're called St Pierre or John Dory when they hit the fishmonger's slab, by which time they look more like Douglas Hurd. (wrong again: John Dory is *Zeus faber*. But anyway...) These creatures are symmetrical and identical: specimens of their species. This lump of clay has no symmetry. This human face has surpassed symmetry. A specimen abstracted from the species is symmetrical, but the unrepeatable individual steals from symmetry. Rubato. My symmetry says I am, and my mark on it says I'm only here the once. How does it go? asymmetry, symmetry, dissymmetry, then either dissolution or higher order symmetry? Maybe. Though we will never really know why, the first known portrait, carved on mammoth ivory about 30,000 years ago and found at Dolní Věstonice, shows a face whose symmetry is broken.[1]

Groups of symmetry

Another cut: having excluded creatures too small to see, we discard symmetries in invisible dimensions, even though that means most of them.

---

[1] Jill Cook, *Ice Age Art: arrival of the modern mind* (London, British Museum Press, 2013), pp. 70-72.

Space	Time/Wave	Particle/Rhythm
Point	Mineral	Logic
Line	Vegetable	Rhyme
Plane	Animal	Metaphor
Body	Human	Naming

Each successive group incorporates the previous one – geometrically in column 1, physically in column 2, and literally in column 3: metaphor can entertain logic, for example, whereas logic, with the law of non-contradiction, cannot accommodate metaphor.

I have extended the 'animal, vegetable and mineral' categories by one at either end: subatomic, which I don't understand, and human, which I haven't really grasped either. In the nineteenth century there would have been a 'superhuman' category, courtesy of Solovyov or Nietzsche, but that hubris has nearly lost us our human specificity. 'God is dead' led to 'I is dead'. I don't think poetry can touch the godhead. It's only human. But human it is.

It would seem that Big-Bang archaeologists are projecting a golden age of supersymmetry in ten dimensions or so. People like John Ellis try to reassemble the Ur-version, rather as classicists infer Orphic cosmology from slighting references in Aristotle, or the way theologians chase through Coptic and Armenian translations for something nearer to the original 'In the beginning' – but the nearest they'll get is Greek. Echoes is all we ever get, the air shaken by speech, the seismograph. There's never a sign but in translation.

Still, if time began, it's always beginning somewhere, quite apart from nostalgic algebra.

I gave my daughter a box of crayons.
First she chewed it
then she rattled it.
This went on for quite some time.

When she did put wax to paper
she just did rhythm,
cardiograms.

Note that none of the above groups could have been extrapolated from its predecessor. There's something miraculous about vegetable from mineral, birds budding from branches. A miracle, true, is that which no rational being can believe in. But then rational beings didn't deduce themselves from cognates in the trees. All they can do in this area is explain themselves away. Showing how something has evolved over time explains it in the etymological sense (it unfolds the thing origamically). It does not explain things in the common sense of saying why they're there. So why are we here? Wait a minute.

Words

What symmetry do we have in letters? numbers? words? This English alphabet (capital letters) has 6 letters without an axis of symmetry, 4 with rotational symmetry – three of them through 180 degrees, one complete, 3 others with two axes of bilateral symmetry, and the rest with one axis of bilateral symmetry: 2 diagonal, 4 horizontal and 7, like us, vertical. Of the digits, 2 have two axes of bilateral symmetry, 1 has a horizontal axis, 1 has full rotational symmetry and 1 rotates through 180 degrees into another. Not much of a pattern. In fact, the distribution is just about random, as though the idea were to get the maximum variety from simple signs, which seems practical.

Words: they are produced by symmetrical organs. The shapes those organs make – the cave of 'ae', the tube of 'oo', the closed gates of 'n', the glug of 'g' – are just as bilaterally symmetrical as us, but there is no symmetry at all in words, not even 'Malayalam': play it backwards, it doesn't sound the same. They're borne on breath, spoken in time, and can't be taken back. A word on time: it seems it was thinking about right and left that led Kant to say that space and time were intuitions. Blinkers, more like. Time is a syndrome quarks may not suffer from, but we do; like speech, it is not a palindrome. It's a *fuite en avant*, the devil in the driving mirror. Symmetry is a sign of ecstasy. Make love, 'the beast with two backs' (in the words of Othello's adviser) and that's another sinuous axis of it. Make love or, better still, play football! Since while the converse goes without saying, it must be emphasized here that thoughts about symmetry or any other activity are at best irrelevant to love-making; also, the rerouting of blood from the brain during intercourse is likely to have an adverse effect on thought. On the other hand, some consideration during your next match with Hamilton (NZ) Academicals ('the beast with two forwards') as to what your opposite number thinks your next move is going to be, and vice versa, might just improve your game. Symmetries, like axioms and the line-up, are for what is settled; the operative part is asymmetric. Some verse doesn't get as far as symmetry: there's only one team on the park, triumphant in its haletotic bardic breath. Some verse can't break out of symmetry, like two collusive teams whiling away 90 minutes. Some transcends it, though, like the human face. 'Soccer isn't a matter of life and death: it's much more important than that.'

Ports of Perception

If something is apprehended on its axis, if the axis is a port of perception, any symmetry it might have would not be directly perceived. You'll see the symmetry in the shape of a leaf, but not in its colour, because you're at the end of a beam that's undergone filtration and reflection in the leaf and in your eyes. You can feel (and hear some) symmetry in forces and objects, but not in their textures, since the axis is at the meeting of (say) fingertip and surface. The same applies to olfactory receptors and taste buds, where molecules join. There aren't symmetrical smells. And smell is intimate with taste. And taste, like speech, runs along the tongue, sweet at the tip, salt on the blade, boiled broccoli at the uvula.

Are we ourselves the axes of some further symmetry, drawn towards a moment of balance, strained and used by it till we have neither shape, nor humanity, nor name? If time were a fourth dimension, desire could be a sixth sense – but it doesn't get us closer than the other five to answering that question. What desire has it doesn't want: itself, this moment, part of me. It yaws like a compass needle when the lode is on a plane it can't turn to. I want to be this, to have that, but not to have been or be had; I want to go and do things, not be gone or done in; I want to stay, I don't want left behind. All the conjugations tell the same story: desire is centrifugal, contradictory, and as absolutely time-bound as speech. What I'm after is something that does with existence what poetry does with utterance: not reduce the world to symmetries but adumbrate the patterns we're in: it's more a prayer than a power game. This spiel is mostly mineral, punctate, logical in its way. It's crystallizing outwards from the word 'symmetry'. It's about to be twisted by the word

Chirality

I can't believe that the spiral – the word itself suggests circle and parallel – isn't symmetrical. Find yourself a spiral staircase. There is a good one on Bridge Street in Glasgow, over the Glaswegian pub, I think. A steep flight of stairs from Nelson Street takes you to the circular floor of a cylindrical stairwell. A hanging stair winds widdershins up the wall. Stand at the top and look down. In fact, raise the building another ten floors to make the point quite clear. The banister spirals in towards the centre of the floor of the stairwell, though the staircase has a circular plan – which gives it infinite rotational or mirror symmetry – and in elevation, if we ignore the fact that this particular example levels out into a landing once in every full turn, it is a sine curve set on its side, which gives it two axes of symmetry for every floor it rises (one for each peak and trough of the sine curve).

You may object that I have found symmetry not in a spiral but in the plan and the elevation of a helix. Very good. What I have said is that the spiral can be analysed into two components that have symmetry. The same is true of other obvious examples: cyclones and snail shells. But before we return to specifics, a word on dimensions. For a long time I exercised my trivial imagination on quadrivial space. I tried to see what happened to a party of particles whizzing up and down the four axes (x, y, z and t) of length, breadth, depth and time. It's only this morning that I have finally realized that that's as pointless as trying to visualise quantities in their progress through a long division sum. Feynman diagrams? I'll no more see a particle in there than I'd see the newscaster's scalp if I sawed the top off my TV (and I don't have one). To me, space is nothing and nothing doesn't have a shape, but I won't be bothered by the next physicist who tells me that space-time is curved: all he means is that his co-ordinate system is warped. If he can live with that, so can I.

Dimensions

But there is still less to dimensions than meets the eye. I cannot visualize one dimension either. Judging from the problems that generations of Greek geometers had in deciding on the nature of the point – Zeno reduced it to the absurd but no-one quite reduced it to unity or set it at naught – there is no shame in that inability. John Burnet thought Leukippos had solved it with the atom, but then Burnet was writing when Rutherford (who visualised atoms as billiard balls) seemed to have done the same. Heisenberg seems to have worried at the same bone (wave or particle? verb or noun?). Worse still – put it down to stereoscopic vision if you like – I am not at all sure that I can see in two dimensions. A line always implies a space. I see nothing but surfaces and I assume, always, that there is depth to them. That is why the spiral is so obviously symmetrical. That is what painters play on: when a surface doesn't make sense the viewer looks into it. When that doesn't make sense either, stay cool: it's that twentieth century. The artist might just be making the point that I am making here: there is no point; don't trust appearances; don't trust realities either.

So if I can't see four dimensions, or one dimension or even two, then what is the point in talking of three? Dimensions are for graph paper. They set things straight: they put vision and dementia behind bars, which isn't always a bad thing, though always is a bad thing: somebody has to take a shillelagh to Occam's razor gang from time to time, and defend different interpretations of the world: a sycamore has one, morning glory has another, the black redstart has a third – to say nothing of barnacle geese, goose barnacles, beautiful hooktips etc.. In other words, respect not only what divides one realm, one science from another (crystals have no pentagonal lattice while cinquefoil plants are common) but what distinguishes each creature from the next. Name them. I do not deny the use of categories: in learning a language, for example, paradigms help distinguish *por* from *para* in Spanish, and indicate when to use which aspect of a double imperfective verb in Russian. But there are so many exceptions to the rules, and flaws in the pattern of exceptions, that you have to choose eventually either language, languages, worn stone stairs, eroded reason, most irregular in the most used words, or the practice of weeding out linguistic illogicalities and ambiguities so you can express things more clearly, make do with clarity, and miss out on symmetries that don't add up (see 'Insomnia' below).

Mirrors

Symmetry round a vertical plane didn't exist before animals. And it wasn't confused before the invention of mirrors. Reflection in water distinguished opposites: up from down, sea from sky, root from branch, sun from seed; reflection in the glass compared and confused similarities: right and left, and wrong; dexterous, gauche and sinister. They can be both similar and opposite, things of the heart, hope and despair. The intimate but unseen schism between handedness and heartedness, heart and hand, and the way that opposites rotate into similes, unsettle. There's a flat contradiction between two senses, sight and touch. Mirror imagery is not to be taken at face value, as Elizabeth Bishop shows:

Insomnia

The moon in the bureau mirror
looks out a million miles
(and perhaps with pride, at herself,
but she never, never smiles)
far and away beyond sleep, or
perhaps she's a daytime sleeper.

By the Universe deserted,
she'd tell it to go to hell,
and she'd find a body of water,
or a mirror, on which to dwell.

So wrap up care in a cobweb
and drop it down the well

into that world inverted
where left is always right,
where the shadows are really the body,
where we stay awake all night,
where the heavens are shallow as the sea
is now deep, and you love me.[1]

Writing is an up-and-down reflection: I think things up and write them down, and there is no more danger of mistaking the words for the world (though it happens), than of taking sea for sky. The cinema, though, is a back-to-front reflection, a mirror image, and film very often is mistaken for life. The mirror is neither me nor you. The word is both of us. So how were we divided?

We could start with two sets of 23 chromosomes, join them up, and follow cell division till it produce up and down, right and left, and another creature with another set of 23 to offer, but that's not really the beginning. I'll take another story. Adam was divided from the earth, Eve from Adam, settler from nomad, hairy Esau from gentle Jacob, builder from planner. Babel! The ziggurat, helical sign of division. With that kind of history between us, any communication is fraught. Clarity isn't the most important quality here, it's charity, trust that ambiguities are honest and illogicalities are true. It's an interpersonal thing and the only important axis of symmetry is the page,

I turned to symmetry hoping for help
in staking out my heart, but it's the knotted
cord itself that sets the measure.
'Quelle que soit la fécondité d'une méthode,
son office est surtout de consolidation
et, si l'on veut, de prolongement,
mais sur un terrain préalablement fixé.

---

[1] Elizabeth Bishop, *Complete Poems* (London, 1991), p. 70

Elle met en ordre l'acquis et, ce faisant,
comble les lacunes et exploite les percées,
mais elle n'inaugure rien d'essentiellement neuf'.[1]

Mozart kicked away the ladder Bach had come up by,
and I've had enough of broken chords and scales.
There's one way and one way only to go about it:
find an angel and pick a fight.

---

[1] Robert Blanché, *l'Axiomatique* (Paris, PUF, 1995 ; 6th ed. 1980) :
'However fertile a method may be, its function is essentially that of
consolidation and, perhaps, extension, but in a predetermined field. It puts
discoveries in order, filling gaps and making use of advances, but it does
not inaugurate anything that is essentially new.'

Seven Rhymes

For a delicious moment, in a cornershop on Orkney, I wondered what this arty snap of Manhattan was doing in the postcard rack:

Yet no one would mistake this next one for the jetties of Stromness:

Which goes to show that some connections are non-commutable. Variations on that archetypal bar chart have been declined and conjugated so exhaustively that you could see it almost anywhere. As though the Manhattan skyline was hard-wired into our brain, in the way that Steven Pinker imagines Chomsky's grammar to be.

The Orkney shot reminds us that the great skyscrapers *were* jetties of a sort: the helicopter from JFK that used to land on the PanAm building; airships docking at Lakehurst in New Jersey. And New York has waterside jetties of its own. Not like Stromness, though. The ships of Franklin and Cook took on water there, and it has the best, the most forlorn and poignant local museum in existence. Or thereabouts. And George Mackay-Brown used to live there, in a little council flat on the main street, which was where I asked him about the martyrdom of Saint Magnus. On my first trip to the Orkneys I had read his *Orkney Tapestry*, and noticed a few odd coincidences with the martyrdom of Saints Boris and Gleb, of Kievan Rus'.

Boris, and then Gleb, had agreed to meet on an island unarmed and parley with a kinsman about the division of their kingdom. So had Magnus. On the way to the meeting, Gleb's horse came a cropper, and he knew he was going to his death. On a calm sea, a wave broke over Magnus's boat, with the same premonition. In both cases, the wicked kinsman landed with a band of armed retainers. The good men prayed and wept before the fact. In the end, Gleb and later Magnus forgave their executioner before the deed was done. Gleb's executioner was his cook, who is named in the text. Magnus's executioner, also identified by name, was his wicked cousin's cook. Each hagiography ends with a list of amazing miracles and an account of the translation of the relics to bigger and bigger churches. The remains of Magnus, cloven skull and all, are kept in St Magnus Cathedral on Orkney. The problem is that the killings of Boris and Gleb, well documented and historically corroborated, took place a century before the martyrdom of Magnus.

I couldn't make much sense of it. Mackay-Brown heard me out in frosty skepticism, and gave me a little reading list that I've just rediscovered in my copy of *A Historical Russian Reader*, edited by

J. Fennell and D. Obolensky (Oxford, OUP, 1969). His list included *The Orkneyinga Saga*. The copy I bought, edited by J. Anderson in 1873 (James Thin, The Mercat Press, 1981), lay on my shelf half-read for twenty years.

The essence of both hagiographies is clear enough: the triumph of the meek over the strong, and the establishment of a new set of values in a way that could harness that strength. For warriors, that was the fortitude of martyrdom. In spite of my huge respect for Shestov, I read the story of Isaac in a similarly conventional way: it is the victory of a higher form of religion, and commemoration of that victory in a powerful story (in Abraham's case, the abolition of human sacrifice). But what has intrigued me, off and on, is not the essence but the details: why the cook? Perhaps because the cook was more of a cardinal character then than now. Painters mixed their pigments as cooks condiments. And look at the violence in cookery: 'Take one capon; hack it into gobbities'. My guess is that recipes for torture and maiming were swapped with the same glee as those for capon kebab. But all the other facts? Surely there is some direct connection between the two stories.

Well, as it happens, there are two. On the web, experts turn up only general links; but a simple answer was sitting on my shelf, in the two books I have just mentioned. The Varangians who caused incidental ructions in the story of Boris and Gleb were Scandinavian mercenaries hired by the martyrs' brother Yaroslav. And according to the Saga, they included at least one Earl of Orkney: Rognvald. Here's the sequence of events: Vladimir of Rus', who had established Orthodox Christianity in his kingdom (after murdering his brother) set his twelve sons up in different parts of the country: Boris in Rostov, Gleb in Murom, Yaroslav in Novgorod, Svyatopolk in Pinsk, and so on. When Vladimir died in 1015, Svyatopolk promptly murdered his half-brothers Boris and Gleb. Yaroslav made his move from Novgorod and – to cut to the happy ending – removed Svyatopolk and reunited Rus' by 1019. Rognvald, who went on to rule Orkney together with his brother, St Magnus's grandfather (until the latter murdered him), served in Novgorod for some years, returning west around 1031. He may therefore have been acquainted with the martyrs' brother Yaroslav, who was, ultimately, his employer.

So one reason for the similarity in the hagiographies is that fratricide was just one of those things that big men got up to on short winter days. The other is that Magnus's family, torn as it was between the old gods and the Christ, shuttling between Russia and Orkney, will surely have known about Boris and Gleb the martyrs. Orcadians in Russian employ will have seen the brothers' cult grow over the years until their relics were translated for the fourth and last time, on the centenary of their death, to the new church in Vyshgorod; this was done with great pomp in the presence of many foreign guests on Saturday the first of May, the second week of Easter 1115, a fortnight and two days – if the chronicles are synchronized – after the murder of St Magnus. The killer, if he had hurried, could have made it to the celebration; after all, he wasn't averse to the idea of a pilgrimage – he certainly went to Jerusalem later in life, and brought back holy relics (a paradoxical trade, when you think of it: supply pushed up demand, since those who were guilty of breaking martyrs' bones made amends by purchasing more that they hadn't broken). And pilgrimage was already a tradition among the earls of Orkney: the fratricide who was grandfather to the murderer *and* to the martyr had gone on pilgrimage to Rome with his friend, the Scottish King, Macbeth.

2

The Roman fresco below is in the Museo Archeologico in Naples. It is entitled Sappho probably because that was the only woman with a pen people could think of. A pen and a book – so we are into the Christian era already. It's a Neapolitan woman, so probably a Greek speaker. Once again, I'm not sure that the connection is commutable: one look at this photograph of Maria João Pires by Patrick de Mervelec on a Schubert CD and I thought of the painting. But would the musician be flattered at the comparison with this face whose features struggle towards symmetry as a thought lurches towards formulation? Not sure.

As with the two hagiographies there are arresting coincidences: the diffused lighting, the bangle earrings, the shape of the hair (in spite of the Roman hair net), the angle of the head, and the uncertain direction of the gaze. But once again, the essence is clear as day: this – the fresco and the photo – is the artist as a beautiful woman. And she is looking blindly for beauty itself. The fact that Pires is Portuguese transports the image from Naples to Lisbon and the Atlantic, like Domenico Scarlatti. The vivacity of southern baroque, heard from a mile off shore, has the cold undertow that affected Schubert.

3

This is the only unambiguously deliberate rhyme of the seven. It is unexpected, accurate and witty. Fortunately, the Basel Art Museum[1] has kept these two paintings by Konrad Witz together. They were painted around 1450. (At the other end of Switzerland, in the delegates' bar of the Palais des Nations in Geneva, a huge mural depicts the same two saints, though the visual pun is not maintained.)

The lady looks on as St George turns from profile on his steed to fillet carefully the dragon he exists for. (He was a real, fifth-century martyr, but the dragon-slaying was grafted onto his CV around the millennium). In the other picture, the poor man in distress looks on as St Martin, with the same *ébrillade*, accurately slices his own cloak in two. I seem to recall that the Vatican did away with St George not too long ago by putting him in limbo with the unbaptised babies and then abolishing limbo: he had been too closely in cahoots with Perseus, Andromeda, Prometheus and other Greeks of the wrong type. And how could you canonize someone for slaying a beast that never was? St Martin, though, really did slay the dragon that haunted the Old Testament and the new: mammon, and other avatars of the dragon's hoard. As Augustine's mentor Ambrose put it brutally – all wealth is the fruit of injustice. One Polynesian king was asked why his people used pigs as legal tender rather than something more portable and less perishable,

---

[1] http://80.74.155.18/eMuseumPlus?service–home .

such as cowries. He explained that once you had a certain number of pigs, all you could do was slaughter them and have a big feast for your friends and neighbours. If it weren't for that, then some people would soon accumulate too much, and great inequity would result. If you don't slay those beasts then by and by there is a hoard and a dragon to be dealt with. Which is what St Martin did: he shared his cloak with a beggar.

4

I started listening to the *Well-Tempered Clavier* when I was living in Argenteuil, already onto the *St Matthew Passion* but still a Bob Dylan fanatic. Not a bad adolescent role model, sardonic Bob, but as big a fake as those he denounced so eloquently. Usually trying to look younger and sound older, to talk poor and be rich. Soon after that I would finally see him in concert, at Earl's Court and at Blackbush where, as he was singing a mean version of *Masters of War*, two police helicopters took off behind the stage, their trajectories crossing in the night air, and I remembered those rumours about Bob chipping in to the Yom Kippur War effort. Which would have been fine if he hadn't written that song. I still like *Watching the River Flow*, probably the first thing of his I heard more or less as it came out. So, in Rueil Malmaison one night I was, for reasons that escape me, alone in someone else's flat and fairly incandescent with rage. Enjoying it. I put on *Highway 61 Revisited* (Dylan's version of the story of Isaac was so much better than Leonard Cohen's), but that couldn't hold it. There weren't many records there that I had time for; I put on the *Well-Tempered Clavier* and realized, with a tremendous jolt, that this music could channel all the anger I would ever muster, and take it in its stride. This music, as I was to find out over time, could absorb just about anything I threw at it. The only reason I ever listened to anything else again was in fear that, as in Stevens's *Un anglais meurt à Florence*, I would find it die on me one day. I had to give it a context to flourish in.

Whenever I hear the 13th prelude I think of Pushkin's 'K ***', and vice versa. In this case, the association is fully commutable. And I have wondered why, and whether there was anything to it. In the Zeitgeist, Pushkin was closer to Mozart than to Bach, and he himself, in *Mozart and Salieri*, nudged the parallel as far as decency would allow. He was one of the pure artists who, perhaps wisely, never mixed his poetry with religion. Still, this prelude, *andantino, delicato e semplice*, innocent of sonorous theology, is Mozart foretold by Bach. And Pushkin's poem – which must be the best thing ever written for a keepsake book – is in the same spirit. What's weird is that it is in the same shape too. I would try to translate it, but even if I succeeded, you wouldn't believe that the triteness of the imagery and the flatness of the vocabulary was his not mine. And given how obviously the shifts in tone are signalled, you wouldn't believe the same man could manipulate rhyme and varied repetition with such simple mastery.

The lyric is in six stanzas; according to Siglind Bruhn[1] the prelude is in six parts too. Let's consider them together (Bruhn's analysis of Bach (in bold) with mine of Pushkin). For Pushkin (all in italics), lower case letters show the rhyme scheme and upper case denotes thematic recurrence (lines 2-4 of the first stanza recur in the 5th; the latter couplet of the 2nd stanza recurs at the same place in the 3rd, and the same trait links stanzas 4 and 6). Here we go.

I : bars 1-6m: tonic to dominant (F# major to C# major). *abab, A: Bright memory of first meeting the woman addressed in the poem.*

II : bars 6m-12d: modulation to the relative minor of the tonic (D# minor). *cbcb, B: In gloomy times thereafter he still remembered her voice, her face.*

III : bars 12-15m: modulation to the relative minor of the dominant (A# minor) *cbcb, B: But the years passed, and he forgot about her.*

IV : bars 15m-18m: modulation to the relative minor of the subdominant (G# minor). *dede, C: He lived in a dull, depressed, alienated routine.*

V : bars 18m-24m: modulation back to the tonic. *abab, A: Then his soul awoke, and he recalled her again*

VI : bars 24m-30: tonic confirmed. *afaf, C: The depression is reversed, and the good of life and love return to him. The initial feminine rhyme is confirmed in triumph, with a new motif, the 'f' rhyme, derived from the 'e' rhyme in stanza 4; the 'e' rhyme features 'lyubvi', the genitive of 'lyubov'', 'love' in the nominative form, the tonic, as it were.*

---

[1] http://www-personal.umich.edu/~siglind/text.htm .

There is a constant to and fro between the male 'I' and the female 'you', never coinciding with the regular masculine and feminine rhymes. In the Bach prelude, the right hand states the theme, but it is the left hand that marks the beat.

There is a similar, almost naïve switch from dominant to relative minor, with 3rd and 4th parts modulating farther and farther from the tonic in a short space, then in the 5th part a sunrise return to tonic, while in the 6th – with arpeggios lent to Beethoven's *Moonlight Sonata* – a trace of the minor mood underlines the confirmation of the bright, initial theme, which is the simplest of broken chords.

It would be possible to use the Pushkin poem as a voice-over to the prelude, particularly since both are very short. But it might sound too much like Gounod's *Ave Maria*.

5

We leave Bach's 13th prelude for Rilke's 5th elegy. Pagan as Pushkin, religious as Bach – not a happy mix with all those angels and all the dead; it's so late Roman that I have to bring on St Augustine (a contemporary of Saints Martin and George). Here he is mocking the gods of the marriage bed:

> The god Jugatinus is brought in when a man and a woman are united in the 'yoke' (*iugum*) of marriage. So far, so good. But the bride has to be escorted home. The god Domiducus is employed to 'lead her home' (*domum ducere*). To install her in the house, the god Domitius sees to her 'going home' (*domum ire*). The goddess Manturna is called in as well, to see that she will 'remain' (*manere*) with her husband. What else is needed? Should we not show consideration for human modesty, and let the sexual desire of flesh and blood achieve the rest, without violation of the secrets of modesty? Why fill the bridal chamber with a mob of divinities, when even the bridal escort retires? And what is the purpose of so crowding it? That the thought of the presence of the gods should make the couple more concerned to preserve decency? Not at all. It is to ensure that with their cooperation, there shall be no difficulty in ravishing the virginity

of a girl who feels the weakness of her sex and is terrified by the strangeness of her situation. For here are the goddess Vierginensis, and Father Subigus (to subdue – *subigere*) and Mother Prema (to press – *premere*) and the goddess Pertunda (to pierce – *pertundere*) as well as Venus and Priapus. What does all this mean? If the husband finds the job altogether too much for him and needs divine assistance, would not one god, or one goddess be enough? Do you mean to tell me that Venus alone would not be adequate? She is, they say, so called (among other reasons) because 'not without violence' (*vi non sine*) can a woman be robbed of her virginity! If there is any modesty in human beings (there seems to be none in the gods!), I feel sure that the belief in the presence of so many divinities of both sexes to urge on the business in hand would so embarrass the couple as to quench the enthusiasm of the one and stiffen the reluctance of the other.[1]

But Rilke doesn't hear him:

Angel: suppose there's a place we know nothing about, and there,
on some indescribable carpet, lovers showed all that here
they're for ever unable to manage – their daring
lofty figures of heart-flight,
their towers of pleasure, their ladders
long since, where ground never was, just quiveringly
propped by each other, - suppose they could manage it there,
would not the dead then fling their last, their for ever reserved,
ever-concealed, unknown to us, ever-valid
coins of happiness down before the at last
truthfully smiling pair on the quietened carpet?[2]

For the good of the couple, I hope the dead in question do not include the Polynesian king quoted above.

There is a cyclical progression in these matters, akin to the cycles of iconoclasm. Augustine reduces the Roman pantheon to unity,

---

[1] *City of God*, book 6, chapter 9; finely translated by David Knowles for Penguin Books, 1972.
[2] Translated by J.Leishman and S.Spender (New York, 1939).

which Mediterranean Catholics then clog with saints. The Lutherans make a further clean sweep, as Gautama had done to the Hindu gods, but the Tantric Buddhists have brought them back. And then in the Ramayana bas-relief in Angkor Wat, some deity demonstrates the perfect freeze-frame golf swing with his sword and so becomes the hero with a hundred arms, just as Shiva had become the god with six, Tamil sculptors having to manage the resultant chubby clefts on either shoulder, in their magnificent bronzes. Thus art is misconstrued by theology.

The Buddha would reduce the heavenly circus to a minimum, but Augustine would set that minimum at one, not zero. I'd maybe stretch it to two. Or, like the Orthodox, just a few essential icons, idealized people or personified ideals, for it must be abstract. But then soon enough, from the bus-station comings and goings of a Moscow church, you find yourself in the spiritual jumble sale of a south Indian temple; it is on the same, vast landmass after all, the same old ladies and regular pilgrims and holy fools; the cloth of gold comes off the priest to drape the statues. In the wreaths of incense you might not notice that the priest has no clothes, like the King he worships.

And so minimalism emerges, once again, from Byzantine finery, in the form of Suprematism, though the standard academic view seems to miss the link, and looks for its meaning in geometry and the avant garde.

There was the Black Square, yes, and then there was the Black Cross:

And there was this next one, because skewed as it is, the Malevich cross is a quote or steal from St Gregory's or any number of other stoles, including those painted in icons of Saints Boris and Gleb.

:

Suprematism was indeed a precursor of minimalism, but it was a child of the icons.

It is possible that, like Aleksandr Blok in the same régime and place, Malevich was discrete about Christian implications of his work. He did, after all, want it to survive. I'll go too far, for the sake of argument, and suggest that Malevich was painting what the master icon painters would have left to their apprentices: geometric designs on apparel. As though a modern painter were unworthy or unable to do what the icon painters had done. Did any painting in that twentieth century achieve the focus or serenity of an icon? Did any of the arts? Architecture, perhaps: guided light on grey concrete.

6

A poster of Malevich's 'An Englishman in Moscow' was on my wall for maybe twenty years, from the time I bought it at the Beaubourg exhibition in 1978. It was cheerful, colourful and weird; it showed I'd seen the exhibition and asserted my allegiance to that phase of Russian art that was quickly put down by the revolution it had longed for. It had replaced, for trivial reasons, an equally weird and wonderful image from Bosch that had accompanied me through adolescence like a transitional toy, allowing an image of Christ to be an object not of reverence but of contemplation.

I do not remember many dreams. Of those I do, I pay attention to the ones that clearly are not simply a digestion of the previous day's impressions; these are rare. Within that number are a few that refer to events that turn out to occur the following day: once a bombing, once an earthquake, usually trivia. I look for an explanation; when I can't find one I'll maybe put it down to coincidence, or forget it, or doubt my memory: the usual techniques to allow me to sleep on both ears, as the French say. It's a survival skill. But when I saw that photo on the front page of *El País* on 30 September 2002, I knew that I'd have trouble filing this one away. Here is the photograph:

And there is that painting. The photograph was taken in 2003; the painting was made 500 years earlier, 1500 years after the scene it depicts (what a jump from Konrad Witz, who had painted only fifty years earlier). The photograph was taken in Jericho, fifteen miles down the Roman road from Jerusalem.

Both images are close cropped around faces and hands that flare on a brackish background along with a few violent bursts of red and blue (in the photo red cloth top right, blue cuff bottom left; in the painting, four patches of flame red, three of cerulean. Huge physical and emotional energy in both: look at the chin of that foreshortened face, beneath the cross; top centre in photo.

The wicked thief painted in left profile, bottom right, echoes a bodyguard, left profile bottom right of the photo. On the left, in right profile, a man with a white moustache touches Arafat's sleeve; we see both his hands. In the painting, on the left, right profile, he is remonstrating with Christ; we see one of his hands reaching towards him.

Behind the forehead of the wicked thief, a man in a wizard's hat is looking down towards his chest; he might be sending a text message to the man who looks similarly absorbed, in the top left of the photograph.

Behind Arafat, a man in uniform, his arms outspread, grasping a wooden spar, is seen in right profile. In the painting at that place, the right profile shows a caricature Roman nose: a civilian, but he was in command of the troops. Arafat too is in uniform; the painting caricatures him in a soldier's helmet, on the right.

In the photo, of course, he wears the famous kaffiyeh that so many students in the West have taken up. It is held in place by a double band of rope; in the painting, Christ's head is uncovered, but he wears a double band of thorns. The cloth, that moments earlier had been applied to his face to wipe away his sweat, is being taken way by Veronica; it bears an image that Eastern Christianity would take up and cherish, which looks directly at you; no one else in the painting does. In the photograph, the only face looking into the lens is that of a second bodyguard whose features – though without the same serenity – resemble those of Bosch's Christ who, eyes closed, abstracted, grasps that long plank of wood; we see both hands.

Apart from hands and faces, clothing and one length of linen, that plank is the only artifact to be seen in the painting. The same is true of the photo. We see Arafat's right hand only, and it grasps the wooden spar.

7

Just as *Chevrefeuille* was based on an episode from Tristan and Isold, just as the *Testament of Cresseid* was written as an appendix to *Troilus and Criseyde*, which ultimately drew on Homer, so was Blok's *Twelve* calqued on a scene from Dante, whose *Inferno* was based on a sketch map in the apocryphal gospel of Nicodemus. (See part III, 'The Harrowing of Hell and Resurrection'.)

It would be nice to believe that we see what we see, but we always see thanks to someone else. It would be good to believe what those people tell us they see, but we have to check. Blok's sighting of

Christ up ahead of the rough red guards came not too long after the Angel of Mons, a retrospective mass hallucination that conflated a short story about St George with an account of the Battle of Mons.

Blok wanted to believe, or he believed, that the mayhem was not the end of the world but the beginning of something others would live to see.

The authors of the account of the descent into hell believed, and wanted others to believe, that the pathetic death of Christ was not the end of the world but the winning of the war. To that end, they located the last battle of Calvary in a cosmic strategy Christ had hardly mentioned, but that every Christian knows.

In the sciences, good metaphors are shrunk to technical terms; in religion they get codified as articles of faith. But the descent into hell was a metaphor for what? For the resurrection recounted flatly and with plausible inconsistencies in the last chapter of three of the four gospels. That is the stone wall we run into with Blok and Dante.

To recap. The hagiography of Boris and Gleb, and that of Magnus, works as an account of how a new interpretation of honour can replace an old one. In order to appreciate that, the reader is not obliged to share the belief of the protagonists (killer or martyr), though both are to be taken seriously. The Pires / Sappho is only a rhyme: the simple pleasure of surprise and recognition. In the St Martin / St George parallel, the simple rhyme has been set to the purpose of honouring valiant deeds – especially that of St Martin, because the simple sharing of wealth, especially for those brought up in the grasping Western tradition, is quite heroic. In Pushkin and Bach we have another simple rhyme and in this case, pure art (remember that, in publishing it, Bach described this first set of preludes and fugues as musical exercises; they are not religious pieces). The 'deity' mentioned in the Pushkin poem is in the nature of the Muse. Readers such as Blok or Solovyov are free to interpret that in a mystical way; they are equally free not to.

We seem to be approaching a conclusion here that rhyme is art and etymology – religion. A rhyme works if the reader acknowledges the resemblance, the chime. There's no need to agree on a system of values: you can hear rhymes in a language you don't know. But if etymology is to work, the buy-in is compulsory. You must assent to the etymology of 'etymology', which asserts its own origin in the origin it seeks. Accept that, and you join a community of faith in the stupendous tautology of the dictionary. Reject a strong ontological consensus, and you're in for trouble, like St Magnus – unless, like Malevich, you keep your head down. Thus Suprematist squares and crosses just happen to resemble the stole of an Orthodox saint, in which case they are pure art; or they derive from those icons, in which case they conceal a humble religious subtext.

Augustine and Rilke contemplate the same accretion of shades around human acts, though with opposite attitudes. Clearly I side with Augustine, though I wouldn't rail against the supremely strange accretions and proliferations in the *Garden of Earthly Delights*, where Bosch seems to have had privileged access to the shenanigans of macrophages and killer cells some centuries before the invention of the appropriate microscope. But his greatness is in putting humanity on the slide, bringing it into looming focus in 'Carrying the Cross'.

I had thought the seventh rhyme was Blok and Dante, but that is etymology because Blok's poem is deliberately based on the Inferno. The last rhyme is Bosch and Blok. There are eighteen figures in the painting, nineteen faces. In Blok – a score of figures in a white-out. Both portray us as a frighteningly violent breed that only a Christ could redeem, starting with the good thief, top right in Bosch, clearly scared to death.

But then rhyme isn't reason, and the Bosch painting rhymes also with that photograph where people are ugly, sure, but not that bad. They get by with a figurehead in place of a saviour. We'll clutch at any spar when the ship goes down; they won't all float.

Part II

Mungo's Hat and Maxwell's Demon

What I was seeking, in part I, was a way of thinking that offers some alternative, especially in an era where we are being told that it's either status quo or the apocalypse. Perhaps (as Broome acknowledges) that goes beyond the scope of philosophy. It's maybe for a community, a culture to reflect on. Hugh MacDiarmid, of course, would have plumped for apocalypse. Just before his death he argued against the 1979 referendum on Scottish devolution, which he saw as offering much too little. Its rejection, though, disappointed some in his grandchildren's generation who for a decade thereafter put more into the long-term of Scottish culture than into the bleak short-term of Scottish politics, which in any case didn't know what was about to hit it. One of the results of this cultural effort was Cairns Craig's four-volume *History of Scottish Literature*, which remains a good platform from which to view its languages, traditions and cross-purposes until the moment when prose took over from verse. It shows the European bent of our culture that was for centuries its only constant. Flashback, then, to the view from 1988.

My first five years were spent in Cessnock naming all the cars on Paisley Road. Then along to Crookston, reading *Here We Go*, *Janet and John*, *Scottish Catechism of Christian Doctrine*, 'To a Mouse', 'To a Louse', 'To a Mountain Daisy', 'Oor Wullie', the *Hotspur*, *Bunty*, *People's Friend*, at seven deciding it was time for books without pictures, starting at the left with *Tom Brown's Schooldays*, *Little Women*, and a hundred pages of some endless Dickensian thing before going back with some relief to Biggles and Enid Blyton until it was time for long trousers, Agatha Christie and Alistair MacLean, commended for his large vocabulary by our English teacher, a Sydney Carton lookalike and bitter antagonist of

Samuel Beckett who gave us Macaulay's *Essays on Warren Hastings*, for at least two years: it was one of the few books there were thirty-eight copies of, and that was because no one, no one would have wanted to pinch it.

That was why I did languages in the end: when you've learnt irregular verbs that's them out of the way; Warren Hastings just kept coming back. At any rate this is how I remember it – but although my copious diaries of the time record that on a given day I had meat round, chips and peas for tea and afterwards read a book, they don't lend to specify what the book was. Sydney Carton confiscated a friend's brother's copy of Six Glasgow Poems by Tom Leonard 'Thaht big shite wiz dayniz nut' – which was from another planet in any case. That was about it: I was at Oxford before I saw *The Cheviot, the Stag and the Black, Black Oil* on the box and started going to the theatre. But it wasn't till I got round to reading *A Drunk Man* after failing to find my way north out of Inversnaid that I got curious about Scottish literature. What is it? Is it what Scottish people read? The only book mentioned in Barbour's Bruce is Ferambrace, a Charlemagne romance Bruce declaims to his men while waiting for the rest of his army to swim or be rowed across Loch Lomond. A later king, James I, knew his Boethius, Gower and Chaucer; Wyntoun knew about monopedes and other monsters from the Mediaeval Id (I've got three odd volumes of his chronicle: they're stamped Trinity College Church of Scotland and they smell like Glasgow Cathedral). And so on. While the Gaelic poets were drawing on Irish tradition, Dunbar was reading Chaucer. Much later, Ramsay is editing Dunbar and returning to Scots, and the gentle shepherd hero of his play reads Shakespeare and Ben Jonson, Drummond of Hawthornden and Cowley. There's good verse in that play:

> Speak on, speak thus, an' still my grief
> Haud up a heart that's sinking under
> Thae fears ...

Soon after that James Thomson sets out his pantheon in 'Summer' and there is not a Scottish poet or philosopher there; his sole attempt at emulating Ramsay shows he has difficulty in writing Scots – even though, as Mary Jane Scott shows, he was a good,

Scottish Latinist.[1] With Burns we are back to Ramsay's fusion of English and Scots (volume II is excellent on strategic use of English by Scottish poets), though here – for the first time? – is work sustained by Scottish tradition, from the recent past of Fergusson and Ramsay, through Montgomerie to Hary; Burns wrote, 'The story of Wallace poured a Scottish prejudice in my veins which will boil along there till the flood-gates of life shut in eternal rest'.[2] M. P. McDiarmid makes big claims for The Wallace in volume I which I could hardly dispute: all I have here in Geneva is a version published in 1722 and subsequently purchased in a jumble sale by my mum. I quote at random:

> And (Wallace) cleverly so laboured their buff,
> Their armour did not signify a snuff.
> The Scotsman there behav'd extremely well,
> As the poor South'ron sensibly did feel:
> Then all the English left the field and fled;
> And Sir John Morton he was killed dead.

That, believe it or not, was the version that inspired Burns. I've been on the lookout for someone, anyone, whose chosen reading was Scottish Literature as we can infer it from *HSL* – which never troubles to define it. Hugh Miller quotes casually from The Bruce, and visits Thomson's grave, but only because it is in Shenstone's garden. In the end there is only this:

> As for literature, he read the classic poets, to be sure, and the Epithalamium of Georgius Buchanan, and Arthur Johnston's Psalms, of a Sunday; and the Deliciae Poetarum Scotorum, and Sir David Lindsay's Works, and Barbour's Bruce, and Blind Harry's Wallace, and the Gentle Shepherd, and the Cherry and the Slae'...

The Sunday reading of a pedantic old Jacobite in *Waverley*.

---

[1] *The History of Scottish Literature*, general editor Cairns Craig (Aberdeen University Press, 1987-1988), Vol. II, p. 85 [from here on a Roman numeral followed by an Arabic is a reference to *HSL*]).
[2] *The Poems and Songs of Robert Burns* ed. by James Kinsley, p. 1078.

What the Scots write, then, is not what the Scots read. The country is small, and linguistically divided. The reading and the writing overlap, but not enough, not on a big enough scale, to get a more or less autonomous literature going – like English or French or Spanish at different times. Everything is dispersed; there is no ready-made tradition. Few Scottish writers hit the ground running and many just hit the ground. The winners make literature, the rest are history, leafmould for later growth. Each writer has to find his or her own traditions – in history, in oral tradition or elsewhere. For this reason cultural and historical background are especially important in study of our literature, and *HSL* is very strong in this respect. It is not quite so strong on 'elsewhere': in a small country, especially if it is culturally subdivided, individual genres tend to overshadow the national literature – it's a literary version of the economic situation in Switzerland, where three or four Swiss multinationals have turnovers larger than the national budget; do you describe the economy in national or corporate terms? Neither should be overlooked, but proper assessment of both requires more knowledge than an individual could manage. This is an interesting situation for the writer (the share dealer) and an impossible one for the critic (economist). *HSL* by definition concentrates on the national view of our literature. In so doing it raises questions of genre worth looking at.

The first is literary history itself. There is something disingenuous about literary histories, which examine other texts and contexts but do not in general subject themselves to the same scrutiny. An analogy may be Thames & Hudson's *World of Art* paperbacks, that present paintings and suggest interpretations, but pass over in silence the composition of the books themselves, the pickling of images, subtraction of texture, addition of context, and removal of any autonomy the work might have had on the wall. I presume that in both cases the justification would be that the books are not designed as things in themselves but as guides for other things – Climbing in Scotland, handholds and techniques for difficult passages, or, if the subject is a text last published in Leyden in 1742, lush illustrations and first-hand accounts: it's the *National Geographic* experience. You can almost smell the dentist's waiting room. The objection to that justification, of course, is that literary histories are things in themselves as well, built for purposes that may or may not accord with the purposes of the authors they discuss, The Guggenheim art gallery in New York was built by Frank Lloyd Wright, who was rumoured to have despised the decorative arts. The visitor begins at the top of the building and descends a helical ramp lined with paintings. Because the floor is sloping it is inconvenient to stop for any length of time in front of a painting. The viewer is kept moving by gravity, and the eye tends to follow the suave lines of the building – which is thus designed to display not paintings, but itself. There is no such grand subversion here, especially since the *HSL* is the work of many hands, but the genre of literary history arose, in one sense, as a justification of British imperialism, and it leaves no tome unturned.

I'll return to that, but first I would like to consider alternative openings. An odd one is Switzerland, which has roughly the same population as Scotland, four (or so) literary languages, one of them Romansh, spoken by about one per cent of the population, in the high valleys to the east, which makes it the demographic equivalent of Gaelic. Writers in each of these languages are consciously and definitely Swiss; as in Scotland, there is the phenomenon of promotion, whereby a good Genevan author writing in French becomes known as a French author (Phillipe Jacottet, for example), but they cope with that more or less as the Scots do. The curious thing, though, is that there seems to be no notion of a single Swiss literature: the Genevans are suspicious not only of cultural colonisation by the French, but also and equally of linguistic colonisation by the German-speaking Swiss. Imagine the Scottish Gaels looking only to Ireland, the Orcadians to Norway, English speakers to England and Scots speakers nowhere in a union that is political but not cultural; for Switzerland, in contrast to Scotland, is a state without a literature.

The most venerable type of literary history is that of the Rig Veda and the Bible, where a collection of texts is accumulated, pruned and approved. Commentaries are kept separate. In the *HSL* we have the commentaries, but too often the texts themselves are not available: a lot of important ones were last issued before the First World War, by the Scottish Texts Society, which caters only for specialists in any case. Try and find the poems of David Lindsay or Gavin Douglas in a bookshop. Try and find W.S. Graham or Hugh MacDiarmid, for that matter. Things must improve, though: if Cairns Craig can produce something on the scale of *HSL* in a short time, then old texts can surely be reproduced more quickly still. Then, in happy contradiction of what I have just written about Switzerland, *l'Age d'Homme* publishes, for the benefit of French speakers, cheap paperbacks of modern Swiss literature in French and in translation from German and Italian.

Another approach is exemplified by Vissarion Belinsky, who was the first to acclaim Gogol and Lermontov, who wrote the earliest full-scale study of Pushkin's work, and who helped Dostoevsky and Tyutchev at the start of their careers. He lived by and for his work, prospecting poetry and prose for answers to his questions: is there a Russian literature? What is it for? What is the function of the writer/citizen? Of the intelligentsia? He lived in Petersburg when great things were being written, when a literature was being born, so the result is not prestigious assertion of culture but urgent questioning of it. George Davie argues that philosophy has been the lynchpin of Scottish culture, though in his notes on MacDiarmid he observes that the vital thinking is not always done by professional philosophers, and alludes to the work on artificial intelligence now being done by psychologists. But the vital questions are in natural intelligence and human responsibility. Over the last half-century, for the first time, all Scots have gained access to the heritage of the entire country – as *HSL* shows clearly. This may be like the close of *One Hundred Years of Solitude*, where someone discovers the aboriginal history of Macondo with its prediction of doom just as the place collapses about his ears; or it may be that something is beginning, in which case those vital questions have to be asked, by critics.

Literary history was an eighteenth-century invention. In 1744 James Thomson sings:

> Happy Britannia! where the Queen of Arts,
> Inspiring vigour, Liberty, abroad
> Walks unconfined even to thy farthests cots,

And scatters plenty with unsparing hand ...
Full are thy cities with the sons of art;
And trade and joy, in every busy street,
Mingling are heard: even Drudgery himself,
As at the car he sweats, or, dusty, hews
The palace stone, looks gay.

In 'The Castle of Indolence' happy Drudgery has been dubbed Sir Industry:

Then towns he quickened by mechanic arts,
And bade the fervent city glow with toil;
Bade social commerce raise renowned marts,
Join land to land, and marry soil to soil,
Unite the poles, and without bloody spoil
Bring home of either Ind the gorgeous stores;
Or, should despotic rage the world embroil,
Bade tyrants tremble on remotest shores,
While oer the encircling deep Britannia's thunder roars.

Without bloody spoil. The shallowness of this view becomes even more apparent in comparison with, say, Adam Smith. (*The Wealth Of Nations*, end of Book 1,1). In 1751, as Robert Crawford tells us,

Adam Smith became the first person to give an official course in English that dealt with the technique and appreciation of modern writers in that language as well as in the classical tongues. Hugh Blair, a Church of Scotland minister who from 1762 became Professor of Rhetoric and Belles Lettres at Edinburgh University, was in effect the world's first professor of English Literature. He built his lectures on Smith's work ... The enterprise of Smith and Blair was to enable the 'provincial' Scots to engage with the culture of England on that culture's own ground.[1]

The seventeenth century made the literature and the Empire, the eighteenth rationalised them. Language, literature and life were put on file, and although Scots made these fields their own in the eighteenth and nineteenth centuries, there is nothing about James Murray's *Oxford English Dictionary* or the Edinburgh-based and

---

[1] 'Ecclefechan and the Stars', *London Review of Books*, 21 January 1988.

edited *Encyclopaedia Britannica* in *HSL*, and nothing about histories of literature.

The Encyclopaedia is the most transparent of the three new genres, but the dictionary is no more objective than history of literature, and at times no less consciously literary. The histories started to appear in book form towards the end of the eighteenth century. Edwin Morgan's list: Thomas Warton, *History of English Poetry from the eleventh to the eighteenth Century* (1781); Dr Johnson *Lives of the Poets*; Hazlitt *Lectures on the English Poets* (1818); Taine, *Histoire de la littérature anglaise* (1864, trans. 1871); in Scotland A. Campbell, *Introduction to the History of Poetry in Scotland* (1799); J. Sibbald, *Chronicle of Scottish Poetry* (1802); D. Irving, *The Lives of the Scottish Poets* (1810), *Lives of Scottish Writers* (1839), and *The History of Scottish Poetry* (1861). Dissenting voices could not drown out Britannia. The Empire was a mammoth project, big enough for anyone to get lost in - and, not knowing whether they were the victors or the vanquished, the Scots got lostest. There's a nice illustration of this in 'Exile and Empire' (Ill. 416): A minor character (in *Tom Cringle's Log*), Don Ricardo, is revealed as being Scottish by birth and upbringing but Spanish in his identification with society in Cuba; yet, 'in his mountain retreat, sole master, his slaves in attendance on him, he was once more an Englishman, in externals, as he always was at heart, and Richie Cloche, from the Lang Toon of Kirkaldy, shone forth in all his glory as the kind-hearted landlord'. James Murray's autobiography is called *Caught in the Web of Words*. This paragraph has lost me, but as policemen learning points duty are told, if it all gets too much for you and you can't keep the traffic under control, just take off your gloves and walk away.

HSL has a fine chapter on the culture of science in the eighteenth century. On Hume and Smith, John R. R. Christie writes, 'Scientific theories were the provisional fictions through which human imagination is obliged to apprehend and control the world'. In considering the division of labour, Adam Ferguson

> ... did not exempt the figure of the 'man of science' from complicity in the divisive process of interest and competition. In modern society, knowledge is commerce. 'The productions of

ingenuity are brought to the market; and men are willing to pay for whatever has a tendency to inform or amuse'. By implication then, science itself is increasingly produced by occupational specialisation, and knowledge, as commodity, feeds into the ascending spiral of desire and gratification which is the psychological principle of market-based society. (11. 301)

This, in spite of Thomas Reid's attempt to bring science back to realism, is still the state of play from particle physics to the professions, which are the locus if not the focus of any power in Scotland today; when society loses the place, cling to professional pride. When you don't want to talk about the morality of a situation, talk about technique. The work of the physicist is easily suborned by the market. The good physicist must be a metaphysician too, asking why he/she wants to know. Literature is perhaps of less use at the moment to expansionist politicians, but artists can be persuaded to perform or conform, or more insidiously, they can be used by literary history. As Walter Benjamin writes: 'Even the dead will not be safe from the enemy ... if he wins'.

It is good to see Ian Hamilton Finlay strike a blow for the arts by turning frigates and tanks into works of art, but the reverse is much more often what happens, and the *Oxford English Dictionary*, the *Britannica* (now American) and the *Oxford History of English Literature* (launched with welders still on board) are flagships of civilization, hidebound cruisers in a world of pink maps. Matthew McDiarmid has been quoted as calling for a grand-scale, prestige-conferring history of Scottish literature. As John MacInnes says of something else: 'There is a perverse, if not downright lunatic, expenditure of energy in the venture, but it is, of course, perfectly understandable'. (III. 393) Please no.

Having done with the history of history of literature, we should note that *HSL* discusses texts not all of which would usually be called literature. Volume I, edited by R. D. S. Jack, is the most traditional in this respect, and pre-Reformation Scots translations of legal texts is as far as it goes from the beaten track; volume II, edited by Andrew Hook, who goes out of his way to call it a (as opp. the) history of Scottish literature in his opening sentence, devotes almost half the chapters to social, historical, aesthetic and scientific work – and it works very well. Douglas Gifford in volume III allocates about a fifth of the chapters to extra-literary context, while Cairns Craig in volume IV gives two or three out of 23 chapters to context. This of course prompts the questions: what are you calling literature? And who cares?

> *Despondent and unable to rest because of the impending execution of some prisoners he had visited in Newgate, Boswell made his barber try to read him to sleep, with David Hume's History of England.* (II.160)

Each literary text is located somewhere in a slow conversation that ranges across countries within languages and across languages within genres. Even the Cantos and other modern epics edited by the grim reaper can be seen to be trying to finish saying something. Blok speaks and MacDiarmid answers – too late for Blok; Olson get wind of something and Morgan picks up on that. MacDiarmid writes Morgan a putdown of raji-rife beat poets, and Hamilton Finlay takes the French minister of culture to court.

Try again. In his introduction to volume II, Andrew Hook indicates 'that the gap between the practice of major historians such as Hume and Robertson, and that of a novelist such as Scott, was not in fact especially wide'. Unfortunately, he does not expand on that. I guess that the gap results from literature's principle of unity. We might regard histories as Hume and Smith regarded scientific theories: provisional fictions through which human imagination is obliged to apprehend and control the world (II. 301). Like scientific theories, they should satisfy the tacit criteria of concision and elegance, which makes them user-friendly. Their worth is neither textual nor contextual, but practical. By inventing characters, historical novelists signal their intention that the work be judged in ultimately aesthetic terms – a combination of credibility and approbation.

For example, when in *The Brownie of Bodsbeck* farmer Laidlaw gets away with manhandling Clavers while minor characters have their ears cut off or are summarily shot for much less, we might think that Hogg just can't resist the opportunity of making Claverhouse look like a small-time bully (at the risk of ruining the plot), whereas the passages Hogg takes from Wodrow on Clavers's persecution of the Covenanters ring all too true: we never have far to look to see a psychopath take power when the law breaks down. But when we turn to Wodrow's work as history, or when we let *HSL* do that for us (though there is no general index to refer from Wodrow to Hogg):

> In the work he reluctantly wrote for publication, his massive two-volume *History of the Sufferings of the Church of Scotland, from the Restoration to the Revolution* (1721), it was not sufficient to report, he had also to convince. Especially he aimed to convince English readers that the proceedings of the Royalists against the Presbyterians had involved religious persecution and denial of civil liberties and not been (as Sir George Mackenzie, for example, alleged) a legitimate suppression of rebellion. So Wodrow's greatest strength as a historian, his commitment to tell a story which he knew to be true, brought him directly up against his dilemma - that those he aimed to convince were the least likely to listen. He discusses his problem in terms of prose style.[1]

Its justification is not aesthetic or textual, but practical: coming across. It might seem futile to pursue questions of genre, especially now that the events are so far in the past that Wodrow's history might read like Caesar's or any other Black Penguin, but what the historical novel has done to history, to Scottish history at least, subjecting it to the pleasure principle of the market, restricts the sphere of moral judgement to the inside of the book – the author need no longer stand by his word and say this is true; it just has to ring true – as though the Never-Never Land of the Pretenders had turned half of historiography into historical romance. One can see the point of Thomas Reid's attempt to reground science (and history with it) in the realism of Common Sense (II. 301). Otherwise literature and history are two packs of lies, the one

---

[1] Douglas Duncan, 'Scholarship and Politeness in the Early Eighteenth Century', *HSL* II. 58

depending upon plausibility and the other on the author's skill as a used-car salesman.

So how do you establish a canon? MacDiarmid's method in *The Golden Treasury of Scottish Poetry* was a kind of parody of the pun at the base of English literature: he claimed everything and everyone who wrote in Gaelic or Scots, who was born or lived in Scotland, who had a Scottish name or who had anything to do with the Norse sagas, because they were really Celtic in origin, and so were the Scots. This is all good anarchy, but if you are looking for legitimacy, as *The History of Scottish Literature* clearly does, then where do you draw the line?

> Then round again to the placid hills of Fife beyond the grey-blue sliver of the Forth. And just below me a landmark which has always held for me a strange attraction, the blunt protuberance of Dalmahoy Hill whence, it was once said, Mynyddawg and Gwlyged led the ill-fated men of Gododdin, still drunk from their year-long feast of mead, on their last long march to Catraeth against the Saxon. (John Herdman, *A Truth Lover*)

Much fine story-telling must have been suppressed, lost, in the conflict of cultures, as is evidenced by the survival of the Gododdin, composed probably beside Dundee, by Neirin, about the year 600, the earliest extant of Europe's heroic poems in a vernacular tongue. (M. P. McDiarmid, I. 27)

Thirteen of the sixteen chapters of volume 1 are on writing in Scots. We have the heroic opening of Barbour and Hary after a chapter on Middle Scots as a literary language, then 'The Alliterative Revival', showing continuity from the mid fifteenth till the late sixteenth centuries, and a fine piece on 'Poetry – James I to Henryson' that focuses on numerology, so that, in the first four chapters, we have information on the language, subject matter, versification and architectonics of Scots Mediaeval verse. This is followed by a chapter each on religious and secular poetry, and a chapter by the editor on 'Poetry under King James VI'. There is little overlap, the sequence is well calculated to emphasise continuity, tradition. The second half shows the other side of the coin. In 'Poetry after the Union 1603-1660' there is little to boast about apart from Urquhart, although there are things that are worthy of attention.

'Vernacular Prose before the Reformation' shows the plain purposive style of the reformers displacing the Latinate prose of the papists. A crucial moment, this, and the problems of Scots in that period tend to distract our attention from Scotland's 'global languages': Latin and the European connection was at its final high point with Buchanan; English was being smuggled into the country in a Bible, like Latin before it. Yesterday Europe, tomorrow, the Empire! The chapter on prose after Knox is mainly on Drummond and Urquhart (so I'd have thought 'The Cypress Grove' would have merited more than two sentences). After that, we have 'Early Scottish Drama', 'Scottish Latin Poetry', 'Latin Prose Literature', 'Gaelic: The Classical Tradition', and 'The Ballad and Popular Tradition to 1660' - all very good, and each left very much to its own devices. Hamish Henderson's chapter on popular tradition takes a line that others might usefully have followed: the work is Scottish, but the tradition knows no bounds and respects no boundaries. 'Latin Prose Literature' is expertly written, but begins with the craziest decision in the entire work: Michael Scot and Duns Scotus are left out of the reckoning because they 'belong primarily to the history of European thought'. Also, if readers are curious enough to read about the author of Historia Abbatum de Kynlos, is it likely they will need to be told that Mary I was 'the ill-fated Catholic queen of a predominantly Protestant Scotland'?

Anyway, the materials relating to Columba and to Kentigern and Merlin are discussed and situated with great clarity. Thomas Innes (discussed in volume II) is mentioned as one source of the story of St Andrew, but once again – no general index, no connection. Incidentally, C. S. Lewis and his 'sixteenth-century' volume of *The Oxford History of Literature* crop up quite often in volume I, but only three references are noted in the index. Drummond, a man of many parts, comes up again in 'Scottish Latin Poetry', which is dominated by George Buchanan. As James MacQueen says, 'if Buchanan's works now seem remote from the mainstream of Scottish creativity, the reason is to be found not in their failure as works of literature but rather in our failure to provide access to them in a changing cultural and educational system. It is to be hoped that a new edition of his poems will soon rectify this.' (I.218)

This is the first time that Latin has been so strongly presented in a history of Scottish literature, and I was left feeling it might even have been pushed a bit further in order to bring the Celtic poems closer in. The classical Gaelic tradition came over from Ireland, and so did the Latin: Columba was a Latinist, but what language did he speak? If St Kentigern christened Merlin, or if St Mungo *was* Merlin (see Nikolal Tolstoy's *The Quest for Merlin*), what language did he talk to himself in? And good as it is to begin on the bright note of Barbour, could we not have had a little more on the Gododdin, and what went down with the dispossessed? I fill the blanks with creatures from Wyntoun's Chronicle.

> *As there was every appearance of a heavy tornado, the Dooty allowed us to sleep in his baloon, and gave us each a bullock's hide for a bed.*
>
> - Mungo Park, *Travels in the Interior Districts of Africa*

In the last chapter of *Waverley* the old Baron Bradwardine, pardoned for having fought in the Jacobite army, has his home restored and returned to him by Talbot, the avuncular English soldier who had saved Waverley from going to the gallows for the same offence. The Hanoverian hit-man shows the old pedant round his house :

> There was one addition to this fine old apartment, however, which drew tears into the Baron's eyes. It was a large and spirited painting, representing Fergus Mac-Ivor and Waverley in their Highland dress; the scene a wild, rocky, and mountainous pass, down which the clan were descending in the background. It was taken from a spirited sketch, drawn while they were in Edinburgh by a young man of high genius, and had been painted on a full length scale by an eminent London artist. Raeburn himself (whose Highland Chiefs do all but walk out of the

canvas) could not have done more justice to the subject; and the ardent, fiery, and impetuous character of the unfortunate Chief of Glennaquoich was finely contrasted with the contemplative, fanciful, and enthusiastic expression of his happier friend. Beside this painting hung the arms which Waverley had borne in the unfortunate civil war. The whole piece was beheld with admiration, and deeper feelings.

Men must, however, eat, in spite both of sentiment and virtue ... The dinner was excellent. Saunderson attended in full costume, with all the former domestics, who had been collected, excepting one or two, that had not been heard of since the affair of Culloden.

The frame of the picture is the frame of the novel. Fergus Maclvor, the chief of Glennaquoich in the story, was one of Charles Edward Stuart's generals in the '45. Scott portrays him as a man of great ambition born into a society that could no longer put ambition to good use: the clan is bankrupt (he gives away the last of the family silver in the traditional gift to the bard) and the insurrection presents the chance to march on London in a colossal cattle-raid. When the enterprise falls, he knows at once that his days are numbered. It is interesting that Scott who did, after all, support the Union, did not take the easy way out and have Maclvor killed in the retreat. Instead, he has him captured and taken to Carlisle, where he is finally hanged, drawn and quartered; his head is then impaled on the gates of Carlisle town. Scott thus points out, gently but emphatically, that for all its positive effects, the Union of parliaments opened Scotland to at least one utterly barbarous practice, which was not removed from the statute book until 1814, when Waverley was published (See Andrew Hook's note in the Penguin edition).

Bradwardine, the old Jacobite pedant whose reading so closely corresponds to a Scottish literature course, also fought in the '45. The Hanoverian authorities in the person of Talbot realise that he fought not for personal ambition but for history – his main concern throughout the campaign was that of reviving the family tradition of pulling off the king's boots after battle. Talbot realises that if he is left with his history – the family trappings and his Scottish literature – he will be perfectly happy and will present no threat to the British State. He is content to remain on his ancestral estate, where his butler is allowed to appear 'in full dress', like a figure in a painting. To paraphrase Douglas Young,

> They libbit Glennaquoich,
> He gart them bleed.
> They dinna libb Bradwardine,
> they dinna need.

Waverley, the hero, is a tourist. He stops at nothing in his lust for local colour: he joins the army, goes over to the other side in a fit of pique when his commanding officer asks him not to fraternise with the enemy, cuts a dash in tartan pantaloons and looks on while said commanding officer is cut to pieces. And while he is trying to decide which of the local lassies he really wants to take back home, the servants who enlisted with him are found guilty of treason, largely by association with him. Never have I been so infuriated when a character didn't get his just desserts – but like every resourceful tourist, all he has to do when the going gets rough is call the consulate or show his American Express card. A word in the right ear (the king's) from Talbot and he's back on the coach.

The author of Waverley is not to be blamed for letting this monster off scot-free: he just showed what was happening. As volume II of *HSL* demonstrates, sentimental jacobitism had been waxing throughout the eighteenth century: Penicuik, one of the engineers of the Union, James ('Rule Britannia') Thomson and James Boswell were all sufferers. It had no outlet in politics, so some kind of 'Disnaeland', to use W. N. Herbert's word, was required. Real people don't die in Disneyland. Tourists don't die on holiday – or even if they do it's just an awful exception that proves the rule. Scotland was now the realm of the tourist – Dr Johnson being the last traveller to have taken any sort of risk in going there. From then on the tourist would be no more threatened by reality than a reader by a novel. So what happened to real life in Scotland? We can consider the lower orders later, but it's interesting at this point to look at another man of ambition, Mungo Park. He undertook his first expedition to the Niger in his early twenties, put up with amazing hardship and returned to Scotland, where, between 1798 and 1804, he was a neighbour of Walter Scott's. Park told Scott a few hair-raising tales that Scott declined to relate to Park's biographer (I wonder where they were used), and said that he would rather brave Africa again and all its horrors than wear out his life in long and toilsome rides over the hills of Scotland, for which the remuneration was hardly enough to keep body and soul together (Introduction to the Everyman edition of Park's *Travels*, 1932). Waverley stayed in Scott's drawer, as it happens, until after the news of Park's death reached Britain. In the course of his travels Park discovers that his predecessor, Major Houghton, had been allowed to die of thirst by the Moors. Park himself is taken prisoner by Ali, the Moorish chief, and spends months in captivity and in fear for his life. He makes his escape when his captor tires of him. It seems plausible that Ali knew exactly what he was doing in his treatment of Park: having killed one infidel, he finds a second coming in search of the first; if he kills this one too, a third will arrive. Better surely to maltreat the second and let him return home to tell his countrymen to steer clear of the area? It only delays the inevitable: first the explorers and missionaries, then the army, then the Paris-Dakar. Mungo Park becomes Waverley sooner later:

> We found the monarch sitting upon a mat, and two attendants with him. I repeated what I had before told him concerning the object of my journey, and my reasons for passing through his country. He seemed, however, but half satisfied. The notion of travelling for curiosity was quite new to him. He thought it impossible, he said, that any man in his senses would undertake so dangerous a journey, merely to look at the country and its inhabitants. (Park, p. 40).

> Donald asked Edward in a very significant manner, whether he had nothing particular to say to him, Waverley, surprised and somewhat startled at this question from such a character, answered he had no motive in visiting him but curiosity to see his extraordinary place of residence. Donald Bean Lean looked him steadily in the face for an instant, and then said, with a significant nod, 'You might as well have confided in me; I am as much worthy of trust as either the Baron of Bradwardine or Vich

Ian Vohr: but you are equally welcome to my house'. (Scott, p. 143)

I related to Tiggity Segoe, in answer to his enquiries, the motives that induced me to explore the country. But he seemed to doubt the truth of what I asserted, thinking, I believe, that I secretly meditated some project which I was afraid to avow. (Park, pp. 55-56)

The Moors, indeed, subsist chiefly on the flesh of their cattle, and are always in the extreme of either gluttony or abstinence. In consequence of the frequent and severe fasts which their religion enjoins, and the toilsome journeys which they sometimes undertake across the Desert, they are able to bear both hunger and thirst with surprising fortitude; but whenever opportunities occur of satisfying their appetite, they generally devour more at one meal than would serve a European for three. (Park, p. 114)

Steaks, roasted on the coals, were supplied in liberal abundance and disappeared before Evan Dhu and their host with a promptitude that seemed like magic, and astonished Waverley, who was much puzzled to reconcile their voracity with what he had heard of the abstemiousness of the Highlanders. He was ignorant that this abstinence was with the lower ranks wholly compulsory and that, like some animals of prey, those who practice it were usually gifted with the power of indemnifying themselves to good purpose, when chance threw plenty in their way. (Scott, p. 142)

If eighteenth-century literature is factions and frictions, the nineteenth century is an explosion: in describing it you try to establish the causes and to say what shape it took. Douglas Gifford's introduction to volume III looks to the social and intellectual causes, while his overview of the novel, 1814-1914, traces the trajectories of various writing careers, managing a fantastic volume of information. The other contributions to volume III are caught in this perspective. In 'Scottish Poetry in the Nineteenth Century' (volume III) Edwin Morgan discusses a lot of fine work by internal and external exiles. He relates that 'Walter Scott who helped to stage-manage the royal progress, produced a celebratory version of an old song, "Carle, now the King's come", and Roger promptly published his anti-celebratory "Sawney, now the King's come", advising ambitious Scots to "kneel and kiss his gracious bum"'. (III. 341) But the rotten egg, unlike the bomber, never gets through. Even Byron's 'English Bards and Scotch Reviewers' ultimately flatters rather than shatters the Edinburgh junta by taking its criticism seriously. A chilling critique by Andrew Noble of 'John Wilson (Christopher North) and the Tory Hegemony' shows just how low Scotland had sunk by the mid nineteenth century: Wilson, 'the head of Scottish literature', saw the growing urban Scotland as a cesspool of sin and was quite unwilling to see its inhabitants as victims of brutal economic pressures (III. 147). The heroes and statesmen with their language that James VI called 'heich, pithie and learned' had gone south; the men of business with their 'commoun and passionate' were shameful philistines, and the 'corrupit and uplandis', had not the leisure to write.

Sentimentality. The problem is that while in the eighteenth century sentimentalism is a literary theory and practice that can be discussed with some precision – as John Mullan does in 'The Language of Sentiment: Hume, Smith and Henry Mackenzie' (II. 73-89), by the twentieth century it seems to have flitted from literary theory to psychopathology:

> It could be argued further that the very strong streak of sentiment in Barrie, which on occasion topples over into sentimentality, is the most Scottish thing about him. Such sentimentality, whose origins must be sought in the emotional distortions produced by Scots Presbyterianism and other factors, fuelled the Kailyard School of novelists and continues to fuel an important strand of Scottish popular fiction.[1]

But sentimentality is not a Scottish prerogative. In fact, the Russians easily outdo us: Esenin, one of their most popular poets, can make Robert Burns sound like Wallace Stevens. Come to think of it, some of the Mexican soaps my mother-in-law watches would make *People's Friend* readers blush. If it is possible to forget about

---

[1] David Hutchison, 'Scottish Drama', IV. 169

nationality for a moment when discussing sentimentality – and popular culture for that matter: another contributor writes of Scottish popular culture as though no other nation had any (IV. 245) – it might be better to consider it in class terms and stop bashing Presbyterianism.

In considering the nineteenth century I want to distinguish between (a) writers who have the technique to avoid it but want above all to be understood as sensitive creatures (by sensitive readers, of course), and (b) those who describe their feelings rather than evoke them, perhaps because life has not given them leisure to distance themselves from their subject, analyse it, select the facts that produce the feeling, and fire them back at the reader.

If so, then sentimentality is a symptom produced by two different ills – a refusal to contemplate prevalent injustice on the one side, and an inability to get clear of it on the other: John Wilson (Christopher North) versus the likes of William Thom and Janet Hamilton.

The production of sentimental writing, though, is only half the problem: its reception is the reader's half. Let's take two extremes: a plangent account of an awful event distracts the audience from the facts, and gets them annoyed at the teller; yet if the teller were to display no emotion at all, the audience would begin to see this as sinister and once again would be distracted from the crux of the matter. The trick is to guess the expectations of the audience and play along with it to a degree. But without critical feedback this can't be done. Why did William Thom, who was capable of expressing radical thoughts, write sentimental stuff for Whistle Binkie? Was he playing along with the editors? Or did he have a notion that the middle classes that produced it, that could let a child of his own starve and that was unmoved by extremes of poverty, had to be given sentimental descriptions of grief and joy, being unable to experience them? If we don't know, then that is partly Thom's fault and partly ours. Automatic rejection in any case is not an escape from the sentimental into more astringent air, but part of the same dialogical problem: the patrician Nabokov's scunner at Dostoevsky's manipulation of sentiment.

So how can Scotland shake off Balmorality? In the words of Neal Ascherson (1979 and 1989): 'Scotland needs democracy more than independence, social justice more than a flag on the ships. Any directly elected parliament is good, however limited its starting powers.' On the one hand there won't be peace until the last national anthem chokes on its own flag – which is maybe just a way of saying that there won't be any peace. In a way it was not bad to belong to a country whose national anthem is uproarious booing and whistling on the terraces, and whose flag is scored out with a big red cross (wrang!). On the other hand, if power corrupts, impotence doesn't do a lot of good either. A wee gold star in the corner of the flag when I gain a say in how my life should be organised.

The double edge to Scottish literature is that each writer (and reader) has had to invent his or her own tradition. The advantage is work like MacDiarmid's; the disadvantage in the constant return to first principles is inability to agree over basic questions.

So it would have been good to see criticism of women's writing attempting an overview, but the divisions in Scottish society break up the study of women's writing in *HSL*: the chapter in volume III concentrates on middle-class women's writing in English, leaving working-class women writing in Scots to the 'local literature' heading, and Mary MacPherson to Gaelic literature. In volume IV Muriel Spark is seen as too big to fit in the women's writing corner, and Naomi Mitchison is put along with Linklater and Grassic Gibbon, which is fine, though she has been active for so long that she might have made the connection between the women novelists of volume III and the present.

In the 1920s it got fashionable to see Roman Catholicism - the auld kirk - as the real national religion: we have MacDiarmid's Alba replying to Thomson's Caledonia, MacColla's anti-Presbyterian works and Muir's scurrilous book on John Knox. As Andrew Noble remarks, 'The tragedy of MacDiarmid's generation was that it was almost wholly out of synchronisation with national consciousness and hence political possibility'. (*Glasgow Herald*, 7 March 1989) After a long period of – indifference – it's Calvinism again. Consider Cairns Craig on the search of Scottish Renaissance writiers for a lost cultural continuity:

> Calvinism also had clear claims, since it had represented the backbone of political and theological power in the society for 400 years. Most writers, however, rejected Calvinism and all its works both because it was identified with nineteenth-century Victorian values which, as good twentieth-century citizens, they were bent on overthrowing, and also because of Calvinism's apparent rejection of literature itself, as 'lies' concealing the true word of God ... Catholicism, too, had its proponents, many of whom looked to Scotland's pre-Reformation past as the real Scotland which was rural, Catholic and creative as compared with the dour, guilt-ridden, inhibited Scotland of the Reformation and after. But Catholicism was not only deeply antagonistic to many Scots because of the long and maintained traditions of Covenanting struggles for the national church; it was also feared by many because of the pressure of Catholic immigration from Ireland and the threat it posed to the local communities and traditions. (Introduction, IV.6.)

A few words of clarification here: the fear and antagonism of Scots towards Irish Catholic immigrants (a quarter of whom were in fact Protestant) took the form of Paddy-bashing on the street and 'Catholics need not apply' in the job adverts. The word for it didn't exist then, but it does now: racism. It cannot be dignified with talk of long and continuing Covenanting struggles. I do not suggest that Catholics of whatever nationality are morally superior: both divisions have ruled in Scotland and both have performed miserably in terms of their beliefs.

Enough of tribal rivalry; on to religion, where some confusion remains. Of Muriel Spark, we are told that 'it would be wrong to see her Catholicism as merely opposing her Edinburgh background,' because it seems that according to Cardinal Newman, Catholicism and Calvinism have points in common. The ensuing discussion of doctrinal niceties omits the staringly obvious point that both are Christian sects. Scottishness is associated with Calvinism, which Spark manages to evince in spite of her Catholicism. And her Jewish origins. And not having lived in Scotland since the 1940s. The 'Four Scottish Novelists of the

1950s and 1960s' chapter speaks of 'the "fallen world" and promised "heaven" of Calvinism' – ideas that are shared with other Christian churches. George Friel is described as being from a Catholic background, yet at the end he is one of four novelists with a Scottish cast of mind, i.e. Calvinist in origins. Alexander Trocchi, distinguished by his absence, couldn't have been squeezed into that framework anyway.

Fortunately, the chapter on 'Recent Scottish Thought' sees Calvinism as a tradition, not a touchstone, and in an article in *Cencrastus* on Alasdair MacIntyre, the same authors show a way forward, asking how MacIntyre's 'Augustinian Christianity' is to be related to Calvinist traditions. (It is also worth looking back beyond Geneva and Rome to Iona, since the Celtic church followed the tradition of the (non-Augustinian) desert fathers. I can't give a reference for that because a hermit from Roslyn ran off with the book.) Duns Scotus, in this connection also, should certainly have been discussed in *HSL*. As *Britannica* notes, 'His strong defence of the papacy against the divine right of kings made him unpopular with the English Reformers of the sixteenth century for whom the word "dunce" (a Dunsman) became a word of obloquy, yet his theory of intuitive cognition suggested to John Calvin, the Genevan Reformer, how God may be "experienced".' John Knox brought that idea home. Also, he was the great voluntarist of scholastic philosophy, arguing the primacy of will over intellect – and that goes well with Barbour (p. 77, against necromancy, and the character of Bruce in general), and surges out again in MacDiarmid's own work, and in his espousal of Shestov.

It was a mistake to break MacDiarmid's work in two. Its unity, though difficult, is valuable. In *HSL* we have a solid, conventional essay by Catherine Kerrigan on MacDiarmid's early poetry and an exciting piece on the late poetry by Alan Riach, who sets out like Mungo Park, not sure if he'll get word back: '... the millennial vision of MacDiarmid's later work has a material analogue only in culture, specifically in literature and most specifically in itself' (IV, 222). Is this like Von Neumann's rueful remark, on the subject of computer models of the brain, that it may transpire that the simplest possible model of the brain is the brain itself? Maybe, though it seems to me to the clearest analogue now to MacDiarmid's later poetry is the utterly incurable computer virus. *In Memoriam James Joyce* is a great poem, while *Marxism and the Problem of Linguistics* is no classic. The two are associated on the pretext that both are Marxist. Riach notes the following from Stalin's book:

> Here we shall have not two languages, one of which is to suffer defeat, while the other is to emerge from the struggle victorious, but hundreds of national languages, out of which, as a result of a prolonged economic, political and cultural co-operation of nations, there will first appear most enriched unified zonal languages, and subsequently the zonal languages will merge into a single international language, which, of course, will be neither German, nor Russian, nor English, but a new language that has absorbed the best elements of the national and zonal languages.

Working as a translator in a number of UN agencies I have seen what happens to languages after prolonged economic, political and cultural cooperation of nations, non-governmental organizations and multinationals. The working languages (they include, of course, and by Stalin's consent, English, Russian and not German but French) are used largely by people who have learned them in adulthood. They converge and become more abstract because when a specific term has no equivalent in another language, it is either borrowed or translated with a generic term. They are sanitised to avoid giving unintended offence (e.g., one place insists on lexical equivalents of 'endogenous' because 'native' has colonial connotations for English speakers, 'autochthonous' has similar problems in Spanish, as 'indigenous' has in French). Denotation is simplified and connotation, the communal aspect of language, is regarded as interference; no community – no epic. What results is not a world language, but an international chewing-gum, Desperanto, and if it is allowed to slash and burn its way through the linguistic rainforests of the world, a lot of people will lose their tongues. The fostering of Scots, and Gaelic, their literatures, and the minority languages of central Scotland, are vital, and not only to the people of Scotland.

HSL does help to reverse this bureaucratic whitening of language and culture – though it must be acknowledged that, with its two layers of delegation (general editor / editor / critic), and the maddening lack of communication between individual contributors, it has true bureaucratic deniability: no one is really responsible for the result, and the only indication the reader has of the relative merits of various works of literature is the number of pages each is allotted – and given that some important writers are not even mentioned, that will not do. *HSL* derives, ironically, from the great projects of empire, and it will affirm the values of Scottish literature at home and abroad; but it questions those values in the best contributions, contemplating the past with a view to the present.

And so back to the present. Cairns Craig's history, and my assessment of it, are history. At the time it looked like a proud summation of Scottish literature, and it is true that there has been no invalidating revision of it since then – nothing to compare, for example, to the thorough re-examination of Russian literature that has happened in the same quarter century, with the publication of banned authors, and the new world that contemporary writers (and their critics) have had to assimilate. But with the revolution in publishing, and the resurgence of Scottish politics, Craig's history appears now as a monument to that grim decade between the 'no-vote' and the poll tax, and his history is one of many. Quite how many was made clear by Alan Riach, who generously provided me with the following list, his personal favourites marked with asterisks.

- John Stuart Blackie, *The Language and Literature of the Scottish Highlands* (Edinburgh, 1876) ***
- John Merry Ross, *Scottish History and Literature to the Period of the Reformation* (Glasgow, 1884)
- Nigel MacNeill, edited with additional chapter by John MacMaster Campbell, *The Literature of the Highlanders: Race, Language, Literature, Poetry and Music* (Stirling, 1892, second edition 1929)
- Hugh Walker, *Three Centuries of Scottish Literature* (London, 1893)

- James Hepburn Millar, *A Literary History of Scotland* (London, 1903)
- T.F. Henderson, *Scottish Vernacular Literature: A Succinct History* (Edinburgh, 1910)
- G. Gregory Smith, *Scottish Literature: Character & Influence* (London, 1919)
- John Speirs, *The Scots Literary Tradition: An Essay in Criticism* (London, 1940)
- Sydney Goodsir Smith, *A Short Introduction to Scottish Literature* (Edinburgh, 1951) ***
- H. Harvey Wood, *Scottish Literature* (London, 1952)
- Kurt Wittig, *The Scottish Tradition in Literature* (Edinburgh, 1958)
- David Craig, *Scottish Literature and the Scottish People 1680-1830* (London, 1961)
- Derick Thomson, *An Introduction to Gaelic Poetry* (London, 1974)
- Maurice Lindsay, *History of Scottish Literature* (London, 1977)
- Roderick Watson, *The Literature of Scotland* (London, 1984)
- Cairns Craig, general editor; R.D.S. Jack, Andrew Hook, Douglas Gifford, co-editors, *The History of Scottish Literature*
- Marshall Walker, *Scottish Literature Since 1707* (London and New York, 1996) ***
- Douglas Gifford and Dorothy McMillan, editors, *A History of Scottish Women's Writing* (Edinburgh University Press, 1997)
- Duncan Glen, *Scottish Literature: A New History from 1299 to 1999* (Kirkcaldy, 1999)
- Alasdair Gray, *A Short Survey of Classic Scottish Writing* (Edinburgh, 2001)
- Douglas Gifford, Sarah Dunnigan and Alan MacGilligvray, editors, *Scottish Literature in English and Scots* (Edinburgh University Press, 2002) ***
- Carla Sassi, *Why Scottish Literature Matters* (Edinburgh, 2005)
- Marco Fazzini, editor, *Alba Literaria: A History of Scottish Literature*, (Venice, 2005) ***
- Roderick Watson, *The Literature of Scotland: Volume 1: The Middle Ages to the Nineteenth Century, The Literature of Scotland: Volume 2: The Twentieth Century* (London, 2007) ***
- Ian Brown, general editor, Thomas Owen Clancy, Susan Manning and Murray Pittock, co-editors, *The Edinburgh History of Scottish Literature* (Edinburgh University Press, 2007) ***

- Robert Crawford, *Scotland's Books: A History of Scottish Literature* (Penguin, 2007)
- Alan Riach, *What Is Scottish Literature?* (Glasgow, 2008)
- Gerard Carruthers, *Scottish Literature* (Edinburgh University Press, 2009).

Hugh MacDiarmid's 'Point of Honour' comes to mind:

> ... So life leaves us. Already gleam
> In the eyes of the young the flicker, the change,
> The free enthusiasm that carries the stream
> Suddenly out of my range. [1]

On the other hand, if you plot the number of histories of Scottish literature per decade on Riach's list, adding Edwin Morgan's list from earlier in this chapter, what you find is not a stream but a tsunami:

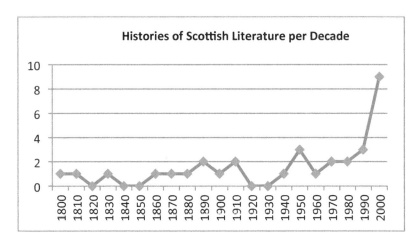

It's time, perhaps, for some Napier to produce a logarithmic, literary meta-history, before things get out of control. On the other hand, over the same two centuries, the school teaching of Scottish literature has had to depend too much on the enthusiasm of individual teachers. This should change now that the Scottish

---

[1] Hugh MacDiarmid, *Stony Limits and Other Poems*, in *The Complete Poems* (London 1978),vol.1, p. 391

Parliament has made it a compulsory subject in Scottish schools. It's time to put individual writers in touch with individual readers, preferably when the readers are still young enough to sing songs and tell their own stories for the sake of it.

Edwin Morgan the Translator

'He pauses in an astounding landscape, almost afraid to move.
When he moves, he is no longer himself. And that is it'
  - Edwin Morgan, 'The Translation of Poetry'[1]

'It's unpleasantly like being drunk.
What's unpleasant about being drunk?
Ask a glass of water.'
      - Douglas Adams, *The Hitch-hiker's Guide to the Galaxy*

It is not just the profusion and variety of Edwin Morgan's translation work that surprises: it is the quality, the rarity of some pieces – the improbable Aigi, the trove of Hungarian poetry done into English. I have set as many of the originals as I could locate and understand against the translations, which leaves plenty of opportunity for further study, since Morgan has translated into English and Scots from Italian, Russian, German, Spanish, French, Portuguese, Anglo-Saxon, ancient Greek, Dutch, Khmer, Armenian and Hungarian – working with cribs on the last three, although latterly he got by in Hungarian.

He is not unique in this respect, but the culmination of a movement in modern Scottish poetry. In the 1920s Donald MacAlister, then Principal of Glasgow University, translated from and into many classical and modern languages; he seemed to have a particular weakness for Welsh Romany. MacAlister contributed to the

---

[1] *The Scottish Review*, 2:5, Winter 1976, p. 23.

Scottish Chapbook, whose editor, C.M. Grieve, was quite a different kind of translator. Lacking MacAlister's gift for foreign languages, he was far more intimate with his own. MacAlister was followed, more or less, by Douglas Young, MacDiarmid by Goodsir Smith. Many Scottish poets then and since have produced fine versions from foreign originals, although none matches Morgan's range or excels him in quality.

This chapter assesses his translation technique, considers his theoretical statements on translation, and asks how his translation work relates to his poetry.

Morgan takes poets at their word. When it comes to a choice, as it does at every turn, he tends to let line-break, rhythm or rhyme, image or argument or syntax go rather than lose the simple sense. Consider the first four verses of a dizain by Maurice Scève in Morgan's version:

> Comme corps mort vagant en haulte Mer,
> esbat des Ventz, & passetemps des Undes,
> j'errois gottant parmy ce Gouffre amer,
> ou mes soucys endent vagues profondes.

> Wanderer: drowned body in the open sea:
> shuttlecock, plaything and mock of wave
> and wind: bitter the gulf: waverer
> buoyed on my own unfathomed misery -
>   (*FR*, 46-7)[1]

In the first verse every semantic load-bearing word has been translated ('Wanderer' does for 'vagant') but the effect is not the same. It comes as a shock in that book, after reading through

---

[1] Abbreviations used in the text: *FR – Fifty Renascence Love-Poems* (Reading, Whiteknights Press, 1975); *P – Poems of Thirty Years* (Manchester, Carcanet, 1982); *MPP – Master Peter Pathelin: An Anonymous 15th Century French Farce*, translated by Edwin Morgan (Glasgow, Third Eye Centre, 1983); *RP – Rites of Passage: Translations* (Manchester, Carcanet, 1976); *WHV – Wi the Haill Voice: 25 poems by Vladimir Mayakovsky*, translated by Edwin Morgan (Oxford, Carcanet, 1972).

poems replete with conceits on evenings and glances, woods and golden locks, to find a corpse floating in the first verse. Morgan does not use a simile to set up the effect, and he breaks it up with a colon. This is almost a caricatural illustration of the points I set out to show: the sense of the verse is kept but line-breaks, rhythm (dodgy first line), image, argument, syntax and rhyme all go by the board as Morgan uses enjambement, punctuation, and expectance of a verb that doesn't show up to make a much more choppy sea than Scève's. It should not be concluded that this is simply a bad translation. Morgan has decided to make the first four verses rough, and that has involved the (regretted) sacrifice of the powerful first line, but the continuation of his version shows he is quite capable of keeping to the shape of the original, and the last line skilfully explains the sense of the French without expanding it: 'tout estourdy point ne me congnoissoys' – 'I am dazzled, struck; I am hidden from my mind'.

These points have to be pursued with a few more examples. In Morgan's translations there are remarkable few unforced errors – by which I mean semantic distortions not made inevitable by rhyme or rhythm. The ones I found were as follows: in 'Goya', by Voznesensky (*RP*, 18), 'voronka' is 'bomb crater' not 'raven' (*vorona*), although since both images are suggested elsewhere in this short poem, it might be simply a shift of emphasis; judging by the grammar, Quasimodo's 'morte di pietà,/morte di pudore' at the end of 'Letter to my Mother' could be either 'compassion is dead, modesty is dead' or 'compassionate death, tactful death' – Morgan's 'Death of compassion,/death of quietness' hardly allows the second alternative; similarly, Montale's description of himself 'uomo che tarda/all'atto, che nessuno, poi, distrugge' might just be 'a man perplexed, /tardy to act when no act is destroyed' (from 'Mediterranean', *RP*, 62) or maybe he is saying that when he gets round to doing something, no one undoes it. There are always such nits for the picking, but in the end the only real mistake I found was in both Morgan's versions of 'A se stesso' by Leopardi, where Morgan has him spurn nature at the end, instead of himself.

Morgan's semantic fidelity sometimes results in too much clarification, something he himself warns against: 'the process of trying to understand the foreign poem always tempts us to make the translation a little clearer or simpler than the original, and this may have a weakening effect.'[1] A Frenchman whom I asked to check Morgan's translations of Maurice Scève found himself returning to the translation on difficult points in the French. Scève has a reputation for obscurity earned by lines such as the following:

> tout lieu distant, du jour et de la nuict,
> tout intervalle, ô qui par trop me nuyt,
> seront rempliz de ta doulce rigueur,

Anyone would expect a 'toi' before the 'qui', and without it the expectation generated by this already long sentence is cranked up still further. Morgan's version gives the game away before the end:

> regions remote from night or turned from day,
> all space, O my too rigourous friend, will be
> filled with your sweet but changeless cruelty.
> (*FR*, 50-51)

It is difficult to see what else could have been done there, but the explicative instinct that irons out the grammar is the same urge that treats semantic ambiguities, such as those mentioned above, with a little too much decision.

Just as he is faithful to the sense of the original, Morgan is quite determined to add nothing of his own. A search for counter-examples produced the following: in Montale's 'Arsenio', '...o troppo noto / delirio, Arsenio, d'immobilità'[2] becomes '...oh delirious / memory, Arsenio, of marmoreality' (*RP*, 65). 'Marmoreality' is a fine, original touch. The penultimate line of Voznesensky's 'Parabolic Ballad', which literally translates as 'he leaves tonight for Siberia' becomes 'Galoshes flounder through a Siberian thaw', so that Voznesensky gains something in translation.

---

[1] *New Hungarian Quarterly*, VIII. 25, Spring 1967, p. 30.
[2] *Ossi di Seppia* (Milan, Mondadori, 28th edn, 1983), p. 116.

But things change. Years after that comment was written, his biographer drew my attention to a poem egregiously traduced by Morgan:

> Well, the infidelity has a Genevan connection! It is in his translation of 'Elegy for John Calvin' by George Buchanan [1506-1582], done for Scottish Religious Poetry: an anthology (eds Meg Bateman, Robert Crawford and James McGonigal [Edinburgh: St Andrew's Press, 2000]. I would need to check how recent the translation was, in his papers, but my impression at the time was that he did it for the occasion. And towards the end of the 90s he was particularly annoyed at the Section 28 nonsense, but annoyed from the anti-church perspective (see also his anti-Souter jibe in the poem contra Winning).
>
> Anyway – for the original's criticism of two Pope Pauls conflated as 'te Pauli duo, flagitis et fraude gemellis' he teases out: 'Paul the Third, that famous pederast, Paul the Fourth, more straightforward in viciousness' whereas Professor Google informs me that the descriptive phrase means 'twins in crime and fraud'. Now this may have been for Buchanan the crime that dare not speak its name, but it did lead EM to depart from his normal piety towards the text.[1]

It's a strange day when Google translates more reliably than Edwin Morgan, and a sour one when Morgan's impiety is trumped by the Church he targets. But to our muttons: because he (usually) refuses to add to the original, Morgan is at times compelled to pad. 'I've closed my balcony' ('He cerrado mi balcon') in Lorca's 'Casida del lianto' becomes 'My balcony I've drawn, I've shut it' *(RP,* 120); 'Terribly silent' in Yevtushenko's poem 'Stalin's Heirs' becomes 'voicelessly loud with dread' *(RP,* 29); similarly, 'O znal by ja',[2] where Pasternak seems to imitate the laconic punch of Raleigh's 'On the Life of Man', with its closure 'Thus march we playing to our latest rest, / Only we dye in earnest, that's no Jest', is neither laconic nor punchy in Morgan's version:

> neither patter nor legerdemain
> nor read-out speech redeems the player

---

[1] James McGonigal, email to PMcC, 19 February 2013.
[2] *Stihotvorenija I Poemy* (Moscow-Leningrad), 1965), p. 371.

> cued for complete decease unfeigned.   (*RP*, 33)

On rare occasions this padding distorts the argument of the poem; here is Morgan's version of Montale's 'Spesso il male' *(Ossi di Seppia*, 54) with brackets round Morgan's interpolations:

> Often I've met the wrong of the world (in my walk:)
> (there by) the strangled brook with its guttural song
> (there with) the puckerings of the (thirsty tongue
> of a) parched leaf, (there by) the horse that fell and shook.
>
> Little I knew but what I saw (in a rune)
> a vision of the divine Unconcern:
> (there by) the statue in the drowsy sun
> at noon, and the cloud, and the heaven-climbing hawk.
>   (*RP*, 59)

The concision of the first stanza has been sacrificed to make it match the second, with its fine, clinching line. To put Morgan's technique in perspective, though, we should compare it with that of William Soutar, or Robert Lowell. Of Morgan's version of 'Verses on Pushkin: Third Variation' by Pasternak, we might quibble that the ink on the manuscript mentioned is drying, not dry; as for Soutar's version, it is not immediately apparent that it is the same poem.[1] In his imitation of Montale's 'Dora Markus II', Lowell is much more exact than Morgan on the mysterious lines

> Ravenna è lontana, distilla
> veleno una fede feroce   (*Le Occasioni*, 1976)
>
> Ravenna is far away, A ferocious faith
> distils its venom   (*Imitations*, 1962)
>
> far off is Ravenna; beliefs
> are fierce and strong with death.   (*RP*, 68)

---

[1] William Soutar, *Collected Poems*, ed. Hugh MacDiarmid (London, 1948), p. 392.

But Ravenna is very far away from Lowell's American Dora, who saunters in her aura of sugar daddies and harmonicas.

This brings us to the least quantifiable point on Morgan's translation technique – his fidelity to the tone of the original. In this field individual examples could hardly convince; we have to try from another angle. It will be admitted that a poem cannot be translated on a word-for-word basis. Something has to inform the whole translation. There are obvious mechanical ways of doing this, but Morgan often neglects them; he is quite capable, in translating a renaissance sonnet, of producing a decasyllable with twelve, thirteen, fourteen or nine syllables (*FR*, 21, 37, 39), and of more or less neglecting the rhythm of a poem for children such as Brecht's 'The Plum-Tree' ('Der Pflaumenbaum', *RP*, 141); compare Michael Hamburger's version[1]. What he never lets go if he can help it is the tone of the original. He even faithfully renders Voznesensky's studies in cool with suitably farout language, of beats and bums, and birds from restaurants, since he would sooner traduce his own voice than that of the original. For the same reason, he avoids hermeneutic translation: he neither naturalises his original (like Lowell's Montale) nor updates it (like Logue's Homer), nor turns it into his own poem (like Goodsir Smith's second version of Sappho). He will, on occasion, 'make it strange', as Shklovsky might have said, but this, I hope to show, is a different matter. Morgan's best translations are from poets whose formal structure can be rendered loosely – Montale, Leopardi, Mayakovsky. The perhaps surprising conclusion is that, as far as translation is concerned, Morgan is not centrally concerned with form, but rather with the sense of the word and the tone of the poem. The rest is instrumental.

Reading Morgan's books of translations after his poems can give the eerie impression of dealing with an identikit poet. He begins conventionally enough with apprenticeship in the sonnet from Petrarch *et al.*, and essays in discursive forms from the Anglo-Saxon onwards. In the 1960s Morgan tries the more eye-catching forms of Braga and Eugen Gomringer. But he takes more than

---

[1] in Bertolt Brecht, *Poems 1913-1956* (London: Methuen, 1981), p. 243.

forms from other poets: there is something familiar in the arbitrary exotica of the Lorca translations ('Live iguanas arrive to gnaw the insomniacs / and the heartbroken man on the run will meet at streetcorners / the quite incredible crocodile beneath the soft protest of the stars', *RP*, 118). In fact, Lorca's 'Asesinato' looks like a blueprint for Morgan's 'The Barrow':

> Murder
> (*Two voices at Dawn in Riverside Drive, New York*)
> - How did it - ?
> - Scratch on the cheek,
> that's all. claw
> pounding on a green
> shoot. Pin plunging
> to meet the root of the scream,
> and the sea stops moving.
>   - But how – how?
> -   Like this.
> - Get away from me! That way?
> - Sure, The heart
> went out alone.
> - Oh no, oh god –   (*RP*, 118)

> . . . The fog was really thick, but then
> someone came up out of the fog
> and I shouted HELP and rattled the barrow,
> and he came up closer and looked at me
> and felt the bars, but not a word,
> and I couldn't really see his face,
> and you know this is when something happened
> -   He robbed you, I knew it, dirty thief,
> it was all a plant, it was a trap to
> -   No he wasn't after my money.
> -   He had something in his hand you see
> -   What do you mean in his hand? his hand?
> -   He had something in his hand. He killed me.
>   (*P*, 258)

Mayakovsky's 'A Richt Respeck for Cuddies' (*WHV*, 30) leads on to a paean for the timber wolf ('The Third Day of the Wolf', *P*, 132), and in the general progression from the isolated observer of nature to the morally committed, political outsider (Leopardi to Voznesensky via Montale, Pasternak and Mayakovsky), there are facets of Morgan the poet. There is even the unpredictable formal trickster in the person of Sandor Weöres, whom Morgan has translated in abundance. It's like the king's clothes, without the king. All that's missing from the translations is the stark simplicity of some of Morgan's love poems.

On the other hand, it is Morgan who chooses what to translate (and what commissions to accept): Montale not Pasolini, Mayakovsky not Mandelshtam, Aigi not Brodsky, Brecht not Rilke. Of course he was not faced with these choices in the form of alternatives, but putting it like this highlights the selections Morgan has made. There is a degree of ventriloquy in verse translation, and at times it is difficult to tell which is the operator and which the dummy. Maybe his own comments on translation policy can help us out. In an article comparing Gavin Douglas and William Drummond as translators, Morgan says:

> Between the times of Douglas and Drummond the Renaissance ideas in Imitation are the great divide. To Douglas, Virgil was Virgil, whether in Latin or in Scots – 'Go, wulgar (i.e. vernacular) Virgill . . .' as he says at the end. But Drummond had no hesitation in publishing as his own a large number of poems which ran the gamut from close translation to loose imitation or paraphrase, taken from Italian, French, Spanish, Latin and even English. Some of his best-known poems are in fact direct translations, though the average reader who comes across them in anthologies will be unaware of the fact. A measure of moral blame has attached to Drummond for this, especially as he quite naughtily does label some poems 'translations', but never the best ones. But this is an area we today have to walk in rather warily. A property-conscious, copyright-conscious world is not the best vantage-point for understanding the subtleties of the communion of European writers, a vast web of ideals and traditions shading off in each country into finer and finer distinctions and measures of vernacular or personal variation. Drummond relished these European blueprints not simply because, as Ben Jonson claimed, he was conservative or old-fashioned, but also because the doctrine suited the subtle and delicate movement of his own mind: the making of small distinctions, the slight renewal or slewing round of established metaphors or comparisons, the

infusion of a personality drop by drop into a tradition – these are what Drummond wanted and got from his habit of translation.[1]

Morgan is like Douglas in that he views the original as the touchstone, the essential constant in the practice of translation. He is like Drummond in that he likes to explore the transmutation effected when the foreign poem comes into his own language. Yet he wants neither literary monuments nor cannibalised texts; he has not tackled the translation of a celebrated classic poem, just as he has avoided hermeneutics, where the kind of fusion that can produce brilliant effects always erodes the boundary between original and translation. Stop at this point and think of a famous translation. Or ten famous translations. The King James Bible? Constance Garnett's Dostoevsky? Urquhart? Fitzgerald? Translations tend to be famous either because the original was a famous classic and the translator was there at the right time, or because the translator left a powerful personal stamp on the work. So what's in it for Morgan? He has made a lot of translations, many of them unpublished. My own, limited experience of verse translation tells me that, given thorough knowledge of the work and its cultural and linguistic nexus, and given the luck to hit on a good approach quickly, a good translation of an eight-line poem might be made in a day. My experience of payment for verse translation is even more limited, though I am told there is not much money in it. Having considered how and what Morgan translates it is probably worth asking why he translates.

In a review of Robin Fulton's translation of Blok's *Twelve*, Morgan alludes to the totally different approach to the poem taken by Sidney Goodsir Smith in his (Scots) version, and comments that there is more than one valid route up the mountain. I have always found this a very suggestive comment and wish Morgan had developed it. Whoever has tried to translate a lyric will know the feeling of nearly getting there and having to abandon the attempt, because a crucial rhyme is missing, or a notion can't be negotiated with the materials to hand. A famous example is Pushkin's 'ja vas

---

[1] 'Gavin Douglas and William Drummond as Translators', in A.J. Aitken, M.P. McDiarmid and D.S. Thomson eds, *Bards and Makars* (University of Glasgow Press, 1977), p. 198.

ljubil' – 'I loed ye but.   Aiblins intil my briest', in Morgan's version *(Voice of Scotland VI:* 1, April 1955). The first three words of the Russian have stymied all attempts: 'I loved you', 'you' in the polite form, whereas love lyrics from Petrarch onwards have used the intimate form.   In those three words the author acknowledges that the intimacy is gone forever. Douglas Young, too, translated it into Scots, and not satisfied with that tried to put it into German (using 'du' for some reason, instead of 'Sie').

The comparison of poem to mountain and translation to route would also seem to suggest that a translation is radically different from a poem: ephemeral and dependent rather than substantial and rooted. This may be connected with what Waiter Benjamin says in 'The Task of the Translator', which Morgan commends in a paper entitled 'The Third Tiger: The Translator as Creative Communicator' (delivered at Glasgow University on 3 June 1988). It may be connected, but since I do not understand Benjamin I turn to Morgan's comments:

> … Is there some interface that makes translation possible? This is what Walter Benjamin thought, in his essay, 'The Task of the Translator' (1923), and I think most translators would agree with him, although it's an elusive and difficult idea. Benjamin wrote: 'If there is such a thing as a language of truth, the tensionless and even silent depository of the ultimate truth which all thought strives for, then this language . . . is concealed in concentrated fashion in translations . . . It is the task of the translator to release in his own language that pure language which is under the spell of another, to liberate the language imprisoned in a work in his re-creation of that work' (trans. Harry Zohn, in *Illuminations,* 1973), It is as if the translator had to get *behind the* words of the foreign poem, through his understanding of them, through his analysis of their meaning and their associations, until he is in touch with a deverbalized poem, a brain pattern (possibly) of nervous or electrical energy which he can then reverbalize into his own language. One is reminded of the search of machine translation for an interlingua, a computer language, or even perhaps a spoken language, like the South

American Indian language Aymara which has been tried out because it has an extremely regular and complex grammatical structure capable of containing other languages as subsets. If there is anything in Benjamin's idea, it makes for a different conception of fidelity in translation, a more creative fidelity if that is not a contradiction in terms. If you are in touch with the mysterious hidden 'real' poem underneath the surface foreign words, you will start your translation on a deeper and less conscious level; things, solutions will fly into your head suddenly and seem right without their being plodding word-for-word equivalents.

Now this is hard to follow, or swallow, accommodating as it does three radically different versions of the 'interface': Benjamin's cabalistic notion of a language of truth in the mind of God, a Chomskian view of 'a deverbalized poem, a brain pattern (possibly) of nervous or electrical energy', and an elusive interlingua, artificial or Amerindian. What this amounts to is that Morgan feels the poem is drawn out of the source language into some other medium, before being reconstructed in the target language. I have heard Morgan say that he doesn't like to delve too much into the sources of his poetry for fear of rationalizing it out of existence. I think it's possible to go a little further into his translation technique without doing any harm. The title of his paper is drawn from a poem by Borges, 'El Otro Tigre', 'The Other Tiger' in Thomas di Giovanni's translation, which Morgan reproduces. The third tiger, as Morgan sees it, the one not caught in the words, is 'the sub-verbal tiger of the interface'. It is as though (forgive a technical translator) the Spanish and English texts were two instruction manuals for a piece of (Platonic) earth-moving equipment, the 'real thing' the words only talk about. The other poem Morgan adduces to illustrate his point is an elegy on the poet's mother by Attila Jozsef. Morgan observes, '...the language is simple and direct, with no punctuation, and the verse is free, but the woman in the poem has such reality that you pierce right through the words and seem to see her and her relationship to the speaker before and after death, all in one pattern of perceptions.' Here we might object that mother, and tiger, are archetypes: the non-verbal unity there is not independent of words, but outwith the poem. The notion doesn't work at all for, say, Mayakovsky's 'Fiddle-ma-Fidgin', or Morgan's own *Newspoems* – most of his work in fact, where the poem, the co-ordinates of the event, are sound, sense, rhythm, rhyme, line, local history etc and most have to be changed to suit the other observer's standpoint; these aren't ghosts waiting to be painted, but pure constructs.

What are we to make of Morgan's 'translation interface'? Is it mystic, physiological, linguistic, Platonic or archetypal? Maybe each of them by turns. For Morgan it works and that's what matters to him. His most entertaining translations make the audience aware of it as well.

La farce de Maître Pierre Pathelin, an anonymous work of the fifteenth century, was translated for the stage by Edwin Morgan. In one scene the draper goes to Pathelin's home to collect the money he is owed. Pathelin feigns madness, uttering a tremendous tirade of flapdoodle, to the consternation of the draper and the amusement of his wife, in about seven different languages or dialects: Limousin, Picardy and Norman French, Flemish, French with a Breton accent, Breton with a French accent, Lorrainese and Latin. Five centuries on, this is probably more fun for scholars than for audiences. The edition I consulted has a footnote for every word of nonsense, which helps us compare the first two parts of Pathelin's diatribe (which I have translated from Limousin and Picardy via modern French) with Morgan's version:

> PATHELIN: Crowned Mother of God, my faith, I want to go away, I renounce God, overseas. God's belly, I say flute! Don't make a racket, do your sums! Don't let him talk to me about money. Do you understand, dear cousin?
>
> GUILLEMETTE (the wife): He had a Limousin uncle, his great-aunt's brother. I'm sure that's why he's blethering in Limousin.
>
> THE DRAPER: Hell! He's gone off his trolley, with my cloth under his oxter!
>
> PATHELIN: Come in, sweet lady. What do all these toads want? Back off, you heap of shite! Quick! I want to be a priest. Come on! Let the devil take his place in this nest of old priests! And

should the priest really be laughing when he ought to be singing his mass?

Morgan's version:

> PATHELIN: Och, the howe-dumb-deid's ay brattlin,
> The ugsom eeries are sae ferlie,
> It's fell the fremd ma tirly-mirly,
> And fient a jouk a jaup the toaly.
> Wee chookie-burdie's melanchoaly.
> Ah cannae smoch the hough an aa.
> Forforchen auchter larder waa.
> Bawbees for kimmers, nane for you.
>
> GUILLEMETTE: You see he lived once at Tamdhu
> With his Scotch uncle, a whisky man
> At the distillery, one of the clan,
> His aunt's husband. So he speaks Scots.
>
> DRAPER: The Devil cannot change his spots
> He's spiriting my cloth to the tomb.
>
> PATHELIN: Wie eine Blume dada zum,
> Und Merz und Herz so kunterbunter,
> Kuckuckverein einander unter,
> Uber alles immer Geld.
> O, was fur ein Haifischfeld!
> Sind Sie Sie von Sinnen siechen
> Rosenkrank und Guldensieben
> Are dead und on ze Toten-pole.   *(MPP, 39)*

And so it continues to custard-pie its way through Italian, Russian and Latin. There won't be a footnote for every word of Morgan's version, because he has brought it back to the theatre: one person is talking to two others; one of them is listening earnestly and the other is enjoying the spectacle.

Is the inscrutable interface anything other than the space between two people, one speaking and the other listening? Whatever their respective languages? It is this specific phase in translation, or

116

translation as a verbal enactment of this fraught transition, that is so central to Morgan's work.

The foreign reader sees a poem shorn of the day-to-day, the ephemeral; its outline is clearer, its context and associations less so, its register and accent might not be caught. (Maybe this helps explain why the likes of Poe and Byron could mean more at times to the French and Germans than to native English speakers.) The situation has its advantages and its drawbacks. At times the reader has the impression of going right to the heart of the poem while being unsure of the tense of a verb or the sense of a noun. Who knows? Maybe the author would have left blanks at those points if he could decently have done so, but felt obliged to fill them in, thus ruining the thing for native speakers. Here is what Edwin Morgan writes on first encounters with poems to be translated:

> But again this early reading ought perhaps to be fairly impressionistic, since it is important to remain faithful to these shocks and splashes of impact, representing as they do one's first sudden glimpses of the foreign poet's world, the poet's foreign world, which one is about to enter. For example, long before one fully understands a difficult poem by Eugenio Montale, his world stirs and reveals itself ... there is a shimmer, a play of light on water and on crumbling buildings, a face glancing in a mirror, an accordion being played in the twilight ... Absorbing this atmosphere is a step in comprehension, and one grasps at this point not only the tone of the particular poem but the signature of the author's style; one begins to sense his 'hand', his way of putting things. At this stage, too, most poems yield more unmistakable pleasure than they do at any later moment of understanding ...[1]

What Morgan does with his Mayakovsky translations is to convey this 'first sudden glimpse of the foreign poet's world'; he gives us not Mayakovsky as an ideal Russian reader would understand him, but Mayakovsky as Morgan found him – full of strange invention, glinting with unfamiliar words. Morgan is not a native speaker of Scots, nor are most of his readers: he introduces the translations, in print and on stage, in English. Consider 'Ay, but can ye?', the first poem in *Wi the haill voice,* and one of Mayakovsky's earliest.

---

[1] 'The Translation of Poetry', p. 21.

Wi a jaup the darg-day map's owre-pentit
I jibbled colour fae a tea-gless;
ashets o jellyteen presentit
to me the great sea's camshach cheek-bleds.
A tin fish, ilka scale a mou –
I've read the cries of a new warld through't.
But you
wi denty thrapple
can ye wheeple
nocturnes fae a rone-pipe flute?

Early Russian audiences, too, must have found these futurist pieces
very foreign. I have a recording of Mayakovsky reading this poem
as late as the mid-1920s: he declaims it in the heroic mode, as
though it were the introduction to 'The Bronze Horseman' rather
than a wry riddle. He made it strange – a practice the Formalists
prized – and he kept it strange. We can see how Morgan works
towards this effect from his rough translation into English:

Hoof beats rang
Apology for a song:
Crap
Crop
Crape
Croup

Drunk in the bluster,
With ice for shoe-leather,
The street slipped along,
The horse came a cropper
Down on its crapper,
and presto
The open mouths mooched together,
Gaper behind gaper, all in a cluster...

(Glasgow University Library, MS Morgan 105)

Horse-cluifs clantert
giein their patter:
crippity
crappity

croupity
crunt.

Bleezed in the blafferts,
wi ice-shoggly bauchles,
the street birled and stachert.
The cuddy cam clunk,
cloitit doon doup-scud,
and wheech
but the muckle-mou'd moochers werna lang
in makin theirsels thrang…   (*WHV*, 30)

Pruning articles and prepositions, grafting on a verb or two, fusing
alliteration with simple sound effects so the sense has to be sought
out, all delivered in street-Scots stiffened with dictionary words, it
now works more like the original:

Bili kopyta,
Peli budto:
- Grib.
Grab.
Grob.
Grub. -

Vetrom opita,
l'dom obuta,
ulitsa skol'zila
loshad' na krup
grohnulas',
i srazu
za zevakoi zcvaka...   (Mayakovsky, II, 10)

In 'The Ballad o the Rid Cadie' (*WHV*, 29), Morgan matches
Mayakovsky in his sound effects, where the sounds of 'Cadet
laddie', 'bluid-rid cadie' proliferate through the first half of the
poem, till 'Like grumphies in claver lived the haill Cadet caboodle,
/ the Cadet and his cadaddy and his grampacadoodle' – then they
are overtaken by the wind and the wowfs of the 'revo-wheesht
though – LUTION', leaving nothing but the moral of the tale. In
'Eupatoria' (*WHV*, 70), Morgan definitely goes one better, ringing

the changes on the title, from sanatorium to Eupatorianity – just as he does in 'Versailles' (*WHV*, 48), where 'Pompadour' engenders Pompadusas, Pompadoris, and Pompadorchester suite.

At the end of 'Mayakonferensky's Anectidote', immediately after a few verses of bureaucratic English (the backward elements in these translations all speak English – bureaucratic, banal or Mills & Boon) there is a send-off in neologised, legal-Latinate Scots:

> I canny sleep for waumlin thochts.
> Nicht's haurdly gane.
> Day loups. I see't aa plain:
> 'Oh for
> yin mair
> sederunt to convene
> to congree to conclude
> to comblasticastraflocate sans avizandum
> ilka sederunt and tap-table-tandem!'   (*WHV*, 44)

The message comes across straight away, but it keeps fizzing and sparking for some time afterwards. We get the delight of engaging with Mayakovsky's work – as when the man himself is praising Brooklyn Bridge:

> It's prood I am
>   o this
>   wan mile o steel,
> my veesions here
> tak vive and forcy form -
> a fecht
> for construction
> abune flims o style,
> a strang,
>   trig-riveted grid,
>   juist whit steel's for!
>   ('Brooklyn Brig', *WHV*, 61)

In the end, though, English is the chosen language of most Morgan's translation work, and in it he pursues a different strategem, aiming for a transparency of language that distracts as

120

little as possible from the original. It works very well, especially in the versions of Weöres and Jozsef, and other Hungarian poets: it also seems to be a good glaze to apply to Pushkin.

At times it may be felt that there is too much self-abnegation on the translator's part: I am sure that the lexis of Edwin Morgan's poems is much larger than that of his translations, and that the direct speech in his poems, which is always, individual, is never so bland as in his translations. His later work, though, has a still finer finish than, for example, the early Scève dizains. Reading Weöres or Joszef in English I hardly think of the translator at all. And that is as it should be.

Beyond the Rant

Leonard's early poems, mostly in Glasgow speech, speak so precisely and with such a fierce, analytical wit that they transcend their status as poems and become part of the shared apparatus we use to think with. I don't know any other contemporary poetry of which that is so true.[1]

Leonard is undoubtedly one of the few writers, perhaps the only writer – in the over-populated eco-kailyard of contemporary Scottish poetry – of unquestionable importance.[2]

If this exceptionally gifted and influential poet is angry, he has very good cause. Abused as a child, afflicted in adulthood by mental illness, humiliated by the authorities at Glasgow University, forever struggling to make a living freelance and never adequately published nor quite given the honoured place he deserved at the acme of Scottish letters, Leonard bit the hands that fed him, fiercely aware of his own extraordinary originality and brilliance. His excoriatingly left wing politics make him dissatisfied with the lies, greed and selfish inhumanity all around him. What he suffered in boyhood is unimaginably awful. He has begun in recent years to speak about it. Denied by a rival and inferior makar, on a jealous and condescending whim, the first class degree he so conspicuously deserved as a mature student, Tom Leonard went on to become an esteemed and important Professor at the very university which had disdained him.[3]

---

[1] Peter Manson, Http://www.petermanson.com/leonard.htm.
[2] John Lyon, *PN Review* 192.
[3] Donny O'Rourke, http://www.scottishleftreview.org/article/reviews-6/.

In the early 80s my wife was studying at the Quaker-funded Bradford School of Peace Studies and I was training as a translator/interpreter. In the bar one evening a bunch of us were vying to come up with the oddest story from our religious upbringing, and we were trumped by an older student who wasn't religious at all, since his parents were and ever had been communists. They had also had one of the first televisions in their part of Glasgow, and it was while the family was gathered before the box to watch Stalin's state funeral that the young lad realised that the man in the picture above the fireplace wasn't actually *his* Uncle Joe.

I had a similar surprise, in reverse, when I asked the editors of the New York magazine *Parnassus* if they might be interested in a review of the work of Tom Leonard, and they said Tom who? I explained that he is big in Scotland, though I did admit that few writers – not even Elizabeth Bishop could compare – had built such a towering national reputation on such exiguous output.

For the record: I met Tom Leonard only once, in 1988 or 89, when he rolled into the Halt Bar in Glasgow just after last orders. I told him how much I'd enjoyed his piece 'How I Became a Sound-Poet' (*Cencrastus*, 22, 1986), the way you could read it either as serious or as seriously crazy and he said yes, that had been the idea. I knew he was researching James Thomson, the Victorian author of 'The City of Dreadful Night', which got Leonard into a rap about 'the fucking city o bastarn dreadful night'. I offered him my copies of Thomson's books on Whitman and Leopardi, but he had them already.

Looking back at that essay on sound poetry, seeing the names that meant nothing to me then, I wonder. I met Rothenburg in Geneva recently; I'd heard of Mac Low the first time I heard Edwin Morgan lecture – that would be in 1977. His account of the Portraits of the American Presidents planted an idea that grew much later, though I didn't actually read the poems till last year. Morgan was of course onto all this stuff, but Leonard took it to extremes that can be inferred from the three quotations above, extremes that I want to test in this essay.

Leonard's work is strictly governed by three filters, or limits, or dimensions: genre, language and affect. I will consider each of them, then very briefly look at what kind of scope they allow his poetry.

Genre

There is an odd absence from Leonard's poetry: nature. I can't think of another poet who never mentions the natural world. No plants, no animals, no skies or mountains. You're right, that's impossible: the very first poem in the book mentions 'a blackbird in the potato patch / the grass full of daisies... / an insect on my arm'... but that's all you get except for, in 'The Psychopath', 'a field in summer heat... trees / obediently still, and the grass, and the sky'. Then a child lying in the grass in 'Storm Damage' and, many years later the same grass and trees in the magnificent 'Remembrance Day':

> I know what it is
> to be powerless
>
> I know what it is
> to be made to lie low
>
> while the unknown enemy
> invades you
>
> what it is
> not to have words
>
> for what is happening
> for grass and tree
>
> and inanimate thing
> to be
> your only witness ...[1]

---

[1] Tom Leonard, *outside the narrative: poems 1965-2009* (Etruscan books, Word Power Books, 2009) (hereafter *otn*), p. 184.

Leonard lives in Glasgow, on the edge of an amazing wilderness, but there is nothing pastoral or bucolic about his work, which could well be the most exclusively urban poetry you will ever find. It must be hard to live in that way, with no respite at all from human categories. Particularly hard for a poet. But he does. On the inadvertently funny side, in a poem he wrote in his early 50s, he tells us:

> ... the sky in the north is translucent like a lake
> translucent like a lake though it is only 3 am
> *otn*, 184-5

Well, yes, but skies *are* translucent: that's how they work. He's so unaccustomed to writing about the elements that he comes out with that tautology and the bathetic 'like a lake' in quick succession. Then repeats them as though that were a discovery.

That first filter – the absence of the natural world from the work – is a simple fact. It doesn't diminish the scope of the poetry in any essential way. The next filter is a different matter entirely.

Language

Hugh MacDiarmid's claims for Scots as a language of modern poetry were established in three books: *Sangschaw, Penny Wheep* and *A Drunk Man Looks at the Thistle*. The poem 'Focherty', from the second book, is typical in its local/cosmic setting, though the language shouldn't send you diving for the *Scottish National Dictionary*, and its persona is unusually humble, the theme more kailyard than metaphysical.

Focherty

Duncan Gibb o' Focherty's
A giant to the likes o' me,
His face is like a roarin' fire
For love o' the barley-bree.

He gangs through this and the neebrin' shire
Like a muckle rootless tree
- And here's a caber for Daith to toss
That'll gi'e his spauld a swee!

His gain was aye a wee man's loss
And he took my lass frae me,
An wi' mony a quean besides
He's ta'en his liberty.

I've had nae chance wi' the likes o' him
And he's tramped me underfit.
- Blaefaced afore the throne o' God
He'll get his fairin' yet.

He'll be like a bull in the sale-ring there,
And I'll lauch lood to see,
Till he looks up and canna mak' oot
Whether it's God – or me![1]

For many Scots there was and still is a shock of recognition in MacDiarmid's metaphysical poetry in Scots. Tom Leonard didn't let his guard down:

> right inuff
> ma language is disgraceful
> ma maw tellt mi
> ma teacher tellt me
> the doactir tellt mi
> the priest tellt mi
> …
> even the introduction tay the Scottish National Dictionary tellt mi…
>> *otn*, 91

The *Scottish National Dictionary* ruled out the Irish patois of Glasgow immigrants from whom Leonard descends, and among

---

[1] Hugh MacDarmid, *Complete Poems* (London, 1978), p. 53.

whom he lives and listens. His voice is distinguished from a nationalist project that denied the value of his means of expression. But much more than by the national language markers, Leonard is concerned by the class divisions, the dividing of the spoils. It is perhaps in his refusal to lose sight of that systemic, systematic cheating that he takes his distance from MacDiarmid, of whom he once wrote:

> MacDiarmid's work ... stands for a life-long advocacy of, and concentration on, lexis itself: anti-existential in its insistence on the validity of the naming process, and through this process deliberately and constantly ignoring the boundaries of what would be considered 'correct' lexis for poetry. These are the lines that I think Edwin Morgan is thinking along when he writes, in his poem 'To Hugh MacDiarmid', 'You took that hazard of naming'.[1]

The quote is from Leonard's essay on William Carlos Williams. I can't be sure, but I guess that 'anti-existential' is double plus ungood in Leonard's book, so he's saying that MacDiarmid did the right thing (introducing 'incorrect' lexis to poetry) for the wrong reason. The essay displays Leonard's extraordinary devotion to voice in his championing of Carlos Williams. It's a faculty that he hones constantly on the class barriers, the linguistic barricades, in the realms of British English. While his ear is subtle, his categories aren't always. 'Under the microscope, the object language tends to separate into its components of lexis, syntax and phonology'. He goes on to associate concrete poetry (especially Iain Hamilton Finlay) with syntax, sound poetry (Bob Cobbing) with phonology and lexis with MacDiarmid. I'd say that's plain wrong as regards syntax, right for phonology and horribly reductive for MacDiarmid. Nor do I agree, at all, that that's how language tends to separate; it's just one of many possible ways of regarding it.

Time and again Leonard's poetry returns to the same question:

> Don't you find
> the use of phonetic urban dialect

---

[1] Tom Leonard, *intimate voices* (Newcastle, 1984), p. 99

rather constrictive?[1]

His best answer is in 'Unrelated Incidents'

> ifyi still
> huvny
> wurkt oot
> the diff-
> rince tween
> yir eyes
> n
> yir ears;
> - geez peace,
> pal!
> fyi stull
> huvny
> thoata lang-
> wij izza
> sound-system;
> fyi huvny
> hudda thingk
> aboot thi dif-
> frince tween
> sound
> n object n
> symbol; well,
> ma innocent
> weeè¨
> friend – iz
> god said ti
> adam:
>
> a doant kerr
> fyi caw it
> an apple
> ur
> an aippl –
> jist leeit
> alane!   *otn*, 77

---

[1] 'Fathers and Sons', *otn*, 54

I don't know how often I have recited that poem in conversation with linguists, but I've only just noticed its filiation with Focherty, where the poet gets to be god at the end. MacDiarmid's god is having a good laugh, but Leonard the poet would be the god of wrath to his worshipful readers, which brings us to the third filter in his work. The first limit – exclusion of pastoral – is a simple boundary to genre; the second – his language – is a chosen constraint, and chosen constraints are one of the things poetry works with; it is productive rather than restrictive. That's not true of the third.

Affect

I saw Tom Leonard perform a couple of years ago, for the first time since I left university, and what stuck in my mind, apart from a wonderfully funny translation from Jean Arp (*otn*, 139), was a rant whose catch-line was 'that cunt was a cop'. It set a suspected (and thus convicted) police spy against a narrator who tells us repeatedly that he likes being free and honest, and that he hates language that isn't free and honest. But why would the government bother to send someone to check his views when they can tap his phone, read his emails, his books and his endless blog? Honestly! What would the report be: 'That prick was a poet'? And even if it were true, so what? The fact of the secret police taking an interest in you doesn't make you an interesting person. It's not something to celebrate in crass alliteration.

It doesn't make you free or honest either. The last poem in the book, 'A Life' and the prose piece 'Honest' would seem to bear that out. In the one he claims he never saw himself as a writer, and in the other he goes nuts when he isn't acknowledged as one. He is a writer.

There's an erratum slip for 'A Life', such that the line, 'the religion of his father was once the religion of the indigenous natives, but they had rejected and overthrown it', instead of being broken after 'rejected' is broken after 'but'. I can't help connecting that with 'the case for lower case' (*otn*, 178), where Leonard tells us what bad things capital letters are ('THE CAPITALIST SENTENCE IS A DEATH SENTENCE', etc). Me, I find them quite handy for showing where a new line in a poem starts, especially these days when texts often migrate from one format or medium to another. Also, if he had to make his printer go to the trouble of inserting an erratum slip in every copy of this book, he might at least have tightened up the writing. 'Indigenous natives'? Aren't all natives indigenous?

I've just re-read an essay I used to love, *The Proof of the Mince Pie* (1973), where Leonard writes:

'By the time I was about eight, like most of the boys of my age, I could tell an elephant from a giraffe, a lion from a tiger, a rhinoceros from a zebra; but as regards the animal life of Glasgow itself, a cat was a cat, a dug was a dug, a burd was a burd – and anything smaller was for stamping on'.[1] He is so hard on the university system that, if I'd read it too early, I wouldn't have done my degree. I'll skip the ripe irony of his jibes at professors (since he became one), and not dwell on how this working-class man was so proud of being rude to a shop girl. What's wrong with the essay, then? It's the anger waiting to pounce if you don't agree with him. Does Leonard know deep down that you can't agree with him? Is that what's making him angry? That you can't agree with his assertion that spending money on education is simply spending money on getting money? Leonard can be a bully when you differ. Look at these two arguments, side by side on his web site:

> There are people who find themselves unable to read Pound's work sympathetically knowing what he believed, wrote, and campaigned for – sometimes in the work itself. The reaction of such people is honest, understandable and not at all to be discredited. But there are others antagonistic to the work whose reactions are not so honest. The 'gargoyles' as Pound called them in London, those lovers of excessive adjectives and poetry of 'boiled oatmeal consistency', have their successors still flourishing today, and the publication of these two books have

---

[1] *intimate voices*, p. 67

given the opportunity once more for these sniffily to dismiss the poetry with the life.[1]

Then this:

> The Elect
> one of those...
> who want all poets to have a sense of 'basic form' and who are always quoting Yeats's 'Under Ben Bulben' about poets having to Learn Their Trade and not be All Out of Shape from Toe to Top who think this has nothing to do with Yeats's views on eugenics – 'the better stocks have not been replacing their numbers' – 'The results are already visible in the degeneration of literature'.

[2]

So to be clear: Tom Leonard is telling you that if you like Yeats, you like him for his politics; if you like Pound, you like him for his art. OK? No, not really.

It's interesting, Pound's dig at lovers of excess adjectives, sticking a pin in Renoir's increasingly corpulent model. Anorexia was in. Now in creative writing schools it's Carver to the bone. But why? What's so wrong with adjectives? Here's Nicolas Bouvier, in his introduction to *Nouvelles asiatiques* by Gobineau.

> Gobineau ... opened the door for me to the great grocery of adjectives, where I have helped myself with all the bad taste I could wish for.
>
> In the literature of the 1950s, which is when I went through school, adjectives were not welcome; not in Sartre's rhetoric or Camus's austerity. Not at all. They were like some box of Turkish delight, a brylcreemed Argentinian tango. A poodle in ringlets that upset Mr Teste's absinthe. The beautiful sentence – like the beautiful soul of provincial confessionals – was virtuous, sober, strong in its one, ineluctable meaning – that was the thing.

---

[1]   http://www.tomleonard.co.uk/online-poetry-a-prose/review-john-tytell-ezra-pound.html.

[2] http://www.tomlconard.co.uk/online-poetry-a-prose/the-elect.html.

And yet I could see clearly that, east of Zagreb, no one knew anything about these sumptuary laws or jansenist edicts; they did know, though, that you can't do justice to the skirl of a bagpipe, to the liquid shimmer of the pipes of Pan or to the heart-rending, chromatic cadence of the Iranian lute without at least three adjectives, stuffed into the sentence with your thumb like marzipan into a cake. Gobineau never forgets this when his characters speak: in the Caucasus, in Armenia, in Turkestan or in Persia, even the humblest and the least fortunate are lifted up and carried along by emphatic, florid, compassionate words that give succour where life gives none, and that are closer to a pious and respectable wish than to a lie, however untrue they might be.

'Outside the narrative', eh? Gobineau is famous as a racialist, which Leonard is emphatically not. But it is Leonard, not Gobineau, who seems unable to relate at all to people he sees in another country. He is so sarcastic about tourists of Glasgow's slums, that he seems terrified of facing the same criticism himself when he goes elsewhere.

> nobody cares if
> the moors or the martians
> lived here
> in the thirteenth century
> …
> the young people here
> for their hole and the beer
> –   they have the right idea
>
> a local mother and her child
> a local man smoking a pipe
> a local dog lying in the shade
> a local somebody going about their work
>
> How *authentic*
> ('Wish you were here', *otn*, 191-3)

Leonard's italic 'authentic' locks him into the Mediterranean tourist trap he was attempting to look down on.

This fear of exhibiting the wrong attitude recurs in various forms. For example:

Have you read Eriugena, the Irish 9th century geezer? Not that
I've learnt him off by heart myself, but he's got some prrretty
interesting things to say about words, thought, all that sort of
trade. He thinks our very own Blessed Trinity, which is to say
Evans Stein and Peacock (sorry, that's facetious) has a structure
that corresponds to the structure of language and its relation to
thought. Reminds me of some of our twentieth century bods in
his own way. Not that I'd ever say anything about him in public
of course you know the way it is unless you can name every stop
between Auchenshuggle and Clydebank you're not supposed to
get on the tram. 'Ignorance of the divine nature is true wisdom;
by not knowing it is best known.' That's Eriugena, or John
Scotus to you.   (*otn*, 114)

The bit about not getting on the tram unless you know the names
of all the stops is very witty, and a waste of time. Why does he
care what you're 'not supposed to' do? Why can he not just get on
and make his point about ignorance and divine nature? Does he
really fear censure from mediaevalists? Or is he afraid of
appearing pretentious? Fear and anger. Here we go again.

> it's difficult to stay angry
> on a full belly
> > ('An Ageing Writer', *otn*, 68)

> the best time was when we shared the same political outlook
> exclusively
> but now

> you've others you can do that with
> the shared anger at injustice
> is to bc had elsewhere
> > (nora's place (*otn*, 147)

That's anger as a social grace, something to be indulged in, like a
wee drink. The damaging restriction to Leonard's poetry, then,
isn't language but anger. When I suggested this to another
Glasgow poet he advised me to drop it, because anger is what Tom
Leonard is about. If that were true, he would be just one more
irascible Glaswegian, and there are plenty of us. Many Glasgow
writers after Leonard have imitated the attitude, which consists of
asserting a working-class identity and defending it with derision of

middle-class hypocrisy – not a difficult thing to do, but clearly quite enough to keep some writers happy and some bourgeois uncomfortable. The next steps are not so simple: write poems worth reading, and develop a useful, rather than just an easily defensible, politics.

A last question before we turn to the quality of the work itself: is the politics essential? Or is it something like choice of lifestyle and management of verse form that is important but dispensable? This rather depends on the poet. MacDiarmid was clearly out to achieve a Dantean level of integration of art and politics, but from a radical angle. It was a magnificent failure in terms of party politics; still, his clever move (tactical historical fiction though it was) of dissociating Scotland from the Empire after the First World War did give Scotland the critical space it needed in order to develop an alternative culture. Edwin Morgan remained a Scottish socialist, but one who accepted various honours from her Britannic majesty; WS Graham was above that and below the radar. Leonard? One of the things that has tormented and antagonized him over the years is the process that the French describe as *recuperation* – the way a dominant class or culture will enlist talent from the lower orders or from the colonies in order both to strengthen the dominant group and remove the threat of a challenge from that uncouth talent. It's clever, insidious, and hard to resist. Impossible to resist unless you have your politics clear, at least in your own head. The TL blog makes his politics abundantly clear, which surely helps him avoid being co-opted, though at the cost of imposing his own reading on his poems.

The Work

For the poetry until 1980, on which much has been written, let's try a little thought experiment, and read it as though it didn't matter whether its author was angry. We find very happy poems about sport; there are deliriously enjoyable poems about the inarticulacy and early sorrows of love; there are riotous poems about the misbehaviour of school children, and tender poems about his parents and their home. 'The Dropout' will ring a loud bell with university children of non-uni parents. There is even a poem that, imitation being its sincerest form, flatters the very cad who cruelly deprived Leonard of that first class honours degree:

> Scotch Education
> I *tellt* you
> I tellt you
> > - (Professor) Alex Scott

> Moral Philosophy
> Whiji *mean* whiji mean…
> > (*otn*, 51)

Sometimes it's sheer celebration – 'Fireworks', about the clinching goal in a football match, is a very short monologue whose language and line breaks score just as good a goal. The prosody of these poems of the 60s and 70s is the work of a keen listener. People who are constantly high on anger *cannot* listen in this way because their ears are buzzing too loud. The rabid write in regular, drumming verse – alexandrines work – so they don't have to listen. People who listen only to their own inner drone will use iambic pentameters, because it makes them and their readers feel that it's poetry. It is comforting and it seems to sell. Tom Leonard doesn't fall into either trap. Early on there is a version of Catullus – and there's more than just a hint of Catullus in Leonard's surprising diversity of theme.

Most of those early poems are happy events and as such don't attract much commentary. The most quoted ones are mordant, both because that's what the angry poet and blogger has led readers to expect, and because they fit in with theories in a way that 'The miracle of the burd and the fishes', for example, doesn't.

Take this one.

> efturryd geenuz iz speel
> iboot whut wuz right
> nwhut waz rang
> boot this nthat
> nthi nix thing

a sayzty thi bloke
nwhut izzit yi caw
yir joab jimmy

am a liason co-ordinator
hi sayz oh good ah sayz
a liason co-ordinator

jist what this erria needs
whut way aw the unimploymint
inaw the bevvyin
nthi boayz runnin amock
nthi hoossyz fawnty bits
nthi wummin n tranquilisers
it last thiv sent uz
a liason co-ordinator

sumdy wia degree
in fuck knows whut
getn peyd fur no known
whut the fuck ti day way it
                (*otn*, 90)

This is not simply a clever response, sharpened with hindsight, to
the inept intervention of the social science graduate in a deprived
area, but a more general statement of how social policy and jargon
deepen the divides they ought to repair. That's how we're
supposed to read it. But wait a minute: this is a man who studied
William Carlos Williams and who attaches such importance to the
nuances of language. How likely is anyone to come out with this
question, however you spell it:

'nwhut izzit yi caw
yir joab jimmy ?'

The whole anecdote is set up to make the social worker look stupid
and the poet cool and clever. Goodness, but I'm beginning to get
angry myself. Let's fast forward a bit.

In *Edinburgh Review* 72, Alan Riach and I published *For What It Is*, a sci-fi spaghetti western set in Glasgow, which includes the following:

> Maybe I should go to the shops. I've nothing left for tonight.
> he turned right towards the corner shop
> Gujerati and Glaswegian. Friendly folk,
> but no tick. I've no money. The bank
> did they close my current account when I went?
> He stopped. Not one more step
> unless it takes me into a new life
> he looked ahead. His brow
> the bough over the park paling.
> The grey road led
> he didn't believe it did.

In *Edinburgh Review* 82, 'nora's place' was published. It begins:

> across the park
> I can't be bothered
> making the dinner, going through
> all the routines and subroutines.

Leonard wasn't copying us. Our choice and treatment of theme was what OULIPO quite seriously categorizes as *plagiat par anticipation*. We had copied Leonard in advance, taking up the kind of character and situation that hadn't snagged in verse until he championed it. He was and is that influential. The important thing is that Leonard's is a much better poem – one of his best, and one that is easily missed because of the prissy subtitle ('a poem is 17 aspects') and the utter understatement of the predicament of a working-class mother who is losing the support of her husband just as the demands of her children, 'all the routines and subroutines' isolate her from the rest of the world too. To call it 'a great poem' is inept, because it avoids all temptation of greatness. I'm at a loss to know how to praise it. Take the precise, flat wisdom of part 7:

> the main thing to have controlled
> contempt for the idea of
> breakdown which is completely

    unromantic and painful despite
    its aura and pseudo visionary crap about
    insights usually obsessive petty

    vanities to do with god and the
    devil and one-dimensional trains
    of thought that go on and on and

    people don't understand you any better
    at the end of it

    (otn, 148)

That was a poem of the Thatcher years. Since then, looking
through this new volume, old fans will find a handful of very fine
poems. There is 'Remembrance Day' (already quoted), and then an
affectionate wedding poem for one of his children, that sets out the
joys and pitfalls of a long life together.

    …There's
    No shortage of busted-up couples out there who would bust a
    gut with grief if you joined them.

– a nicely turned suasion, that.
There is a surprisingly gentle poem, short enough to quote in full:

    From *Myths in These Parts*

    They say in these parts
    'When you die,
    you go to your granny's.'

    Your granny sits in the sky
    with a bag of white peppermint lumps.
    'Come on in,' she says,
    'You made an awful fuss of it.
    We were wondering
    when you were coming to see us.'   (*otn*, 106)

And there is 'An Ayrshire Mother', a touching and fine memorial
to the poet's mother, on a par with 'nora's place' in terms of
quality, and I certainly recognize much of my own mother's

unsung life in it, for which I am grateful. There's a short coda to it, entitled *In Memoriam*:

> the sacred heart
> above the winterdykes
> set roon the fire

I had not come across that magical word 'winterdykes' to denote the folding wooden clothes-horse on which the washing is stretched out to dry when the weather doesn't allow it to be dried in the sun (ie most of the time; small Glasgow living rooms got fairly foggy). The footnotes don't tell you that the image of the Sacred Heart, set above the hearth like Uncle Joe, shows a heart on fire, with a crown of thorns like the winterdykes.

There can be no doubt that recognitions of this sort, available to a couple of generations in parts of Glasgow, add salt to the enjoyment of Leonard's work. Outsiders can register it with amusement, but they can also find a way in to this poetry which, like that of so many threatened languages, speaks in a voice you may not hear again.

A Gathering for Gael Turnbull

He was sitting against the wall of Tweeddale Court absorbing the sunshine and the voices at one of the Scottish Poetry Library free-for-all readings. 'There's always something of interest', he said. I was over to read at the Edinburgh Book Festival (this was in 1995). When I got back to Geneva I told my wife I'd invited a poet called Gael Turnbull to come for the weekend to break his stay at Besançon in the autumn. She was surprised, in that inviting strangers to stay was her trick, not mine. He duly turned up. My younger daughter explained to him at breakfast that he ought to use the chipped plates since the good ones were for guests (he didn't seem like a guest). We wandered downtown, and bumped into a friend. Gael heard her children speaking Swedish and it turned out he was a quarter Swedish himself. We went on to look at the monument to the Reformation. His father had been a minister, the author of several books, a hard act to follow. Gael brought us a couple of his own, and I began to piece his work together. He is more of a listener than a talker, but he talked a lot that weekend, as happens when you return to your own tongue after living for weeks in a strange language: where he'd lived, who he'd known, how he wrote. On the Sunday I took him up Mont Hirmentaz, just south of the lake, looking south-east to Mont Blanc – and again one walk brings others to mind and his poems are full of hills. He said that in the Lake District there were some derelict mineshafts that had been roughly capped but never mapped. So someone out walking on his own might go through a rotten board and never be heard of again.

> So now, in stages, over several years, I have walked from Berwick-upon-Tweed to Iona, from the town hall steps where I

was made a Freeman of the Borough all those years ago (it has been in our family since at least the 1790s) to the little bay on the south of Iona where Columba is said to have come ashore, by way of Dunbar, North Berwick, Haddington, here (Edinburgh), Linlithgow, Falkirk, Bannockburn, Stirling, then across to the southern end of Loch Lomond, up the west highland way as far as the Bridge of Orchy, down Glen Orchy, eventually to Oban (mostly along the route used to carry the dead etc) and so by the ferry across to Mull.[1]

He has walked through Scotland and he has stood for Scotland in the epic vigil for a parliament. Ken Cockburn writes, 'incidentally, the last time I saw Gael was the morning after the referendum, at the Calton Hill parliament vigil, when he was high as a kite...'[2] Oddly enough, the walking and the standing connect with the Morris dancing (which will never look the same to me after Edwin Morgan's poem). Consider the following, from *A Year and a Day*:

May 1: 6.30 a.m., at just 1,300 feet, wind driving the rain, anoraks flapping, six men, on highest point of the Malverns, with even sheep looking miserable in the swirling clouds, dancing 'The Rose'.

July 12: in a slash of sunshine, dancing 'Steve's Lass', Glyn leading, the other men cheering, and then, clowning, half drunk, down the middle of the High Street, on a Worcester Saturday.

October 11: in a chill drizzle, watched by three bewildered children, two shopping ladies and an old gaffer in a grubby raincoat, dancing in our top hats and sky blue tabards, between the old parish church and the brand new shopping centre.[3]

These are some of the songlines (not songlines – singing lines: he favours the present participle) that take Gael Turnbull back beyond his Scots Presbyterian and Swedish Lutheran heritage to 'An Irish

---

[1] Letter from G.T. to P.McC., 1 October 1996.
[2] Letter to P.McC., 29 September 1997.
[3] Gael Turnbull, *A Year and a Day* (Glasgow, Mariscat Press, 1985), pp 27,33 and 42.

Monk on Lindisfarne' and 'Five from the Sagas'[1], then on to a world where Christianity is not in evidence but Hel, goddess of death, still is, in 'Residues: Down the Sluice of Time', in 'Impellings' and in 'Scarcely I speak', the beautiful rendering of 'Son's Wreck' by Egil Skallagrimson. He's a skald, a poet of community rather than an individual.

So what is community to a man who has moved around so much? Well, this book is part of the answer. Note that it is entitled 'A' not 'The' Gathering; I contacted as many of Gael's writing friends as I could, and I'm left with the impression that there could easily be another gathering just as bright in his honour.

Let the poems speak for the poets. Here, I will point out only a few connections. Gael Turnbull is Roy Fisher's oldest literary friend – they go back over 40 years. Jonathan Williams has known Gael almost as long. Along with Eli Mandel, Phyllis Webb made up the 'Trio' of Gael's first pamphlet (Toronto, Contact Press, 1954). Charles Tomlinson writes, 'Gael turned my attention to the here and now in poetry... he pointed out the existence of W.C. Williams to me.'[2] Through his magazine *Origin* Cid Corman put Gael Turnbull in touch with the Black Mountain poets in 1953. Gael's Migrant Press published work by Roy Fisher, Ian Hamilton Finlay, Edwin Morgan and Matthew Mead between 1960 and 1966.[3] I believe Gael also published Edward Dorn's first pamphlet. Eliot Weinberger's magazine *Montemara* regularly featured Gael Turnbull in the 1970s. Hamish Whyte's Mariscat and Duncan Glen's Akros are Gael's present publishers.[4] Tony Baker, on the other hand, has been published by Gael in his 'Minimal Missives' series.

---

[1] Poems printed in *A Trampoline* (London, Cape Goliard Press, 1968), reprinted in *A Gathering of Poems 1950-1980* (London, Anvil Press, 1983).

[2] Letter to P.McC., 5 September 1997.

[3] See David Miller, 'Heart of Saying: The Poetry of Gael Turnbull', in *New British Poetries*, edited by Robert Hampson and Peter Barry (Manchester University Press, 1993), pp. 183-195.

[4] *For Whose Delight* (Glasgow, Mariscat Press, 1995) ; *A Rattle of Scree* (Akros, 1997) ; *To the Tune of Annie Laurie* (Akros, 1995).

August Kleinzahler writes:

> There is a clarity and directness in Gael Turnbull's poetry which, I suspect, is why his poetry has not been more widely taken up and celebrated. There is nothing counterfeit about it, nor can it be counterfeited. Its 'presence and pressure' continually challenge one's own way of registering the world, in language, in life.
>
> He is the most various of poets, a man of uncommonly wide sympathies (and clearly articulated dislikes), and I cannot recall ever coming across an inflated sentiment, an extraneous flourish, a false turn. I have taken great refreshment from these poems for over 25 years, which dates us both but doesn't preclude another 25.[1]

As Carl Rakosi demonstrates, that is not beyond the pale of possibility.

---

[1] Letter to P.McC., 3 July 1997.

Language, Kitsch and Country

As far as I am aware, Alan Riach and Iain Bamforth have never met – though both have travelled to Samoa and to Geneva, where I recorded them reading their poems.[1]

To both of them, Samoa meant Stevenson. To Bamforth, Geneva means Calvin and Rousseau; to Riach it's Conrad and Frankenstein. For one of them, Europe speaks basically German and French; for the other, world literature is written mostly in English.

Country
Re-reading these books[2] gave me a flashback to the last time the English press confronted the prospect of Scottish independence – just before Riach and Bamforth started writing. It was when Tom Nairn published 'Old Nationalism and New Nationalism' in *The Red Paper on Scotland*.[3] He was a bit hard on MacDiarmid, ruthless on Scottish kitsch and dead wrong, for my money, only on the locus of English kitsch: not the *New Statesman* and the *TLS*, but the royals.[4] The editor of that *Red Paper on Scotland* (one Gordon Brown) was deferential to MacDiarmid; but if Nairn provides an exemplary analysis, this man shows another kind of

---

[1] Extracts at http://www.knot.ch/sound.htm.
[2] Alan Riach, *Representing Scotland in Literature, Popular Culture and Iconography: The Masks of the Modern Nation* (Basingstoke, Palgrave, 2005); Iain Bamforth, *The Good European* (Manchester, Carcanet, 2006).
[3] Edinburgh, EUSPB, 1975.
[4] Nairn more than made up for that later. See *The Enchanted Glass: Britain and its Monarchy* (London, Radius, 1988).

example: keep talking, dilute your Scotch, forget Europe and go easy on the socialism. Power is in London, in trust, and Scots have known all about stewardship for a long, long time.

Being a Scot is a matter of embarrassment: some, such as Gordon Brown, are embarrassed by Scotland; others by Britain. In most countries I've worked in, when people ask where I'm from, it's best when they've never heard of the place, because otherwise the word Scotland, in whatever language, is a source of mirth. Among intellectuals paid to know these things, let's take Etienne Balibar, who concludes (though the reader is not privy to his reasoning) that Scottish is a regressive form of nationalism[1]... 'et s'il n'y a pas d'Etat il n'y a pas de nation' (and if there is no State there is no nation).[2]

As the Berlin Wall came down in 1989, Bamforth noted: 'Some wit has even daubed a Scottish Saltire alongside the Joseph Beuys and Keith Haring exhibits: no lost cause lost enough, it would seem.'[3] Eleven years later, he notes:

> Musil, a man of many qualities, could have been describing the break-up of Ukania, our United Kingdom. (Substitute 'England' for Musil's Austria, and 'Scotland' for Hungary and you get this observation: 'Britain,' he nearly wrote, 'did not consist of an English part and a Scottish part that ... combined to form a unity, but of a whole and a part: namely, of a Scottish and a

---

[1] 'Some nations or groups of nations must cross the "threshold" of post-nationality; some societies must gradually "denationalize" or "transnationalize". Some traditional nations will break up in a more or less drastic way. Once again, as a result, we see progress and regression, expansion and decline. The former is to be seen in Western Europe, prefigured in the project of the European Union. We fear the latter in the case of Great Britan (see the brilliant essay by Tom Nairn)...' Etienne Balibar, *Nous, citoyens d'Europe? Les frontières, l'Etat, le peuple* (We, Citizens of Europe ? Frontiers, State and People) (Paris, Editions la découverte, 2001), p. 34.

[2] Balibar, p. 41.

[3] Bamforth, *The Good European*, Berlin Diary, p. 55. Since all further Bamforth references are to this book, the rest will note only the chapter title and page quoted.

British sense of nationhood, and the latter was at home in England, whereby the English sense of nationhood actually became homeless.' But not for much longer, it seems.)[1]

Times change, and since 2000 they have changed some more. I would therefore have hoped from guidance from Riach's book; here's what we get: 'Whether or not a completely devolved or indeed independent parliament would offer resolution remains debatable…'[2]

> Scottish writers are frequently writers for whom their own land has become foreign in a specific sense. After 1603 and 1707, the project of the British Empire led to many of Scotland's writers travelling abroad. This literally meant that the land of their childhood became far-away, never to be returned to … Scotland's status within the United Kingdom relegates the idea of an autonomous national identity to the realm of fantasy … A nation without statehood is the condition of childhood, and children, like Scots, are both the victims and the perpetrators of empire.[3]

Is Riach telling the Scots to grow up or suggesting that arrested development is part of being Scottish? I hope the former and fear the latter. Though he acknowledges (for example) 'the atrocities of Scottish slave-owners in the West Indies'[4], his heart is with the good losers, 'the Celtic hero defiant even in the face of destruction, the Dying Gaul, hounded by empire to the edges of Europe, then finding on the other side of the Atlantic a regenerated myth of the furthering frontier in America'.[5] But the Scots on the other side of the Atlantic *were* the empire, and it was a Scot who, as lieutenant general and commander in chief for America, wrote the following

---

[1] 'You must change your life'; pp. 95-6. Bamforth does not mention Tom Nairn, who made a similar point in *After Britain* (London, Granta, 2001); great minds, perhaps?
[2] Riach, *Representing Scotland*, introduction; p. 11. Since all further Riach references are to this book, the rest will note only the chapter title and page quoted.
[3] 'Treasure Island and Time'; pp. 92-4.
[4] 'The International Brigade'; p. 150.
[5] 'Conclusion'; p. 234.

to London, shortly after his arrival at New York with 6000 extra troops (including the Black Watch):

'Opposition [to royal authority] seems not to come from the *lower* people, but from the *leading* people, who raise the dispute, in order to have a merit with the others, by defending their Liberties, as they call them'.[1] Freedom was a noble thing once, what? That was John Campbell, fourth Earl of Loudoun; the National Galleries of Scotland hold a portrait of him by Allan Ramsay that must have been painted just prior to the '45. The Scots weren't just the outlaws; they were City Hall too. We ripped through the place like smallpox (incidentally – Anderson's book[2] shows that Paul Muldoon's 'Meeting the British' might equally have been written as 'Eating the British'). Riach wonders, here and there, why Scottish literature doesn't seem to hold the same attraction as Irish lit, for critics. It's simple: the glass slipper doesn't fit.

Bamforth again: 'The peoples of Christendom, having been caught up, for much of their history, in the growth of the state power, are being taught, in the face of intensifying globalisation, the lessons of the Talmudic tradition, and living their identity, not in the absolutism of statehood but in the portable Jerusalem that wandered with the Jews through time.'[3]

A dream State? Perhaps. Can it guard against a nightmare nation?

Language

Under this heading I note that Bamforth's book, though entitled *The Good European*, eschews any attempt at definition, and its Strasbourg focus is announced at the outset; by Strasbourg he means the city, not the Parliament. The heavy emphasis on German and French culture, and the total absence of Italy, cannot

---

[1] Fred Anderson, *Crucible of War: The Seven Years' War and the Fate of Empire in British North America 1754-1766* (New York, Vintage, 2001), p. 148.
[2] Fred Anderson, p. 199.
[3] 'Next Year in Jerusalem', p. 214.

be read as a judgment. (Riach's book, though it does assay definition, is not judgmental either – a virtue I'll return to.) On subjects he has less direct knowledge of, such as Russian literature, Bamforth can be a little wikipaedic, but he was writing before the wiki was available, providing the reader with essential background.

With Alan Riach, I return to a dispute that was pursued from the Corona Bar, Langside to the snug of the Mitre, whose demolition has not resolved the matter.

'Because English is the international language of modernisation, the mask is also the modern world'.[1]

That is Riach quoting Tim Cribb. When Cribb made the statement in 1992, there was truth in it. (I'm talking about the international language of modernisation, not about the mask business, which I don't understand.) By the time Riach quotes it in 2005, much of that truth had seeped away; the English language accounted for roughly one third, and falling, of internet traffic. My guess is that Anglophonia peaked around the millennium and is gently going the way of French and Latin. There is no immediate need to invest in Chinese or Bahasa; English will see us out. But that's part of the problem.

When I see Riach endorsing Marshall Walker's comment, 'Poems look different after Pound',[2] I can almost hear Pound say 'I mean HAVE you ever heard of a language called French, or a man called Mallarmé?' (The very next page of Riach's book says almost that, and misses the link; the accompanying overview of modernism is totally anglophone).

Riach acknowledges the issue, when he mentions 'Aimé Césaire's monoglot Prospero, foreclosing dialogue through the assertion of his own authoritative ignorance of other languages',[3] but is still capable of writing this: 'The point [about satirical alienation and

---

[1] T.J. Cribb, quoted in Riach, 'Introduction'; p. 3.
[2] The International Brigade; p. 126.
[3] 'Shakespeare and Scotland'; p. 39.

non-standard forms of English] is as apt in terms of Scots as it is of Gaelic and its long-term application has been international in the establishment of the centrality of the English language in our approaches to literature. American, Australian or New Zealand writing in English remains more approachable to an international readership in English than writing translated from native American Indian, Australian Aboriginal or Maori languages – or, until very recently, Gaelic.[1] There is something awfully presumptuous about that 'our'. It certainly doesn't embrace the likes of Bamforth, whose work is an essential part of Scottish literature today.

Riach's book does show an openness to non-anglophone cultures, but something more systematic will be needed, whether in terms of joint projects with other departments in the faculty of arts, or in terms of collaboration with literary historians in other countries, preferably countries that have had to come to terms with very powerful neighbours. Viet Nam is perhaps the most spectacular in terms of resilience against the odds, but there are plenty closer to home.

In such work, we all are at the mercy of translators (I say that more ruefully than most). Thereanent, I was struck by Riach's quote from Tacitus; we have Calgacus in the field with his warriors before him, saying, 'We, the last men on earth, the last of the free, have been shielded till to-day by the very remoteness and the seclusion for which we are famed.' [The lads realise they're getting this through Roman relay interpretation, so they make allowances. Calgacus continues:] 'We have enjoyed the impressiveness of the unknown.'[2]

'The impressiveness of the unknown?' Each man raises an eyebrow and looks at the other. They check their earpiece and look round at the interpreter. There in the booth, with the earphones and microphone, is a penguin. A penguin classic, but all the same. They draw their bows. Since then they've never strayed from the Antarctic. Which brings us on to the next theme.

---

[1] 'Foundation texts of Modern Scottish Literature'; p. 66.
[2] 'Conclusion'; p. 232. Square brackets mine.

Kitsch

On the power of popular culture, Riach notes: 'We need to keep the value and danger of this potential in all art keenly in mind. Elitist disdain of ephemeral, populist, mass-produced work, or philistine disregard of high art and difficult work are equally inappropriate here'.[1] Agreed.

'Not despite the kitsch to which it is drawn is Mahler's music great, but because its construction unties the tongue of kitsch, unfetters the longing that is merely exploited by the commerce that the kitsch serves'

That is Theodor W. Adorno[2], quoted by Riach, who later paraphrases Adorno thus:

> one of the major reasons why Mahler's music is great is not *in despite of* the kitsch to which it is attracted, the melodrama, the whole range of what we mean by 'sound effects' – but because *the construction* of Mahler's music allows us to understand the language of kitsch. It is crucially performative, utilizing masks and descriptive gestures of all kinds, yet it is also profoundly informed by an intuitive feel for Austro-Hungarian folk-echoes, the rhythms and phrases of the Alps. He helps us to live in a world recognisably modern and contemporary precisely because of the saturation levels this language has reached. Mahler's art – and that of others – allows us to see into the real human desire that is represented in clichés, caricatures and conventional pieties, which is summed up in kitsch and merely exploited by the commerce it serves.[3]

At this point, I don't know whether I'm taking issue with Adorno or with Riach, but in any case – is the reader being asked to take 'Austro-Hungarian folk-echoes, the rhythms and phrases of the Alps' as elements of kitsch? If so, then the whole concept of popular culture purveyed in this book is suspect. At their best, the rhythms and phrases of the Alps keep company with popular music

---

[1] 'Conclusion', p. 231.
[2] 'Introduction'; p. 3 The Adorno text is "Mahler: A Musical Physiognomy".
[3] 'Introduction', p. 31.

and balladry anywhere. Kitsch is not inherent in them. Let me counter-define the term.

If PoMo is today's impression of yesterday's dreams of tomorrow (and the architecture looks that way), then kitsch is how the middle classes present the lower orders to their superiors. The word is German, and the Scottish locus classicus is Walter Scott's presentation of Edinburgh to King George IV, a German tourist. That, at any rate, was the first big set-piece. Thereafter it is a matter of entrepreneurs purveying local colour (the lower orders) to any tourists at all. I notice that the Swiss, in this respect, send themselves up quite nicely – and *that* is where the rhythms of the Alps become kitsch. Kitsch is not exploited by commerce; it *is* commerce, conducted under a tartan pelmet. Artists don't use kitsch: it uses them, and I would suggest that it thrives in situations where artists find themselves representing, or selling, one people to another. This requires commercial connection and cultural disjunction; empires are perfect for the purpose.

James Hogg on Walter Scott: 'Yes, I say and aver, it was that which broke his heart, deranged his whole constitution and murdered him … a dread of revolution had long preyed on his mind; he withstood it to the last; he fled from it, but it affected his brain, and killed him. From the moment he perceived the veto of democracy prevailing, he lost all hope of the prosperity and ascendancy of the British Empire'. [1]

On the Austro-Hungarian, alpine connection, see Bamforth on Joseph Roth's funeral:

> Roth's real faith being the Empire, an imperal aide-de-camp then stepped forward and laid a black and yellow wreath bearing the simple legend 'Otto'. It was a token of recognition from the Habsburgs to one of their most faithful subjects. The aide-de-camp recalled Roth warmly as 'a true fighter for the Monarchy', whereupon consternation broke out among Roth's socialist friends, all of whom tried to shout the speaker down.

---

[1] James Hogg, *The Domestic Manners and Private Life of Sir Walter Scott* (1882 edition), pp. 95-6; quoted from Nairn op cit., p. 34.

Nostalgia can make of history itself a pathetic fallacy. Today the Austrian capital looks as if it had been put in aspic since Franz Josef's glory days; Roth himself is not immune to the charge of high kitsch.[1]

Which brings us back to Riach's paragon of Scottish popular culture, James Bond – who of course is on *Her Majesty's* Secret Service, following Walter Scott in shamming potency for the amusement of the real power. As Riach puts it: 'As British imperial authority declines, the imperial power of America grows, but Britain – and Bond – rises in mythic status as models of benign patriarchal protectiveness for the American cousins.'[2] And again: 'My point is that it is only and exactly by providing him with a Scottish background that such rooted identity could be transcended in his "image" or mask – because, in the history of the British Empire, the Scottish nation had "transcended" itself. Bond's only functional identity in that context is one of service.'[3] Tom Nairn had put it rather more harshly: 'It is true that political castration was the main ingredient in this rather pathological complex (such was the point of the Union), and that intellectuals have been unable to contemplate it for a long time without inexpressible pain. Still, there it was: the one thing which the Scots can never be said to have lacked is identity.'[4]

In this connection it is particularly interesting to read Chalmers Johnson on the dilemma confronting the United States today:

> If we choose to keep our empire, as the Roman republic did, we will certainly lose our democracy and grimly await the eventual blowback that imperialism generates. There is an alternative, however. We could, like the British Empire after World War II, keep our democracy by giving up our empire.[5]

Kitsch flatters the ambitions of emperors, consoles them in their dotage and reconciles the subject peoples to their lot, if they're not

---

[1] 'Scheherezade in Vienna'; p. 47.

[2] 'Nobody's Children'; p. 175.

[3] 'Nobody's Children', p. 181.

[4] Tom Nairn, 'Old Nationalism and New Nationalism', p. 25.

[5] http://www.tomdispatch.com/index.mhtml?pid=160594.

careful. Elitist disdain for kitsch would indeed be inappropriate: it is much too dangerous.

Canon

So what is worth reading, and why? This is the question at the heart of books such as these, and we are now in a position to consider the answers of Riach and Bamforth. In doing so, I must again focus on their approach, not the content, since both range very widely indeed – Riach examining several branches of the arts (including orchestral music, comic books and television drama), Bamforth considering several cultures. Let's begin with one of the usual suspects.

'It was once remarked, in a university English department, that Shakespeare was the real torso, the centre of English studies – everything else mere limbs and appendages. The metaphor is flippant but the centrality of Shakespeare to the critical *oeuvre* of, for example, Harold Bloom, demonstrates a more serious truth about the way the pivotal position he occupies is understood and reproduced in the Anglo-American critical establishment.'[1] Note the shadow of Frankenstein behind that circular Anglo-argument, and now consider Riach on David Hume.

It transpires that Riach is at his weakest when approvingly quoting others; I find myself quarrelling more with the house guests than with mein host. In the section entitled 'The Enlightenment and its Discontents'[2], he endorses a trio of other critics, starting by agreeing with Adrian Poole, who reckons that there was something bloody odd about Hume's equanimity in the face of death. Why couldn't he take Dylan Thomas's advice and rage a bit? All this enlightenment stuff surely means that you're afraid of the dark. And why would a good atheist want to face death like some kind of Christian saint? Another suspicious thing about Hume: like Macbeth, he had no children or other such possessions. (Children – possessions?!) Now Riach quotes Nahum Tate, then Michael Long

---

[1] Riach, 'Introduction'; p. 9.
[2] pp. 54-7.

for the coup de grace (delivered several times, as though the corpse was refusing to be impressed):

> The neo-classic answer to the radical incomprehension which is the Enlightenment's response to the pleasure of tragedy, is given by Hume, and as Long says, it 'derives from a mentality which has no way of allowing that the contemplation of the uncontrollably destructive in life might be something in which a civilized mind would willingly engage. Hume therefore must reduce the impact of tragedy, modulate its passion into sentiment and its despair into elegy, and claim it as the function of "art" thus to present what is difficult in life in a form suited to the undisturbed entertainment of civilized men...'.

Long's conclusion [says Riach] is crucial: 'The failure is catastrophic. There is an entire dimension missing from the moral thought of both Johnson and Hume...'

Conclusion? Shakespeare is confirmed the top torso, and Hume is relegated to somewhere near Scott.

To keep things brief, let's set aside 'the pleasure of tragedy' – Riach's phrase, which sits ill with the argument of Long, who's not talking about pleasure at all, but about tragedy as a means of confronting the unacceptable. Long claims that Hume simply pretended nothing was wrong. Now, as any attentive reader of Hume will know – and Riach says it himself – Hume was at times 'a tormented spirit'. And what Hume discovered in the course of his work gave him no consolation whatsoever. He was, after all, the one who dismantled the notion of causality. In part III section 14 of the Treatise, he writes:

> Thus, as the necessity, which makes two times two equal to four, or three angles of a triangle equal to two right ones, lies only in the act of the understanding, by which we consider and compare these ideas; in like manner the necessity of power, which unites causes and effects, lies in the determination of the mind to pass from the one to the other. ... I am sensible that of all the paradoxes which I have had, or shall hereafter have occasion to

advance in the course of this Treatise, the present one is the most violent...[1]

'Violent' is the word. No causality means no grounds for reason, and no possibility of objective agreement between humans on any point. No science, no tragedy either, including Shakespeare's, because the entire inevitability of action is exposed as arbitrary, along with everything else. This is something that Shakespeare could not help with.

So did Hume, as Long suggests, play at never heed? See Bamforth:

> Nietzsche wanted to stand indomitable alone. David Hume had also attempted to 'redeem' pride, but made no secret of the fact that having dissolved all causal bonds solely by sceptical introspection he needed to play a round of backgammon with friends in order to restore him to equilibrium. Nietzsche, on the other hand, felt obliged to repudiate all qualities that implied mutuality: the most perfect enemy was the friend.[2]

David Hume had proven what others have intuited – that reason is grounded on convention, not on existence. Riach later refers to a novel by Patrick White in which the affective implications of the situation are set out: 'The heart of this vision is a barren rock, its attitude to European culture so massively indifferent that it annihilates every member of the expedition'.[3] Given the same choice as Nietzsche – return to the fold or accept that existence (which includes the stuff you're made of) is utterly indifferent to your being – Hume chose human company. To return there, he used the simple, rough magic of backgammon, in which players agree on a meaning to bits of matter, the counters and patterns on a board. It is not true, but if we agree on it, it works. That's human culture. In short, Hume mapped out the borders of the abyss and flagged the danger. He did indeed retreat, and saved his sanity. I can't see that as a catastrophic failure, but then again I'm looking

---

[1] David Hume, *A Treatise of Human Nature*, book one, edited by D.G.C. Macnabb (Glasgow, Fontana, 1965) p 217.
[2] The Good European; pp. 272-3.
[3] 'The Internatioanl Brigade'; p. 156.

at Hume in the context of European philosophy, not English studies.

Hume apart, Riach's is an epicurean, permissive approach to Scottish culture that can only encourage students to explore and connect areas that had not previously been linked or, in some cases, seriously studied. This is a great and good thing. The sovereign virtue in Alan Riach's critical approach, which must make him an excellent teacher, is that he really *enjoys* reading, and that pleasure is very important to him, and he wants to convey it, in spite of everything. When there is something clearly reprehensible about the authors he reads, he confronts it. In his discussion of Conan Doyle, he quotes what I guess is the most blatant, caricatural racism in the book, showing what is wrong and putting it in context. His approach to the heavily-flawed Fleming is similar. For Ezra Pound, Riach brings in Michael Long again to administer chastisement, and he points out how much more acceptable are the politics of Tom Leonard, but he refuses to pretend that Pound is therefore a worse poet. Riach never solves the problem, but he never hides it.

The general refusal to stand in moral judgment comes with a reluctance to pronounce aesthetic judgment on the work of living authors. Two examples: he mentions Maurice Lindsay's *Pocket Guide to Scottish Culture* (1947) in the same breath as Sydney Goodsir Smith's magnificent *Short Introduction to Scottish Literature* (1951),[1] which will cause sore disappointment in those who read Goodsir Smith first. Later, he devotes several hundred words to Ian Banks's *The Business*, describing it as 'a thoroughly refreshing satire' and 'a risky book'.[2] On the strength of that, I went out and bought it. The way I see it, Riach owes me nine quid, since it's *Mills & Boon* for boys, with a dash of socialist homiletics. Two hundred and forty pages in, I have yet to find a hint of narrative tension, or indeed of satire.

Cut to the sublime. Bamforth ventures: 'Surely no one can imagine visiting the Louvre and being smitten with an aura like … Rainer

---

[1] 'Introduction', p. 22.
[2] 'Nobody's Children', p. 185.

Maria Rilke, who in 1906 saw an early fifth-century BC torso of a youth from Miletus and wrote a poem – about the Word made not so much flesh as work of art – in which he instructed the reader: "You must change your life".[1] Well, this reader can, and he's not unique. Also, though I don't know German, I'm fairly sure that the injunction is not from Rilke to reader, but blindingly impersonal, the torso itself, and so much the more powerful for that.

One doctor on another, Bamforth notes that 'Chekhov made no mention of his impending death, and insisted in letters to his friends he was getting better'. Lev Shestov was scandalised by Chekhov's calm in the face of death, and snapped: 'No man can admit right off that there is no way out.' (Odd how this deeply religious philosopher echoes the secular critics of Hume above.) Bamforth continues:

'He was unmistakably a dying man, but a man who lacked the rancour which Nietzsche, whom he read with interest around 1900, thought the sick foster against the living…'[2]

Bamforth is always judicious on Nietzsche, stern on Céline, whose '… rhetoric, with its harping on extirpation as a *therapeutic* necessity, is part of a biomedical vision that in Germany legitimised Nazi doctrine: the medical profession as a whole played a significant role in obliterating the barrier between healing and killing.'[3]

Now it is Bamforth's turn to use a presumptuous plural: 'The real scandal about Céline, according to Godard, is that we take pleasure reading an author whose ideas we condemn'.[4] But Bamforth is no epicurean: he is more of a stoic, or cynic, and the pleasure principle is not central to his take on literature. Such are the dangers of critical ventriloquy.

---

[1] 'You Must Change Your Life', pp. 98-99.
[2] See "Five Postcards from Badenweiler for Zinovy Zinik"; pp. 241-2.
[3] 'Candour and Hygiene'; p. 137.
[4] 'Candour and Hygiene', p. 139.

I would suggest, in any case, that the scandal of Céline is not one of complicity in evil notions; it's a scandal of stupidity. In the astounding first 200 pages of *Voyage au bout de la nuit*, the narrator whips up an intoxicating contempt for the civilization that produced and prosecuted the Great War. It is a healthy reaction to industrialised madness. That contempt veers to paranoia later in the book, as the narrator takes ship for Cameroon, and it settles into dull misanthropy towards the end of the narrative, back in France between the two wars. By that stage, this reader's pleasure in the work had abated to the extent that I was not inclined to proceed to the later novels, far less the tirades of idiot invective that Bamforth analyses for us. I might return to the novels, but they are long, life is short, and there are other great writers, and greater, that I haven't got around to yet.

There is a secondary satisfaction in tracing the genealogy of such stories. Might Céline have read Kafka's *Amerika* before writing the American episode of the *Voyage*? Had both of them seen Charlie Chaplin? How does Céline's Cameroon compare with Conrad's Congo? Without Céline's take on the war, would *Catch 22*, *Slaughterhouse Five* or Herr's *Dispatches* have been conceivable? Unlikely. For sheer verve, Céline beats them all. But the others all – even Michael Herr – get over the scandal of war one way or another, reaffirming life with other people in a way that doesn't reek of cabbage. As Riach and Bamforth show us in very different ways, that's not easy. But this is as close as cynic and epicurean, intellectual and academic will come to agreeing on a canon. If you consider the poetry that these two have produced – look at Riach's *Homecomings* and Bamforth's *A Place in the World* – you will understand why. Though it will remain surprising that Scotland could be big enough for the both of them.

Bye Bye Bakhtin

Alasdair Renfrew begins his article 'Brief Encounters, Long Farewells' by saying that

> The first textual engagement between Bakhtin and Scottish literature came in David Morris's 1987 article 'Burns and Heteroglossia', published six years after Bakhtin's vogue had been seriously enabled by the English translation of 'Discourse in the Novel'.

In fact, that first textual engagement occurred a good six years earlier, in a piece on Dostoevsky, MacDiarmid and Bakhtin that was read and discussed at the time by Edwin Morgan Alan Riach, Kenneth Buthlay and others, published in a PhD in 1984 and then in book form by the Scottish Academic Press in 1987.[1] The book was called *Hugh MacDiarmid and the Russians*, and the work on Bakhtin had been done at Leningrad University in 1980, when I was preparing the PhD. The publisher's reader was Roderick Watson, and the book was reviewed by Robert Crawford (in the *LRB*) and Christopher Whyte (in the *SLJ*); all of them went on to publish on Bakhtin and Scottish literature. Crawford wrote to me 'It may amuse you to know I'm trying to do a conference paper involving Bakhtin. I wish you'd had more on him in your book. Surely all his dialogic ideas are a godsend to Scottish lit?' That was on 23 June 1992: I remember because I used the quote in a

---

[1] Peter McCarey, *Hugh MacDiarmid and the Russians: Dostoevsky, Solovyov and Blok, Mayakovsky and Shestov; with a preliminary chapter on Ossian, Scott and Byron in Russian Literature* (University of Glasgow, 1984).

cut-up poem shortly after that. I don't claim responsibility or influence, just precedence: I am the man who signed Mikhail Bakhtin for Scotland, and in that capacity I would like to make the following comments.

The Bakhtin I brought back from Leningrad to Glasgow was not about 'prestige and exposure' as Renfrew puts it. He was the critic who, for me and for many others following Professor Byaly's seminar at Leningrad University, had lifted discussion of Dostoevsky out of the undecidable ambiguities of psychology, using analysis of form to get at other aspects of the novelist's work. The Bakhtin I brought away with me spoke of 'polyphony' (the break-out from solipsism into acknowledgment that someone else exists), 'carnival' (other social arrangements are thinkable) and Menippean satire. I simplify grossly; you would need to read the book.

I had not much use for the polyphony: I was working on MacDiarmid, who had little dramatic sense and never saw solipsism as a problem. The critics discussed by Renfrew tend to latch onto polyphony and heteroglossia as something particularly important in Scotland. I'm sure that's true. But I'm struggling to think of a country for which it is not true.

The carnival business struck me as dubious, though I could not have told you why. Alasdair Renfrew does, rather clearly, in his article, though he seems to miss the mark in one sense: although Bakhtin writes with relish of a mediaeval culture where the great cities were on holiday for three to four months in the year, I do not believe he idealised carnival; after all, some of the scenes he describes as carnivalesque in Dostoevsky's novels are violent in every way.

Menippean satire – to summarise Bakhtin's description of it – contains more comedy than the Socratic dialogue, more thematic and philosophical invention; fantastic episodes are introduced to test the philosophical ideas. Mystical and religious themes are prominent, but the action is often set in bars, brothels and highways. Academic philosophy is dropped and only the ultimate ethical questions remain. Abnormal moral and psychological states are depicted in dreams and madness that disrupt epic and tragic integrity. (By contrast, dreams in the epic are prophetic or minatory structural devices; they do not disintegrate the character.) The Menippean features scandal and disruption of accepted codes, and abrupt changes of tone and subject; it incorporates other genres and topical issues.

The Menippean satire as defined by Bakhtin seemed to me to be greatly contrived, but contrived with such candour and ingenuity that it won me over. Little or nothing remains of the eponymous Menippus; and no one claims that Dostoevsky had ever heard of him or of his satire. What this virtual genre did was to allow strong connections to be made among works that, on the face of it, had little to do with one another. What it can do for readers in Scotland (and this is where I want to endorse Renfrew's third conclusion, on the subject of genre) is to locate subterranean connections, and to discard spurious links: *A Drunk Man Looks at the Thistle* is an example of the Menippean genre, and *Cain's Book*, perhaps surprisingly, fits the bill. But *Trainspotting*, which has its points in common with *Cain's Book*, owes more to Ealing comedy.

Another point to consider in this light is the remarkable migration from verse to prose in Scottish literature over the last generation. If, to shortcut the argument, the verse/prose distinction is in fact a superficial trait, then the generic shift might have more to do with the market than with anything else. If readers are looking for work that has the deep affinities we find between certain of these writers, they must learn to reach past Menippus to the presocratic philosophers who, as it happens, tended to write in verse; or to that blinding shock when Greek and Jewish cultures collided. Indeed, they can go back to the first recorded epic – for Gilgamesh is not an epic at all, but a Menippean satire before the fact. Scottish *writers* too could take a harder look at genre: there has been heavy concentration on diction, voice and attitude – to brilliant effect. But where is it going?

Recognition of the Menippean genre that Bakhtin adumbrates depends perhaps too much on the reader seeing a Rorschach test the same way he does. It might be worth taking a step back and viewing this genre less as something transmitted from one practitioner to another and gradually transformed, like the sestina and the sonnet, and more as the result of a set of circumstances which repeat themselves in various situations down the ages, in much the same way as creole languages (some of which are worlds apart from the others) tend to share certain linguistic features such as the double negative, subject-verb-object word order, doubling of nouns for plurals and doubling of adjectives or adverbs as intensifiers.

Creoles are clash languages – often a slaving language mixed with a local one to cope with the basic imperatives of communication; the redundancy built into every language is reinforced, the initial vocabulary is simplified. The Menippean is a clash genre where authors try to deal with the imperatives of survival as a human being or community. When authors are in full command of the media of their tribe, they use and adapt the classical genres. In crises where either those genres can no longer cope or the classes that mastered them have lost the place, something like the Menippean satire is likely to arise: a forceful, impatient and often profane attack on central questions of existence.

Is this where we plug into post-coloniality? I rather hope not. We are far beyond that now, in a world where university-educated domestics wire home enough of their paltry earnings to fuel entire economies (even as their ruling classes siphon off liquidity and bank it abroad). Also, there is a certain slyness in the way the Scots have told themselves their histories. MacDiarmid was very astute in his separatist take, which got us off Scot-free from the Empire. If academia is now selling Scotland as the archetypal colonised coloniser, then astute is not the word; it should simply not be done until we are sure that school history books are revised so as to include the Scottish Opium Wars along with the Union of Parliaments. If not, then we are having our cake, eating it, and selling tickets for the performance.

The People of the Opium

(A virtual installation that was commissioned for the new parliament building)

At the front door of Parliament House, a flowerbed. Its centre shows the Scottish flag – the blue in Scottish bluebells, plastic, made in Hong Kong, the saltire picked out in bits of silver cash. This is the flag that flew on the ships of Dr Jardine and Mr Mathieson when they peddled opium in the Pearl River Estuary. Let there be a silver skull in the top quadrant of the saltire.

Silver was the only commodity the Chinese wanted from the West, so when the Peruvian mines ran out, a new need was created for them. A patch of Remembrance Day poppies at the bottom right corner of the flower bed represents Hong Kong Island.

In the 1830s the opium trade was going so well that Jardine and Mathieson were taking on all the tonnage they could. A model of the Psyche, bottom left, sailing towards Hong Kong: it was converted from a slaver on the Atlantic run to an opium clipper in the South China Sea.

When he retired to Scotland, Mathieson bought the Isle of Lewis. Not long after that, its inhabitants were threatened with famine by the potato blight. Mathieson bought enough grain to feed the islanders, and that earned him a baronetcy. A patch of potatoes top left represents Lewis. This may also remind MSPs of the Tory parliamentarian who suggested that Hong Kong residents with right of abode who wished to migrate to the United Kingdom in 1997 be sent to a Scottish island.

Top right, a black marble stele inscribed with the letter from Governor Lin of Canton to Queen Victoria. The inscription is in Chinese characters, in the Governor's calligraphy. There is no need for an English translation since (a) the message did not get through, or was not acted upon, and (b) every Scot will know it better than the Declaration of Arbroath:

> ... Let us ask, where is your conscience? I have heard that the smoking of opium is very strictly forbidden in your country; that is because the harm caused by opium is clearly understood. Since it is not permitted to do harm to your own country, then even less should you let it be passed on to the harm of other countries - how much less to China! Of all that China exports to foreign countries, there is not a single thing which is not of benefit when resold: all are beneficial. Is there a single article from China which has done any harm to foreign countries? Take tea and rhubarb, for example; the foreign countries cannot get along for a single day without them. If China cuts off these benefits with no sympathy for those who are to suffer, then what can the barbarians rely upon to keep themselves alive? ...

Behind the flowerbed stands a very large billboard. The message on the hoarding will of course change from time to time, but the first might appear as follows: an image of Monument Valley, Arizona ; on the valley floor, tens of thousands of coolies are smoking hookahs. The legend reads: WARNING: WELCOME TO THE BIG COUNTRY.

Part III

Another Informationist Manifesto

'... The musk ox
has no musk and it is not an ox.'
        - Marianne Moore

Hugh MacDiarmid once wrote: it is a lie that the sum of human knowledge has outrun the individual consciousness till only a small part of it is available to any one person. No it isn't. It's not a lie. True, I need not be overwhelmed by this now digital universe, but true also it will not be mastered by me. Isn't it odd that, in the attempt to control the world, we have created a parallel one of fax and info which, too, is beyond our control. Just like a poem, a golem. Consider the surgeon, whose scalpel opens the senseless body to the corpus of medical literature – neither of which that surgeon will ever fathom. Now there's an informationist for you.

André Leroi-Gourhan had a neat way of measuring progress, in the making of tools: cutting edge per kilogram. For a million years or so, there was the pebble tool (10cm /kg). The next million years managed to improve that to 40cm, with biface tools. The volume of the hominid brain doubled in the same period. So tools got lighter and heads got heavier until suddenly, 100,000 years ago, people started decorating their bodies and burying their dead – behaviour that gets termed progressive only by association with prodigious advances in cutlery. Odd, I know, but let's go along with it for another 95 millennia, till they start using those sharp points to make signs on wax tablets. Almost immediately, they hit upon the method of communication which, in terms of cutting edge per kilogram, manoeuvrability and density, has yet to be surpassed: verse. Ah, but what about the digital universe? How many reams

167

and quires of Rilke's angels can jig on the head of a pin-sized chip? That's your cutting edge, like the laser: all cut and no crush.

True in part: it may have no weight, or all the weight of the means of its production, which, once again, is too much for one to handle. In any case, as I hinted in the last paragraph, I am sceptical of progress as applied to art and religion, and advocate a tool that suits me. It isn't the ancient, oral poetry that lives by society, it isn't a modern medium that depends on technology; it was a fair age by canto ten of the Paradiso, where Dante says all right, that was a tough passage: go back and read it again before we press on. It's written verse. It's small, capacious, tough, patient; not, in my domestic experience, fickle: just difficult and demanding (I prefer difficulty to danger when there's a choice).

I am an informationist inasmuch as a butcher is a chickenist. Essentially I am neither a dictioneer nor an encyclopaedist. Sure, there are odd words and facts in my poems but, like the things in W.N. Herbert's 'Some things found in sharks' their value derives from their astounding surroundings. I don't want New World or other eclecticism. Kenneth White asks for Pascal without the anguish. Pascal without the anguish? After the Nth plane crash of the year someone wrote to a newspaper suggesting they build aircraft as tough as the black boxes that protect the flight recorders. Of course it can be done, but then the planes don't get off the ground. And what is Pascal without the anguish? The Marquis de Sade? There's been one already. (Faut-il brûler Sade? Faut-il noyer Beauvoir?) On the other hand, the proposition 'I am doing absolutely nothing therefore I am a Zen master' is fine by me: there's nothing like the sound of one name dropping – except perhaps the sound of a brand name hitting the glass of a TV screen. I'll have no virtual reality or other forms of sensory deprivation for me or my children. Not till Oor Wullie installs a video game in his bucket and sticks it on his heid, Ned Kelly style. Who'd need bread and circuses? Here's a plastic bag, son: away and play at spacemen.

So how do I tell you what? The good, simple words hold only nostalgia. If the people I live with intimate older meanings, I'll not

convey them in wooden toys with iambic feet and sonnet form. I'd
rather use a tax return, a set of instructions, a copyright warning -
starting from scratch every time, because
Tradition is a civil service. This
is politics. Politics of the impossible.

The Harrowing of Hell and Resurrection: Dante's Inferno and Blok's Dvenadtsat'

Co-written with Mariarosaria Cardines

I

Throughout *Dvenadtsat'* (Twelve), Blok refers to Dante's *Inferno*. This important reference does not seem to be discussed in any criticism of *Dvenadtsat'*,[1] and, more surprisingly, it is not mentioned in either of the longish works devoted to Dante and Blok.[2] But Christ's appearance at the head of the Twelve can't be properly understood without Dante. And even extant criticism comes into sharper focus in this context, for just as Blok's line 'The road to heaven must be open/ for those who walk the paths of evil'[3] loses its paradoxical nature when we consider the relevance

---

[1] Works consulted include: E. Bazzarelli, Aleksandr Blok, *L'Armonia ed il caos nel suo mondo poetico* (Milan, 1968); D. Bergstraesser, *Al. Blok und 'Die Zwölf'* (Heidelberg, 1979); R. Dieter-Kluge, *Westeuropa und Russland im Weltbild Aleksandr Bloks* (Munich, 1967); L. Vogel, *Blok's Journey to Italy* (Ithaca, 1973); A. Yakobson, *Konets tragedii* (New York, 1973); L. I. Yeryomina, 'K istolkovaniyu finala poemy A. A. Bloka Dvenadtsat'' in *Nauchnyye doklady vysshey shkoly, Filologicheskiye nauki*, 6, 1980, pp. 3-9, as well as standard works on the subject.
[2] N. Minsky, *Ot Dante k Bloku*, Berlin, 1922; and R. I. Khlodovsky, 'Blok i Dante' in *Dante i vsemirnaya literatura* (Moscow, 1967), pp. 176-249.
[3]: A. A. Blok, *Sobraniye sochineniy v vos'mi tomakh* (Moscow-Leningrad), 1960-63 vol. II, p. 216. References are to this edition and will be given in parentheses with volume numbers in roman followed by page numbers in Arabic numerals. The companion *Zapisnyye knizhki* (notebooks) volume (Moscow, 1965) is referred to as *ZK*. The section and verse numbers of *Dvenadtsat'* are given in Arabic numerals.

of Dante's journey through Hell to Heaven, so Maksimov's essay on *put'* (the way) and on spiral forms in Blok takes on new meaning.[1] Those who ask what Christ is doing in *Dvenadtsat'* are often tempted to turn to the Apocalypse. Sergei Hackel develops the apocalyptic argument at length,[2] using the words of Blok himself, of Bely, Beketova, Merezhkovsky, and referring to the last works of V. Solovyov. The result is a fine, broad reading which somewhat overstates the importance of the Apocalypse. Hackel demonstrates that there are many echoes of the Apocalypse in *Dvenadtsat'*, but the central concern of the Apocalypse – God's judgement that punishes and rewards – is not central to *Dvenadtsat'*, and the Christ of *Dvenadtsat'* is not the Christ who comes to judge. The Apocalypse is a vision of the last age, and *Dvenadtsat'* proclaims the new age – Blok's prose confirms the point. In 'Catilina' (April-May 1918), for example, he explains why he chose to write about that period: 'I...choose that epoch which, in the process of history, corresponds most closely to mine'.[3] Blok saw the present as the beginning of an age. In 'Istoricheskiye kartiny' (August 1919), he refers to the present as 'our new beginning'.[4] The central theme of *Dvenadtsat'* is not the Apocalypse, but Resurrection – the sign of a new age. In April 1918, Bely wrote the poem Khristos voskres (Christ is Risen) which, as Armin Knigge has observed, can be read as an interpretation of *Dvenadtsat'*.[5]

Long before *Dvenadtsat'*, we can detect Dante's Inferno behind Blok's vision of the city. In his notebook on 19 May 1906 Blok writes: 'The city is grey boredom. In the first circle of Dante's Hell there is no pain, but only anguished longing. And this is considered "a favour of heaven". We seek pain to escape anguished longing.

---

[1] D. E. Maksimov, *Ideya puti v poeticheskom soznanii A. Bloka* in *Blokovskiy sbornik* II, Tartu, 1972.
[2] S. Hackel, *The Poet and the Revolution*, Oxford, 1975.
[3] VI, 86.
[4] VI, 425.
[5] A. Knigge, *'Ein Tropfen Politik. Zur Rezeption des Poems Die Zwölf von Aleksandr Blok'* (Zeitschrijt für slavische Philologie, XLI, Heidelberg, 1980, pp. 306-49); on Bely's poem *Khristos voskres*, see p. 323.

And then again the longing in Dante is bright, "the air is still and quiet" – what could be more horrible for us?'[1]

One escape from the 'anguished longing' of the first circle was in the pain of the second, that of those damned for sins of the flesh. The tale of Paolo and Francesca da Rimini (Inferno, V) occurs in three of Blok's poems: in a poem of January 1903 (I, 527), the incident is vaguely related as by a neighbour who has heard what was happening through the wall. It is worked into the *Faina* cycle in 'Ona prishla s moroza' (II, p. 290, February 1908), and it appears again in the *Strashnyy mir* cycle in 'Pesn' ada' (111, p. 15, October 1909). Z. G. Mints identifies the lyrical hero of this poem with Dante.[2]

While the situation and the versification of Dante's *Inferno* are recognizable, and the first lyrical hero in 'Pesn' ada' is treading Dante's path, nevertheless he should not be identified with Dante. Moreover, the *dvoynik* (double) who tells his story to the initial narrator is the modern, vampire-like counterpart not of Dante, but of Paolo da Rimini. Both lyrical hero and double in this poem, while finding themselves in the situation of Dante's *Inferno*, answer the description of Alexander Blok. Of 'Pesn' ada', Blok wrote:

> The Canticle of Hell is an attempt to represent the infernality {Dostoyevsky's term), the vampirism of our age in the style of The Inferno, as is evident from the first words, 'The day was dying' ('Lo giorno se ne andava' – the beginning of the second canto of the *Inferno*). 'Where is my companion? Oh, where are you, Beatrice? – I go alone. ..' Our era is not only without a heavenly companion, Divine Wisdom, but it lacks also the earthly wisdom of the pagan Virgil who accompanied Dante through Hell and handed him over to Beatrice at the gates of Paradise (Inferno, I, 112-14).[3]

Where Blok encounters the incident of Paolo and Francesca (*Inferno*, V) is not relevant to this argument, but it is of interest

[1] ZK, p. 85.
[2] Z. G. Mints, *Lirika Bloka*, IV, Tartu, 197 5, p. 111.
[3] III, 502.

that by the time he wrote *Dvenadtsat'* Blok had long been familiar with the *Inferno* in Italian;[1] and that he had possessed a Russian translation since around 1901-02 when he bought Glazunov's edition.[2]

Before examining the influence of the *Inferno* on *Dvenadtsat'* we should note that in both poems the elements are symbolic of hidden forces:

> I came to a place, where every light was mute, which roars like a sea in tempest beaten by conflicting winds. The hellish storm that never rests clutches and drives the spirits, and torments them with whirling and smiting. When they come before its ruinous force there are cries, moans and lamentation, and there they blaspheme the power of God. (*Inferno*, V, 28-36.)[3]

Blok's lines parallel Dante's:

> Black the nightfall.
> White the snow.
> Wind, wind!
> Not a one that can stand on his own two feet. Wind, wind
> on all God's world!
>> (*Dvenadtsat'*, 1, 1-6)

> 'Freedom, freedom, / hey, hey, with no cross!'
>> (*Dvenadtsat'*, 2, 7-8)

In Dante there are precise connections between the blasphemy and the storm: the storm is the eternal consequence of a moral reaction; divine justice subjects these sinners to the very element which they had allowed to rule their lives. The storm of passion that raged inside them is now around them, too. Condemned never to see God through the storm, they blaspheme in their despair. Blok's storm

---

[1] R. I. Khlodovsky, op. cit., p. 190.
[2] ZK, p. 26.
[3] The text of *Inferno* used and referred to is Scartazzini's edition (Leipzig, 1874). In these references, the Roman numeral gives the number of the canto, and the Arabic numerals are verse numbers.

cannot be defined in Dante's terms of good and evil, but it ranges over similar heights and depths. The physical storm described in the poem wreaks havoc; the political storm is destroying the old order, and in this context the blasphemy of the Twelve is political subversion. But of course the storm described is more than physical and political. As Blok says:

> ...the poem was written in that exceptional and always brief moment when the cyclone of revolution produces a storm on every sea – the seas of nature, life, art; – on the sea of human life there is a certain little backwater, something like the Marquisa's Pond [the Gulf of Finland], which is called politics; and at that time, there was also a storm in that tea cup.[1]

The problem of blasphemy recurs in canto XXI, which is recalled in various ways in *Dvenadtsat'* .The Twelve march through the snow and ice where the people in the street are floundering, and the ten devils with Dante and Virgil go among the barrators who are submerged in the boiling pitch. In this connection Blok's comment on those who see *Dvenadtsat'* as a political poem is relevant: he wrote that they are '... sitting up to their ears in political mud'.[2]

When Dante and Virgil come upon the devils, one is throwing a new arrival down into the tar. As the sinner surfaces, a crowd of devils falls on him shouting 'This isn't the place for the Holy Face.' (*Inferno*, XXI, 48) The Holy Face, 'il Santo Volto' is an ancient Byzantine crucifix in Lucca Cathedral – and Dante sees Lucca as a centre of deceit – so that the devils' exclamation has an interesting ambiguity: its ironic import is that the sinner will no longer be able to make empty obeisance to his favourite icon; its second meaning is that the sinner will not see the face of God here (he might have hoped to see God in the afterlife), and would not be able to pray even if he really wanted to. The ambiguity arises from the fact that the thing – the Santo Volto, Holy Face of Christ – and its representation – the Santo Volto, that particular crucifix – are designated by the same word. This is a particularly important

---

[1] From 'Zapiski o "Dvenadtsati"' III, p. 474.
[2] *loc. cit.*

ambiguity in the Byzantine tradition, where the icons themselves often became the objects of the prayer they were fashioned to focus. The representation, icon or word, can be the mistaken object of worship, and it can also be the target of blasphemy; a church could worship empty representations, and iconoclasts such as the Twelve could be led by the one the icons represent. Thus a devil, who is part of God's plan, though he doesn't understand this, can say 'This isn't the place for the Holy Face', and one of the Twelve, led by Christ, can say to the miserable sinner, Petrukha,

'What did the gold iconostasis
ever save you from ?'

(Dvenadtsat', 10, 9-10)

In Dante's description of the troupe of devils their leader says:

'Go with them, they'll behave themselves. Here, Alichino and Calcabrina', he said, 'and you, Cagnazzo, and Barbariccia to lead the squad. Libicocco goes too, and Draghignazzo, tusky Ciriatto, and Graffiacane, and Farfarello, and mad Rubicante. Cast about the boiling pitch. Safe passage for these two as far as the next ridge, that goes unbroken right across the dens.' 'But, Master, what is this?' I said, 'If you know the way, let us go alone, without escort, for I don't want one. If you are as wary as usual, don't you see how they are grinding their teeth and exchanging mischievous looks?' *(Inferno*, XXI, 117-32)

Blok introduces the Twelve in Section Two of the poem:

The wind is on the town, the snow flutters.
Twelve men are on the move.
Black straps on rifles,
around them- fires, burn, burn...
chewing cheroots, their caps aslant,
all that's missing is the ball and the stripes!
Freedom, freedom,
hey, hey, with no cross!
Tra ta ta!
It's cold, comrades, cold!

(Dvenadtsat', 2, 1-10)

Barbariccia leads a squad of ten, *la decina*, and is called *decurio* ('captain').[1] The Twelve, too, form a military squad, and both squads are remarkable for their lack of military discipline. (It is interesting to recall, in this context, Chukovsky's report that Blok said he saw angels' wings on the Red Guards[2]: it is clear now that he meant fallen angels.) More similarities between the devils and the Twelve are revealed in their wanton violence. In *Dvenadtsat'*, one of the Twelve threatens the dog:

> 'Clear off, mutt,
> Or it's the bayonet tickle!
> Old world, like a mangy mongrel,
> disappear or else!'
>   (12, 9-12)

The dog had earlier been described thus as mangy:

> A mangy tike with a hang-dog look
> presses its wiry coat against him:
>   (9, 7-8)

In the *Inferno*, one of the devils drags a sinner from the boiling pitch and Dante says:

> And Graffiacane, who was nearest to him, hooked his tarry locks
> and hoisted him. He looked like an otter.   (XXII, 34-36)

The emphasis is on its tarry fur. The other devils shout:

'Hey Rubicante, see that you put your claws in him, and skin him!'
        (XXII, 40-4)

Both the Twelve and the devils relish the language of violence. Lines 9-12 of the last section of *Dvenadtsat'*, may be compared with the point in canto twenty-one where the devils are discussing the terrified Dante:

---

[1] *Inferno*, XXII, 74.
[2] See Hackel, op. cit., p. 130.

They readied their hooks, and one said, 'Shall I touch him on the rump?'
And others answered, 'Yes, see that you notch it for him.' (XXI, 101-02)

The Red Guard would 'tickle' with his bayonet, and the devil
would 'touch' with his hook: gentle euphemisms of the chronically
violent. Another comic example of such language is where the
above-mentioned sinner, when he is speaking to Dante, says:

> 'Oh no! see that one grinding his teeth:
> I would say more, but I am afraid
> he's getting ready to scratch my scurf'.
> $\qquad$ (XXII, 91-93)

The last expression, 'to scratch my scurf' (to beat mercilessly),
brings to mind section eight of *Dvenadtsat'*, where the devil-sinner
relationship is echoed in the Red Guard's words to the bourgeois:

> Well, I'll scratch my pate,
> I'll scratch a bit
> $\qquad$ (8, 6-7)

> And with my knife
> I'll slash and slash!
> Fly away, bourgeois, like a sparrow!
> I'll drink your blood.
> $\qquad$ (8, 10-13)

Neither the Twelve nor the devils are in control of their violence;
they are swept along in its element: the devils walk by the black,
boiling pitch, the Twelve walk in black, boiling wrath
(*Dvenadtsat'*, I, 79-8 I) .The violent element interferes with their
objectives so that Kat'ka is killed by mistake, and two devils fall
fighting into the tar (at the end of canto twenty-two). This
apparently aimless violence takes on meaning outside the level of
individual characters, in the overall contexts of *Dvenadtsat'* and
The Inferno: the cyclone of revolution and the will of God,
respectively, which are led through St Petersburg and Hell by the
figure of Christ. This is the crux of the comparison: in both poems
the complex, fleeting image of Christ gives sense and direction to

the action of the characters, but the meaning of the image derives largely from outside The Inferno, outside *Dvenadtsat'*.

2

The provenance of Dante's Christ is well understood: he comes to Dante through the Bible, the Church Fathers, etc. The provenance of the Christ of *Dvenadtsat'* is not yet clear, so we must consider His antecedents, first of all in Blok's own poems. Three particular features are of interest, illustrated in three lyrics. The first is Christ of the storms:

> From legends, from stories and mysteries
> The one, the victorious Christ
> On the waste, and in random day-dreaming
> Made his mark, and in whirlwinds, moved on.
>> (I, 225; September 1902)

The main point of interest is that, as early as 1902, Blok linked Christ with blizzards. We must also note the epithet 'Vsepobednyy' ('all-conquering') .The second aspect is the gentle, radiant Christ, saviour of those who follow Him:

> There He is – Christ – in chains and roses,
> beyond my prison bars.
> There is the gentle lamb in white garments…
> until you fade, like the dead grain.
>> (II, 84; October 1905)

The connection between meekness and salvation through death and resurrection, as in John, XII, 24, is most important for this discussion. The third relevant aspect is the violent Christ, the fierce God of the Old Believers:

> And so – deciduous, rusty water
> Drops that well in the glades of night
> Bring to a frightened Russia news
> Of an incendiary Christ.
>> (III, 248; 1907-14)

The combination of these three aspects in *Dvenadtsat'*, can be traced to a theme whose Western counterpart is the Harrowing of Hell, but whose Byzantine name is 'Anastasis', in Russian icons – 'voskresen'ye' (also known as 'soshestviye vo ad': Descent into Hell). Eastern and Western traditions originate in the Apocryphal Gospel of Nicodemus, written early in the third century. The second half of this document presents the basic story of the descent of Christ into Hell. Different manuscript versions of this gospel testify to a growing difference between Eastern and Western Churches: while the Western Church maintained that Christ rescued only a certain number from Hell, the Eastern Church left it in Christ's power to rescue everyone.[1] For the medieval West, Christ's descent into Hell was principally a triumph, a victory over Satan. The Eastern Church saw this event as the rescue of souls from the kingdom of death. For the East, the breaking of the gates of Hell – and the opening of Heaven's gates – came to symbolize Christ's Resurrection. The representation of Christ in Russian icons of the Descent into Hell is significant. He is shown as a dynamic figure (the only common icon of Christ in vigorous movement – who holds his cross like a banner, whose robe blows in the wind like a flag. He has sown destruction in Hell: He is Christ of the storms. Sometimes dressed in white, He is the gentle Saviour who leads His people from death. Finally, He has broken down the gates of Hell and cast Satan into the pit. A later development (appropriated from Revelation, XX, 1-3) shows His angels completing the rout of the devils. This is the fearsome Christ beloved of the Old Believers, and the 'Vsepobednyy Khristos' ('all-conquering Christ'). The theme of fire which is linked with Christ in *Dvenadtsat'* does not feature in the icons. Its religious source is to be found in the writings of the same Old Believers. In these three aspects, Christ in the mandorla visiting Hell can be recognized at the end of *Dvenadtsat'*:

> Up ahead, with the bloody ensign
> Unseen beyond the blizzard
> Unscathed by any bullet
> Gently treading the storm
> With a pearly dusting of snow

---

[1] J .Monnier, La Descente aux enfers,Paris, 1905.

In a crown of white roses
- up ahead: Christ Jesus.
            (12,33-39)

3

From Resurrection let us return to Dante and the Harrowing of Hell. We have noted parallels between Blok's *Dvenadtsat'* and the *Inferno*, especially cantos XXI and XXII. It is worth asking why the pilgrims Dante and Virgil found themselves walking with ten devils. When Dante and Virgil encounter these devils, their leader, Malacoda, says to Virgil:

> It is not possible to go further by this ridge because the sixth arch lies all broken up at the bottom, but if you would still go onward, make your way along these rocks that lead to another ridge, which forms a path. Yesterday, five hours later than this, completed one thousand, two hundred and sixty-six years since the road here was broken. (*Inferno*, XXI, 106-14)

An earthquake has been caused by a force unnamed, unknown to the devils, but known to the reader. The ten devils help Dante and Virgil cross from one circle to the next through the destruction caused by the death of Christ, just as the Twelve are crossing the divide between one era and the next. Virgil makes more precise reference to the cataclysm in canto IV. Dante and Virgil are passing through the First Circle, the circle of the 'Virtuous Heathen', when Dante asks Virgil:

> 'Did ever anyone go out of here and come to bliss, whether on his own merit or by another's?' And he, who understood my veiled speech, replied, 'I was new in this Condition when I saw a mighty one come here, crowned with the sign of victory. From among us he took the shade of our first parent, the shades of Abel his son, of Noah, of Moses the Lawgiver, the obedient, Abraham the patriarch and David the king, Israel with his father and his sons, and Rachel, for whom he wrought so much, and many others, and he made them blest. And I wish you to know that, before these, no human spirits were saved.' (*Inferno* IV, 49-63)

Here we have the classical expression of the medieval Western Church, with the emphasis on the salvation of a limited number of souls, and on Christ's victory. Compare the image of 'un possente con segno di vittoria coronato' ('a mighty one, crowned with the sign of victory') with Blok's 'v belom venchike iz roz' ('in a white crown of roses'), which seems in the context to signify not so much victory as resurrection and new life: the crown of thorns in miraculous bloom. Note, too, that even the wise Virgil does not know who Christ is. Christ is unnamed and unknown in the *Inferno*, and he is glimpsed only this once, through the past in the Harrowing of Hell. This accords with the Christ of *Dvenadtsat'*, 'za v'yugoy nevidim' ('unseen beyond the blizzard'). The other reference to the Harrowing of Hell is in canto twelve. Here Virgil describes the cataclysm in Hell at Christ's death:

> But certainly a little time (if I discern aright) before He came who carried off from Dis the spoil of the uppermost circle, the deep, foul valley trembled on every side, so that I thought the universe felt love by which, as some believe, the world has more than once been turned to Chaos.   (*Inferno* XII, 37-45)

The words on chaos and love refer to Empedocles's theory of the universe. Briefly, this states that the universe consists of four basic elements (earth, air, fire, and water), acted upon alternately by two forces – love and hate. Hate tends to separate the universe into its constituent elements, and love tends to fuse them. When the universe is totally under the influence of love, all the elements are fused, confused. In spite of the terms 'love' and 'hate', this was a physical theory, devoid of ethical content. It is unclear what the Italian verses mean: there seems to be confusion between Empedocles and Aristotle's criticism of Empedocles, and critics are unsure whether the confusion belongs to Dante or Virgil or Virgil's informers, but the effect of the verses is clear and poignant: the Harrowing of Hell is an event in the spiritual world, and Dante gives it tremendous resonance by linking Empedocles's theory to it. He does it very simply by 'misconstruing' Empedocles's term 'love' to give the word every possible sense, beginning with the spiritual. Putting this expression in the mouth of Virgil, who did not know what was happening, emphasizes the awe and mystery of a cataclysm that shook every sphere of the universe.

This brings us to Blok's note on *Dvenadtsat'*: '... the poem was written in that exceptional and always brief moment when the cyclone of revolution produces a storm on every sea – the seas of nature, life, art ...'[1] which reveals the depth of the similarity between Blok and Dante: Dante from the Middle Ages and Blok from the era of Humanism look forward to a New Age. Both are great seers, and both invoke a greater one as a guide for the new times. Blok's words in his notebook of 1901-02 evoke Dante and the early Christians:

> When kindred beings meet across the centuries, the event is always mystical. Thus Pushkin came up against Peter. When he begins to speak of Peter, straight away, we sense mystery. The same happens with truly practising Christians, when they meet Christ – Dostoevsky in the teaching of Starets Zosima (and all the Karamazovs!). 'Herein is mystery', for the truly kindred have come together across centuries, like clouds that merge, releasing lightning. Other worlds exist.[2]

---

[1] III, 474.
[2] ZK, 21-22.

Tintin in Hell

Sapristi!
Mistah Kurtz,
I presume.[1]

----

[1] The first word is a mild imprecation, a corruption of 'sacristi'; the second, though it could be read as mimicry of standard southern English, is meant to mark the accent as coming from beyond the pale. The name Kurtz (German for 'short') reinforces the salient feature of the narrative. Imprecation, address, deduction: line by line the story goes back in time, and across the equator from west to east, against the course of the sun.

'I presume' refers to the meeting of Stanley and Livingstone in 1871 on the shore of Lake Tanganyika. Livingstone, wandering like a river, was so low on supplies that he would soon have had to borrow from the very slave traders whose activity justified his presence. He was on the wrong side of the watershed, bogged at the source of the Congo, not the Nile. Stanley had been sent by James Gordon Bennett, editor of the *New York Herald*, to get a story. Though no one in Britain knew where Livingstone was, the consul at Zanzibar knew how to reach him, so the scoop was something of a sham (most of this information is to be found in *David Livingstone and the Victorian Encounter with Africa*, ed. J.M. MacKenzie (London, 1996)). It did bolster Stanley's name, though, and started him on a career that took him down the Congo for King Leopold of Belgium, baptizing the font with much African blood. Joseph Conrad's *Heart of Darkness*, published in

1901, recalls a journey he himself had made on the Congo in 1890. The bloody Kurtz and the calculating manager of the ivory business are two sides of Stanley. They meet not at the source of the river, but well downstream, at Stanley Falls. The phrase 'Mistah Kurtz' is pronounced on a boat returning to what must have been Leopoldville, now Kinshasa. The boat is next seen heading up the Mekong with Martin Sheen on board, looking to terminate Marlon Brando with extreme prejudice. So far, so good. Sapristi, though the word does occur in Agatha Christie (perhaps as a private joke: the blood of Christie), is much more common in Hergé. *Death on the Nile* doesn't fit: this is *Tintin au Congo* (alternative translation: Nothing Doing on the Congo), where Tintin, a foreign correspondent, like Stanley, and indeed like Michael Herr who wrote the screenplay of *Apocalypse Now* (see above), is there for a story. Tintin is Belgian, though he doesn't boast about it. As a journalist he hits the Dark Continent well after the missionaries and just ahead of the diamond smugglers. He declines big money from American, British and Portuguese agencies – he may be in cahoots with the French – and takes over a country that looks like a Kenyan game park, not a Congolese forest, peopled with Robertson's Gollies. His methods are those of Prospero and Mistah Kurtz. Like them he can be defeated by no one but himself. He's a loose cannon that gets airlifted out to his next assignment before Conrad's cycles of desire, temptation and surrender can so much as skew his quiff.

Where are the women? All I recall in Tintin is an exceptionally glaikit looking mamma on a train; not a speaking part. The comic is the land of the grunt (see Michael Herr again, his book *Dispatches* on the Vietnam war). The mysterious stranger is geography, even in the other Rambo, 'je est un autre' (the other one-liner of 1871). Mistah Kurtz? It's the same for him. There only are two women: his intended back in Brussels and the African queen - again not a speaking part, more a figurehead. The narrator says, 'Girl! What? Did I mention a girl? Oh, she is out of it – completely. They – the women I mean – are out of it – should be out of it. We must help them to stay in that beautiful world of their own, lest ours gets worse.'

I presume the moral is clear: Livingstone was living in a cartoon strip. A funny hat instead of a Tintin quiff, but similar tuppence-coloured pictures of him being attacked by a lion, and folksy photos of his attendants in pantomime African dress. Meanwhile Livingstone's wife, too often pregnant, explored the rooming houses of London. Hers should have been a non-speaking role too, but she joined him on his penultimate trip, and she drank and she drank and she told him she didn't believe anymore in any of the religion he had been pushing in Africa, then she died on him.

That appeared to be that: another piece of fiction explained away, an open-and-shut case, till what did I see on the front page on 4 December 1996? 'Terrorist Bomb on Paris Train Kills 2'. Yes yes, that too, but this: '*International Herald Tribune* - Frozen Water Found on the Moon'.

> Pentagon scientists, speaking at a news conference, said that radar soundings by the Clementine, an unmanned spacecraft, had confirmed the existence of a large mass of ice in an area of permanent shadow near the lunar south pole ... The southern crater, known as the South Pole-Aitken basin, is 12 kilometres (more than 7 miles) deep, which makes it the deepest yet discovered in the solar system. The lake is estimated to be tens of feet deep.

The Times, 4 December 1996:
> ...material at the bottom of a crater nearly 8 miles deep is frozen water. The guess is that the water was carried there by a comet which crashed into the moon 3.6 billion years ago, creating the South Pole-Aitken crater... The ice lake is estimated to be 25 feet deep and 200 yards wide.

The source is an article in *Science* (Vol 274, 29 November 1996, 1495-8). It begins: 'The possibility of ice on the moon was suggested in 1961.' In fact, it was suggested 7 years earlier, in *On a marché sur la lune* (Hergé, Les aventures de Tintin, Paris/Tournai, 1954), where Tintin and Captain Haddock find some in a cave.

But earlier in that book Tintin as he leaves the rocket describes '...a nightmare landscape, a landscape of death, of terrifying desolation... Not a single tree or flower or blade of grass...' Dante likens the scene to the River Adige as it passes through Trento, though he saw not a comet but Satan crashed into the middle of it, for geographically the Inferno looks like nothing so much as this crater on the moon with a frozen pond at the bottom. In Dante, though, the moon is a nebula, outermost suburb of paradise.

But why am I telling you all this? And which of you is Mistah Kurtz? Is Conrad's heart of darkness on the Congo or on the Thames? T.S. Eliot thought he knew when he wrote 'The Hollow Men': 'We are the hollow men ... Headpieces filled with straw...'
'It seemed to me that if I tried I could poke my forefinger through him, and would find nothing inside but a little loose dirt, maybe.' That was Conrad's narrator on an employee of the ivory export company. Of the company manager, Conrad's narrator says, 'It seemed to me I had never breathed an atmosphere so vile, and I turned mentally to Kurtz for relief – positively for relief... it was something to have at least a choice of nightmares'. Eliot, I guess, was afraid of being like them; his fear was proof he wasn't. (Later, when he found the Church, he lost that fear.) When Tintin did London (*The Waste Land*, Faber & Faber, 1922), the ace reporter dedicated his text to Captain Haddock 'il miglior fabbro', thus likening the dedicatee to Arnault Daniel and himself to Dante. Quite a double act. There they were up country, like Romans in darkest Britain at the start of Conrad's story. It's nice to get on with the natives, but if that's too much trouble, you make a wasteland and you call it peace. You know, shantih, shantih, shantih, the peace that passeth understanding unless you read the footnotes.

> It was morning and Belacqua was stuck in the first of the canti in the moon. He was so bogged that he could move neither backward nor forward. Blissful Beatrice was there, Dante also, and she explained the spots on the moon to him. She showed him in the first place where he was at fault, then she put up her own explanation. She had it from God, therefore he could rely on its being accurate in every particular. All he had to do was to follow her step by step. Part one, the refutation, was plain sailing. She made her point clearly, she said what she had to say without fuss or loss of time. But part two, the demonstration,

was so dense that Belacqua could not make head or tail of it. The disproof, the reproof, that was patent. But then came the proof, a rapid shorthand of the real facts. A bistatic radar experiment measured the magnitude and polarization of the radar echo versus bistatic angle B, for selected lunar areas. Observations of the lunar south pole yield a same-sense polarization enhancement around B=0. Analysis shows that the observed enhancement is localized to the permanently shadowed regions of the lunar south pole. Radar observations of periodically solar-illuminated lunar surfaces, including the north pole, yielded no such enhancement. A probable explanation for these differences is the presence of low-loss volume scatterers, such as water ice, in the permanently shadowed region at the south pole. Belacqua was bogged indeed. Bored also, impatient to get on to Piccarda. Still he pored over the enigma, he would not concede himself conquered, he would understand at least the meanings of the words, the order in which they were spoken and the nature of the satisfaction that they conferred on the misinformed poet, so that when they were ended he was refreshed and could raise his heavy head, intending to return thanks and make formal retraction of his old opinion.

I've spiked that first paragraph of Beckett's 'Dante and the Lobster' with the abstract of the *Science* article mentioned above, trusting you can distinguish God from the Pentagon. Piccarda? Piccarda, most beautiful of women, more beautiful than ever. Your father put you in a convent, your suitor removed you. The vows you were obliged to make you were compelled to break. That lost you your place in the front stalls of heaven, though you are happy there in the pale outer reaches as you were in the convent, as you were at home. But the spots on the moon are gabbroid basalt, the rest is granite. You can't float there like sunlight in a raindrop. Mary Livingstone, ugly as an aardvark, uglier still when a miscarriage partly paralysed your face. Your father had given you to a fellow-missionary, who sent you home to squalor. That lost you your faith and drove you to drink. A decadent and a heretic. You're not even a poet. Miranda, there are not so many stories in the end; this is a tale of misappropriation. Nothing I can tell you will prepare you for the day. *Heart of Darkness* is only *The Tempest* told by an upstart duke, who arrives just as his brother's act is finally coming apart (the magic does get very rough at times). There's a beautiful Ariel poem where Eliot at first can do no wrong:

> What seas what shores what grey rocks and what islands
> What water lapping at the bow
> And scent of pine and the woodthrush singing through the fog
> What images return
> O my daughter.

then he lapses into another bloody sermon.

I give the floor to Sebastian Barker and the *Long Poem Group Newsletter* (No.2, February 1996):

> When, after a period of seven years' composition (1935-1942), Eliot finally managed, in the face of the Blitz, to complete Four Quartets, he made what Lyndall Gordon in *Eliot's New Life* (OUP 1988) called his 'Nijinsky leap': 'Poised over the turning rim of the wheel (of time), he now made for the hub, the still point (of timelessness).' In making this leap (an inescapable act of courage if the poem were to cohere as a whole), it appears he felt obliged to make a conscious, irrevocable, public commitment to mystical Christianity, albeit tempered and made steadfast by the Presocratic philosophy of Heraclitus. In Eliot's case, it is this core of indubitable sincere belief which helps to hold the disparate parts of the poem together. The successful reception of the poem gives us a transparency of a good part of western consciousness at the time, that is to say in the jaws of totalitarian terror. Further horrors were to come to Eliot's mind: the death camps, the atomic bomb. What kind of Nijinsky leap, we might wonder, must be attempted, following Eliot's example, to reconcile human pain and divine love now?

Holy smoke.

There's a painting by Henry Raeburn on the cover of Tom Scott's *Penguin Book of Scottish Verse*, the one my generation grew up with: The Reverend Robert Walker skating on Duddingston Loch. (If you can't see the picture, read the poem by David Kinloch.) Arms folded, one leg stretched out behind him, he has just completed the pirouette that drew the painter's attention to him. That minister has eyes you could skate across. Duddingston Loch is a mirror of oil and canvas. He slices the freeze-dried faces of Dante's traitors bedunk kaschlikk, splitting them like kail and cauliflower. Recongeal. It says the Rev. Robert Walker. But I'm not sure.

Sapristi!
Mistah Kurtz.

The Tum-ti-tum Epithet

> Slowly along the munching English lane,
> Like cows to the old shrine, until you lose
> Track of your dragging pain.

That should be 'mulching', shouldn't it? (Did nobody proofread *Robert Lowell's Poems: A Selection*, ed. Jonathan Raban?) though the dragging pain and big beasts might hint at anthropophagy rather than bacteriophages.

Looking up the page from 'Our Lady of Walsingham' to 'The Holy Innocents' I notice a 'clinkered hill' up which the year lumbers with losses. Shouldn't that be 'clinkered hull'? ... No. But I'm on my guard now. Next is the corpse in 'The Quaker Graveyard in Nantucket', 'its heel-bent deity'? surely, surely that should be 'hell-bent'? And 'the coiled, hurdling muscles of his thighs'? Could it be 'curdling muscles'? Makes just a bit more sense to me. Maybe 'eel-bent deity'; I'll let anything pass after the 'ale-wife run' of the first poem.

A decent edition wouldn't solve the problem, which is that Lowell once said he hoped people would read his work and say 'that was one heck of a poet' or something of the sort (sorry, can't find the reference). He is one heck of poet. And he's always trying hard to stay one, putting an adjectival spin on nouns that would otherwise have been plainer. He polishes his work till the reader can see his face in it. Lowell's.

What is it about adjectives? Their syntactic redundancy (take them all away and the sentences still work), their prosthetic virtues (for dragging rhythms), the fact that they know their place and rarely come wide. All this was a boon to bards and other oral improvisers, giving poet and audience a moment's rest: the berry-brown gown or, south and east, the rosy-fingered dawn. People who read poetry, though, take their own time off. While the adjective still serves as a rhythmic and syntactic rest, it often takes a lot of semantic weight, or strain. Like when Ezra Pound alludes (in Greek) to the rosy-fingered dawn, telling us to think of Homer before breakfast, or when Lowell hits us with the above examples.

Fear not, this isn't a grand unified theory of epithets. It's just interesting to see that the disconcerting effect of Lowell's bravura is what language poets contrive by other means. Astounding adjective and noun pairs may be produced by the Poet of Genius ('the gun-blue swingle' or whatever you like); they may also be produced by various algorithms, which nicely sabotages the ego as the source of all poetry. It leads the unwary to conclude that the text, however produced, is all we should look at. Which is nonsense. I don't like feeling that a poet I'm reading is spending too much effort on impressing me; but better that than a nihilistic purveyor of text and nothing but the text (Ashbery). I've more sympathy for some of the language poets, but in the end 'change the language' is not what it's about. A quick look at three poets who could tell them.

> Ah how bright the mantel
> Brass shines over me.
> Black-lead at my elbow,
> Pipe-clay at my feet.   (W.S. Graham)

This whole business of epithets can intervene at a late (prolonged and tedious) stage of the poem's formation, when the plasma settles down into little nuclear families and the charges get distributed. 'Mantel' gives the brass an ingot shape, 'black' combines with lead to form a shining compound, 'pipe' reacts with 'clay' as candour, the honest ornament. There isn't an adjective in sight. The colours are all substantive. Remove them and the sentences collapse, the hearth with them.

How can adjectives be used in an essential way? Let's see if that's a fair question. Even in Graham's weird first collection, the adjectives aren't responsible for much of the disorientation: true there are bloodshot pennies, myrtle gospels and a nettle forefinger, but there are also limestone viaducts, a boatless sea, blushing joy and a gentle queen, all as reassuring as the conventional sentence structure. Adjectives are weak parts of speech and Graham doesn't overload them. Indeed, until 'The Nightfishing' he's a bit too easy on them. And while 'sheerhulk', 'girlflowering' 'mastertask' and the other Anglosaxoid shunts are looking for integrity, the epithets – high, bright, new, black, white, blue, green, dry, terrible, dead, drowned – are trying to forge the elements that he struck in the later 'Malcolm Mooney's Land'. Sleekit metaphor, not fair at all; it's just a way of saying I don't completely trust his words until then. And anyway, where's the law against putting a semantic load on a weak part of speech? It isn't a matter of law, but discretion. Lowell bends everything to his purpose – that's his way. Graham tries to discern the language's purpose and go its way.

> Outside the tent endless
> Drifting hummock crests.
> Words drifting on words.
> The real unabstract snow.
> > (end of 'Malcolm Mooney's Land')

> It must be abstract
> > (Wallace Stevens).

Randell Jarrell tells us bad poetry is not good and abstract poetry is not poetry (the latter a propos of Wallace Stevens, whose earlier work he praises highly). Well (A) most poetry is bad: it's a mug's game, and (B) the rest can be as it pleases: 'The real unabstract snow' is utter abstraction, lyophilized.

Each Stevens poem is an abstraction, an architectural model on computer. The components can be either images or ideas, but the plan's the thing. 'Poetry is the supreme fiction, madame. Take the moral law and make a nave of it. And from the nave build haunted heaven. Thus,' thank you. Epithets. There are two distinctive tribes in Stevens, the colours and the quizzicals. The colours are primary, and lights rather than pigments (the reverse is true of Graham), slanting in and suffusing the things – golden floor, red bird, pool of pink, bright chromes, colored purple, white moonlight, green shade – to look no further than the first twenty pages of the collected poems. And while the colour epithets show, the quizzicals see (light source and viewpoint respectively, in the computer image). 'The Doctor of Geneva' has a swatch of them, as the good doctor is seen reacting to a new location: lacustrine man, multifarious heavens, simmering mind, unburgherly apocalypse. Stevens quickly escapes anything as crass as a scanning of his epithets, though the exercise confirms that he isn't content with making his poems: in his tremendous ambition that poetry succeed religion, he lets there be light on them with his 'purple' adjectives, and he doubts and believes in them with his quirky epithets.

I had in mind a further manic leap, to Mandelshtam, but the chasm is wide. If Anglosax was W.S. Graham's handicap, then Greek (and Homeric epithets) was Mandelshtam's. Still, it's nice to see how in the poem to JSB he sets up 'O ratiocinatory Bach' (or 'Most reasonable, judicious Bach') to increase the thrill of the punchline, with Bach 'exulting like Isaiah', and in 'I washed in the courtyard at night', how the epithet 'coarse' applied to stars prepares for 'In the rain-butt a star melts like salt'. As he progresses, though, I can't easily distinguish what he's planned from what the language serves him. There are, for me, terrible difficulties in 'The Slate Ode', because although Mandelshtam's (anybody's) rhyme is exogamy that breaks the dominion of familiar etymological association, Mandelshtam seems to reach far into the past of his words as well, where family is not familiar at all. Thus a lot of his weird findings, that have neither rhyme nor reason in a foreign language like English, turn out to have semantic precedents at home.

> Flint meets water and ring joins horseshoe;
> On the soft shale of the clouds
> A milky slate-grey sketch is drawn.[1]

---

[1] *Osip Mandelshtam: Fifty Poems*, translated by Bernard Meares, with an introduction by Joseph Brodsky (New York, Persea Books, 1977).

Now 'persten'' (signet ring) is cognate with 'perst'' (breast) (the ring being a nipple substitute, apparently), that goes with the 'milk slate sketch' of the following line. And 'kremen'' – (flint) is cognate with 'shram' (scratch or scar), so that when at the end he writes:

> I want to place my fingers
> In the flinty path from the older song
> As in a lesion

the thing begins to make sense. Begins to. Enough. I am now in a position to conclude that there are at least four ways of skinning a cat, and that that conclusion gets me no nearer the rough taxonomy I was out to establish. I don't think, anyway, that taxonomy would have shed any light on the light shed by certain poems, or that that would have been useful or possible.

When We Don't Need to Know

Having glanced at the function of epithets, I'd like to drive past allusion before the common ground for it disappears.

Take Basil Bunting's

'How Duke Valentine Contrived

(the murder of Vitellozzo Vitelli, Oliverotto da Fermo, Mr Pagolo and the Duke of Gravina Orsini) according to Macchiavelli'

which mentions a Mister Anthony of Venafro.

I went to Santa Maria Novella railway station in Florence and asked for a ticket to Venafro. 'Where?' Venafro. Never heard of it. Checks screen, checks dog-eared almanack. Oh, right. Rome, then local train south, three hours, two changes. That's right. Siena is easy enough, but your Florentine railway clerk can't place Venafrum, as Horace called it in his odes. Did Messer Antonio di Venafro know his Horace? Because centuries after Macchiavelli they were still using handsome Roman stones as doorposts - you have to read them sideways. It had been a place the patricians patronised. It is now an overgrown village with overgrown villas jostling out the light on what was once a fertile plain. No sign of Horace. Did Basil Bunting know? During the war, when it was a beautiful little village, with a big hole knocked in it by Flying Fortresses that had been trying to hit Monte Cassino 20 miles away? They were so high up it's a wonder the bombs landed at all.

My question is obvious: what do we have to know?

Take the first poem in Muldoon's *Hay*. I'd told a friend it was worth a read, though there was some principle of organisation behind it that the poet dangles in front of the reader's nose too close to focus. Some kind of sestina, maybe. The friend phoned up, all pleased, saying he'd especially liked the poem about the Morbier cheese. Well, I didn't recall that one. He explained, though, that the whole caper with goats, the Jura mountains and the cinder path that runs through the poem, even the Zephyr hubcaps (q.v.) is from the shape of the Morbier cheese, a round thing that gets cut in half so they can put a layer of ash in it, god knows why. He's right. It does leave the puzzle of those odd pairs of words from adjacent spots in the dictionary, but the man deserves a cash prize nevertheless. Perhaps provision is made on the Paul Muldoon website. My friend said that when he saw in the same poem reference to 'the worst excesses of Conlon Nancarrow' he felt immensely pleased to be part of the miniscule élite that could pick up both references. He and Paul, I reckon. And now us too, gentle reader. And did we need to know? No. But we weren't to know that.

Now take the train from Florence to Sienna. There is no train, so take the bus. The city has put up plaques here and there, very discretely, quotations from Dante that I was able to check up in the bookshops:
'Siena mi fè, disfecemi Maremma' on a thirteenth century palace in the middle of town, the words of a young woman who speaks to Dante in paradise (see 'Tintin in Hell'). It sounds like an epitaph, like

'Norfolk sprung thee, Lambeth holds thee dead,
Clare of the county of Claremont, though hight'…

and of course it reads like an epitaph, set in stone there.
Then at the bottom of the hill there's an old covered reservoir – very old, because it's mentioned in the Inferno – 'Per fonte Branda non darei la vista': someone who's landed in hell partly because he

was double-crossed; he's tortured by thirst, but he says, 'If I could see down here the two who got me into this place, I wouldn't swap that satisfaction for Fonte Branda!'

Of course Dante uses bits of this world to make his own: when he describes bits of hell as being like the river Adige at Trento it's earth, not heaven, that is real. But he does it so coherently that, when you're sitting by a pond where three big whiskered carp are enjoying the shade on a July afternoon, you might feel for a moment that you've crossed into the metaphoric level of Dante's real eternity. Everything you learn about Dante's words gets you closer to his purpose.

My language teacher asks a question. I don't know how to reply. He says, just give me an answer: it doesn't have to be true, it just has to make sense. Frank Kermode once described poetry as a higher-level grammar. In some ways it's an antigrammar: it doesn't have to make sense, it just has to be true. And the truth can be difficult even when it is banal. So Bunting hedges it round with reconditry, the worst excesses of which he then has to mend in those hilariously prim footnotes (Attis : 'Parodies of Lucretius and Cino da Pistoia can do no damage and intend no disrespect').

So what's the answer from Macchiavelli, Bunting and Abu'abdulla Ja'far bin Mahmud Rudaki of Samarakand? For he puts himself there among them, their languages and worldly ways.

> Ille mi par esse deo videtur
>
> O, it is godlike to sit selfpossessed
> When her chin rises and she turns to smile;
> But my tongue thickens, my ears ring,
> What I see is hazy.
>   - Odes II, 7.

Knowing Latin is not much consolation. And some allusion, when chased down, is mere distraction.

Squink

I first noticed the work of J.H. Prynne in an *Observer* review of his
Poems (1982) and of Edwin Morgan's *Poems of Thirty Years* (also
1982). The reviewer was much more impressed by Prynne, and
one key change caught me as so strange that I wanted to know
where it came from:

> To return, this is an
> intimately physical place,
> picked out of the air like
> forbidden fruit. So much air and so close I
> can feel the lunar caustic I once used in
> a lab note-book headed 'analysis'. Now
> it's Laforgue again, the evening a deep city
> of velvet and the Parisian nitrates washed off
> into the gutters with the storm water...

I bought the book, relocated the phrase, but apart from The Kirghiz
Disasters and the first line from the poem on Paul Celan – 'Fire
and honey oozes from cracks in the earth' – and the last lines of
'Glove Timing' ('...If you still want to come / in like that, take off
your word for shoes') didn't retain much. And yet I bought the
Bloodaxe in 1999 and went through it again. Which means it's
been on a backburner for thirty years, and I still don't know what to
make of it.

What follows is a reading in three parts. The first approach is
through recent critics of Prynne's work; the second is a secular,
subjective and perhaps naïve recollection of one particular poem;

the third proposes a way of reading that neither rejects nor over-interprets the work.

MetaPrynne

Critics, especially critics of poets they fear are undervalued, can develop similar attitudes to their subjects. I can't sum up the MacDiarmid squad, since I was of their number; Geoffrey Hill instils a religious hush in his exegetes; Kelman evokes a Beckettish stress on the total integrity of the writing, Edwin Morgan's proponents don't understand why he doesn't have the same respect outside Scotland; all of them are on the defensive about something, the thing they suspect is causing the blockage. In Prynne's case it's the *difficulty*.

If you open *A Manner of Utterance: The Poetry of J.H. Prynne*, edited by Ian Brinton (Exeter, Shearsman, 2009) I suggest you go straight to the composer John Douglas Templeton's 'Many Voices: *Singing*', which praises these 'unusual creations rich with possibility'. He says 'Music is often spoken of as a language. Often it seems to be some kind of overheard language of another species where we can only guess at the significance of the utterances.' 'The poems push to the limit the amount of information my brain can hold on to: and so I can't hold on. This is similar to what the composers I am interested in do with music. Your choice is to either embrace this or remain in a paralysis of the "fear of misunderstanding"'.

Prynne's work is as near to pure lyric poetry as we are likely to find today. It aspires to the condition of music. It isn't music. It refuses to be protest poetry and embodies that refusal; if his followers approve of that strategy then protest on his behalf, Prynne can't be blamed. On the other hand, there is a cultic air to his support that Prynne encouraged in the 1960s and 70s, when he was published in small presses that were often run by other poets. This was an exclusive coterie: 'I'm really not interested in the casual reader & his hot little coin.., I don't want a lot of fashion-conscious undergraduates writing for copies that they don't really need. This is serious business'.[1] Prynne did not write manifestoes but he did write letters that were subsequently published and are referred to in this book of essays as 'the Letter to Andrew Duncan', the 'Letters to Drew Milne', and others. Rather like Saint Paul, often with a chiliastic ring, 'The time will come and pour down like a libation, it will flow like oil into the ground'[2], always with the same implicit get-out: this isn't addressed to *you*. 'How can you give, unless you are to present merely symptomatic malnutrition, what you claim to have taken away – the wheat from beneath the iron.' (The Letter to Andrew Duncan, quoted on p. 87)

A cultic consequence of this is the way in which the subject divides opinion. Many are dismissive, but enthusiasts invest great hope and trust in the poetry and in the poet. A few quotes from the book show the tenor of praise for Prynne.

'Prynne has no doubt read every significant poem written in English. I do not know about his multilingual strengths or otherwise.'   – the artist Ian Friend, p. 46.

(Readers of Hugh MacDiarmid's later work might recognise in this the super-poet from 'The Kind of Poetry I Want'. MacDiarmid wanted poetry to cover the gamut of human experience, which meant that the poet would have to know everything. He didn't claim to (though I believe he did claim in *Lucky Poet* to have read every poet of significance – and not just in English). And Prynne doesn't claim to either; his disciples do that for him. MacDiarmid's pseudonymous super-poet *was* a fiction, an aspiration. Prynne isn't.)

'Prynne continues to challenge his readers: there is a poem in runes, another in Chinese calligraphy, pages of complex equations, all still waiting for readers and responses.' Nigel Wheale, p. 164.

This, once again, is reminiscent of MacDiarmid, who in the early days had people believe that he knew every European language

---

[1] Prynne to Andrew Crozier on publication of *Prospect* in February 1964; see Ian Brinton, 'A Common Meeting Point', *PN Review* 203, p. 54.
[2] Same letter.

and a lot more besides. In his case it didn't ultimately matter, it was a journalistic ploy to get attention. Prynne is different and more serious, because the big claims are made by the poetry itself. I ran the Chinese poem past my teacher. She gave me a transcription and word-for-word translation of it, but the most instructive thing was to watch her face as she read.[1] It seems to be better than Eliot's French verse, but here's the strangest thing: it isn't difficult, not even faintly or slightly. It's as conventional as could be (though it doesn't achieve the conventional symmetries), and centuries behind what contemporary Chinese poets are doing. How does that square with the rest of his oeuvre? Eliot's published verse in French approximated to his English, clearly modernist in style. But Prynne's Chinese resembles his English poetry only in being difficult for the average English speaker to understand.

---

[1] 结伴觅石湖
jiē bàn mì shí hú
together seek stone lake

上桥推古载
shàng qiáo tuī gǔ zài
upon bridge infer old time
桥头古景看
qiáo tóu gǔ jǐng kàn
bridge end old landscape see
青苔遮荒苑
qīng tái zhē huāng yuàn
green moss conceal abandoned garden
伴友谈心意
bàn yǒu tán xīn yì
with friend talk heart sense
雨天杯香叶
yǔ tiān bēi xiāng yè
rain day glass fragrant leaf
久回享心间
jiǔ huí xiǎng xīn jiān
long return appreciate heart within

'What a reader needs to do is to enjoy... and not necessarily to have the abstruse knowledge or skills that Prynne has acquired.' – Li Zhimin, p. 59.

Trust him, he's an expert. In what? Prynne is a fine Sinologist, but his Chinese verse is a school exercise, not something for publication on a par with his poetry. What about the sciences? What is the place of science in poetry? Science connects with poetry in one of three ways. Either the poet is a specialist who wants to bring his working experience into his verse along with the rest of what he thinks and feels (several physicians come to mind, but there are also mathematicians, chemists and biologists); or a poet wishes to get to grips with the sciences from the layman's point of view ('On a Raised Beach' is one of the summits on this approach), or the poet wishes to convey the emotional appeal of uncommon fields of research. Prynne's familiarity with the sciences may well exceed MacDiarmid's, but his knowledge and skills in the hard sciences remain those of an amateur. And unlike MacDiarmid he uses science primarily for emotional sophistication; the tonal estrangement that he draws from it and deploys shows he is not writing science from the inside. This ought not to need saying, but if you want science, you ought to go someplace else.

'In the face of difficult poetry, there certainly should be a change of attitude towards "understanding" itself, so that one can feel confident to understand an 'obscure' poem in an "obscure" way.' – Li Zhimin, quoted by Ian Brinton, p. 8

This is where MacDiarmid decisively parts company with Prynne, because the former *did* want his readers and his ideal poet to understand everything. If Li Zhimin is correct in his suggestion, he is correct also in the adjectives: Prynne's verse is not difficult but obscure – a conclusion that would displease the poet himself; let's suspend that one for the moment.

'And sometimes in China one may often memorize a poem one does not understand; only dozens of months or dozens of years later to experience a sudden enlightenment and full enjoyment of the poem' – Li Zhimin, quoted by Ian Brinton, p. 8

Chinese people who memorize poems they don't understand usually do so at school, under duress, at the age of about six. The poems they learn are short T'ang classics. This trains their memory and probably their calligraphic skills. If they recall the poems when they grow up, it is likely that they will indeed understand what they hadn't at the time. Perhaps one could put *Her Weasels Wild Returning* on the primary-school curriculum with the same effect in view, but only perhaps.

Keston Sutherland's essay, 'XL Prynne', starts with three pointed questions: 'What is radical thinking? Is there radical thinking in J.H. Prynne's poems? What is anyone looking for?' After a three-page digression on Marx, he gets back to the point: 'If we are looking for radical thinking in Prynne, should we not start with the realities of injustice and the material distribution of power, and ask what is in fact thought about them by this poetry?' Having considered that question in some depth he is led to a further question: 'What is this frustration of eloquence by its own particles *for*?' In answer, he narrates Prynne's estrangement from Olson, an early influence – ultimately because he came to see Olson's as an imperialist venture that he could not condone or in any way follow. A central act in Prynne would seem to be this pointed refusal to speak falsely. As Perril puts it, 'Prynne's haunted sense that we have induced moral mutation of the species has resulted in poetic utterance's cleft palate' (p.95). Sutherland makes much of Prynne's injunction to shrink: in opposition to the grandness of Olson, the poet should be small. I'm not sure that's the operative shrinkage in Prynne's verse; it's more that he shrinks away from the reader and flings up screens – these poems in runes, in Chinese, the formulae, the strange scientific language, and programmatic statements to the reading public that are made only indirectly, through various friends who share with him a history that the general readership does not. Such are the blatant signs of what happens in every stanza of the poems: they cut and run, jinking more intricately with the passing years, to the extent that even one of the addressees of the early letters says, with a wink at 'The Hollow Men':

> 'Of course, Prynne's aesthetic of difficulty often causes
> panic anxiety, feels like sensory deprivation, and invites

> misconstruction . . . people have different perceptions
> of what 'good pattern' is, and may experience
> incompleteness as anxiety as well as cognitive freedom.
> I know I can't understand late Prynne, and attempts by
> other people to explain it seem dishonest and like
> fistfuls of straw.   (Duncan 2003), p. 164.

As a result, whilst there is unanimity on what Prynne is *not*
prepared to say, no one seems to know what he *does* say. On
radicalism, I counted three different views in the book:

Sutherland: 'Prynne describes communism as "a sort of primal
nostalgia", "a prelapsarian dialect, to describe the unattainable". If
Prynne's poetry is radical, it is not radical Marxism.' (p. 112).

Perril: 'Prynne accepts the aptness of the model of market
economics for discussing contemporary avant-garde poetics, but
not from a perspective of "resistance" to that model.' (p. 100).

Mengham, meanwhile, reads Prynne's *Word Order* (1989) as
praise of a radical alternative to capitalist economy, based on the
gift – though there is no indication of how the gift economy, which
can work in a society where everyone knows everyone else, might
operate throughout a large state (far less is there any sense that a
gift economy is what *does* operate in the controlling echelons of
capitalist and other societies). Given the references to economics
throughout Prynne's work, I find this lack of clarity disappointing.

Prynne has an answer to that, and of course he is free to write a
poem that 'teaches readers to be suspicious of the desire for
translucency aroused by its own complexity' (Jennifer Cooke,
'Warring Inscriptions', quoted in a footnote on p.126). One
consequence of this – whether readers assimilate that message or
not – is that there can be no confidence in what is said, or indeed in
whether anything is being said at all. This gives critics unlimited
licence for free-association. Three examples:

> 'Clean' and 'slain' are not only half-rhymes, they also
> recall the separation of Western and Eastern branches
> of the Indo-European family of languages according to
> the *centum/satem* test'. (Rod Mengham, p. 81)

In the poem in question, they are adjacent words in a line, and so not rhymes at all. Furthermore, the poem makes not the faintest reference to the Indo-European family. As Mia said to Vince, 'That's a little bit more information than I needed'.

On reading the expression 'in no time at all' Simon Perril goes into a long history of the expression 'in the nick of time', which does not occur in the poem. On reading 'A halo of grey cinders' the same author tells us that the 'Gray' is a unit of radiation dose, and that it alludes to the nuclear accident in Russia (it was not in Russia, and Prynne could have chosen to spell the adjective 'gray' but did not).

Of another poem in the collection *Bands around the Throat*, the same author notes, 'The title "Marzipan" remains obscure.' He ventures the following:

> In this publication, Prynne's poem was accompanied by a translation of the poem into French ... titled 'massepain'. It seems likely that Prynne's title itself becomes a pun on its French equivalent as 'mass pain'. Its status as luxury foodstuff – literally the icing on the cake – returns to the ambiguous status of the 'bands' of the whole collection's title as being both constrictions and adornment. 'Marzipan' as a title is part of the book's scrutiny of the lyric rhetoric of pained outcry as being dubiously confectionary: and of the capacity of such rhetoric to complicitly sweeten the pill that it claims to be spitting out. Hence the irony in the title of the final poem of the collection: 'Swallow Your Pride'. (P.96)

He could have added that the French for 'swallow' is 'hirondelle', the name of a cheap French wine that was sold in Britain at the time. Mass pain, indeed. And of course, the title of the collection, *Bands around the Throat*, might allude to the Jacques Brel song, 'Quand je pense à Fernande, je bande, je bande'. But enough of this. 'Marzipan' is a fine poem; leave it be.

Perhaps the strangest feature of such random-access response is that it should ever produce consensus on the work. Yet several authors agree that rubbish is a good thing – Prynne's rubbish, at least.

The apparently destructive effect of this accentuated montage, this 'verbal smash-up', destroys recognizable forms of order and coherence, produces debris, produces rubbish. But the production of rubbish is essential since it is the inevitable outcome of testing the limits of the sequential procedures of an ideologizing rationality. (Mengham, p. 73, citing Marcel Mauss)

'On "Gibberish": David Marriott, An Introduction to the Poetry of J.H. Prynne' (footnoted on p. 130)

> Rubbish provokes complex and intimate congress among hitherto separate discourses and levels of experience... (Erik Ulman, p. 150).

> I have learned much not only from Prynne's interest in rubbish, but also from the sound of his verse... (Ulman, p. 151)

> In context Prynne's variety of diction is another instance of positive rubbish, manifesting both dissonance and fusion within its heterogeneity, both common and conflicting lines of force, rhymes. (Ulman, p. 155)

Words fail me.

Simon Perril raises two points that several critics focus on: centrally, Prynne's rejection of the bad faith implicit in poetry that uses the power of language to speak against power, thus accruing power on its own account; peripherally – the problem of irony and (I would add) how irony might be perceived as such in Prynne's work. He quotes Prynne's Letter to Andrew Duncan, as follows: 'But nonetheless the reader has to maintain a particular alertness to make out, within the ironical and self-parodic interplay of tones, the differences between the right and the righteous, the pain of loss and the power of pain.'(p. 87).

Two authors quote Prynne's diffident ambition for his poetry: 'It has mostly been my own aspiration, for example, to establish relations not personally with the reader, but with the world and its layers of shifted but recognizable usage, and thereby with the reader's own position within this world'. (p. 145)

Self-parody, though, and irony, rely on at least the illusion of a presented self, a persona. Without that, there is no basis from which irony can comprehensibly deviate; given that the self in question shrinks from the reader, or runs like the clappers, we're not offered that stable basis. So what is my complaint? That the author doesn't tell me what to think? Or that he doesn't take responsibility for what he says? And are these two different things?

He doesn't tell me what to think and he does take responsibility for the poems, at least in the sense that he subscribes to them. But that signature is contractual; it doesn't legitimize the authorial fallacy. And even if I have heard good things about the man behind the verse (I'm always pleased that someone who writes like this was broad-minded enough to welcome Douglas Oliver and Barry MacSweeney into the club), I'm not joining a cult of personality. The irony has to be pinned to the paper, not to the person. Back, then, to the question: can irony and self-parody function without a figured self? Self-parody, logically, cannot. What about irony? Characters in a Shakespeare play can deploy irony without committing their author to the point of view in question. But tones (as in the 'self-parodic interplay of tones' referred to above) are not agents and cannot deploy anything at all: they are deployed immediately by the author. And if that author abjures the temptation to turn tonal rhetoric on political reality – then we are in the realm of pure poetry, which turns in its own sphere, disengaged. It's a tenable position: Mallarmé seems to have lived by it.

> The warning signs in *Red D Gypsum* alert poet and reader alike that the 'lyric interior' is not a redoubt, or vantage, from which the all consuming Other can be viewed. Rather, Prynne appears to suggest that the experience of self-negation demands the relocation of subjectivity in a third space beyond the reflexive dyad of self and other. (Nolan 2003, quoted on p. 178).

That's the brighter side of it, though I see no indication as to how that might happen, or where that space might be. And then the same Nolan says also of the same sequence 'It is, perhaps, the most unsparing demonstration of Prynne's constant suspicion that poetry, like Prospero's castle, has been little more than an ego-fortress shielding the arbitrary whims of an icy, autocratic decisionism'. (quoted on p. 172)

Bertolt Brecht, it seems, suspected Shakespeare of not caring about what happens in the world. You couldn't accuse Prynne of that, because there's a continual undertow of anxiety. At moments, it is all that seems to distinguish him from the antic affect of John Ashbery. The result is poetry of great lyric charm, made poignant by what appears, on this meta-reading, to be meticulous authorial disengagement from whatever it might have said.

Is the political defensiveness described by Prynne's exegetes anything more than squeamishness? It seems more a matter of decorum, a refusal on the part of someone who has won prominence in his profession to speak on behalf of the powerless. Fair enough. In its hermeticism it refuses even more forcefully to speak *to* the powerless or the masses. That, too, is fair enough, and consistent to boot. A donnish scorn for the *polloi* is clearly voiced betimes. That – though not so fair – is up to him; readers who don't like it can simply set the book aside. Prynne's remaining readers, then, will not expect explicit political statements or indeed explicit anything else, with the exception of technical fragments whose purpose in context seems more tonal than expository anyway.

Acquaintance
How should this kind of poetry be read? A willingness to take the work at face value, crediting what you don't understand, seems preferable to heavy digging. The two composers who contributed to *A Manner of Utterance* seem to me to present Prynne in a better light than do the explicators and exegetes.

What about a reader who does not take the obscurities on trust but who will never have the leisure or the patience to hunt them all down to source?

There would be nothing wrong with examining Prynne's poetry in the way that *Guardian* journalists investigate Tony Blair's philanthropic and political activities, concluding that whereas it is possible that good work is being done, it is certain that Mr Blair's accountants obfuscate his financial dealings in a scuttle of holding companies and off-shore havens. Instead of asking what Mr Blair is doing, they wonder what he is hiding.

It seems equally fair to adopt a less aggressive stance and deal with the poems rather in the way that you might treat the discretion, secrecy or evasiveness of an acquaintance: take it as a given, as a right to privacy that is being exercised, and engage with the rest.

To check whether such an approach might be tenable, I return to the poem that caught my eye on a first reading of Prynne, and that I still enjoy 30 years later: 'The Kirghiz Disasters'.

From memory, without the text in front of me, I like the title and the tone, the rough hendecasyllabic structure, the deftness of the line breaks, the way it moves in on the accident from several physical, geographic and economic angles till we find ourselves in a freezing train, blocked on the rails. It suggests, in convincing detail, a bit of the world I don't know at all, and that's a joy. With the passing years such glimpses of something really new become rare. I must have read the poem for the first time within a year of waking up on a Soviet train one morning, sixty hours into the journey from Leningrad, to see the first real mountains I had witnessed in five years, and the fertile and glorious spring weather of Georgia, the unfathomable warmth and mirth of the world that was drifting along the rails. I like the way Prynne gets inside the situation, even to the point of realizing the questions that would arise spontaneously: 'Can smoke freeze?' How did he think that up without being in the carriage? I like what Richard Price calls the decorum of his verse, the play of images in the prosody.

I don't like 'the heart/has its excuses', a sad little joke on Pascal's 'Le coeur a ses raisons, que la raison ne connaît point'. That dictum was transmitted in Burns's 'Epistle to Davy': 'The heart's aye the part aye that maks us richt or wrang'. It goes through a declension in John Anderson's 'We believe what eases our minds'

– a declension because, though this is another philosopher acknowledging the de facto primacy of the heart over reason, Anderson does not recognize its sovereignty. By the time it gets to Prynne, it has neither sovereignty nor legitimacy, but only excuses - and excuses made to what? Is a poet subjugating the heart to reason? And am I making heavy exegetical weather of this? But that's one of the problems with Prynne: how do you tell a tawdry joke from some radical critique? Answer: you don't (unless, of course, the joke is so very lame that there's no mistaking it. Did Prynne *really* write: 'With blood on their hands is a terror attack / on the Jewish state. Antrim west bank, / lemon Kurds'? I'm afraid he did – in that book *Triodes*, the one with all the formulae).

So let's get back to what is good about the sequence. There is the cartoon comedy of part 5 – more Miyazaki than Disney, though the poems predate the Japanese animator. It's very well visualized; just as the first part was well sensed, down to the interaction of cold, fire, damp and smoke, this midget with the rolling eyes, the little birds making off with a glove, is all visual drollery. The whole section seems to set up the non-sequitable quip with which the sequence ends.

Checking the book, I am amused by the line

'Hell, not water creeping like afflicted soup into / the park…'

and pleased by 'And at that the fringes wither / with tight credal echoes…' – though the main effect seems to be from the adjective 'credal'.

Also the finale: '… She next stuffs her little crown into a / bag and runs daintily upstairs, she nauseates everyone.'

I notice that two of the strongest associations provoked in me by the sequence were not intended by Prynne. He buries his treasures in the field; in hunting for them, I dig up my own.

Compare that subjective take with a critical exposition of the same poem:

The Kirghiz Disasters dramatises this process of silencing at some length by re-enacting a particular process, the historical destruction of the Kirghizian language not once but twice. A disaster is 'star damage' but no longer 'at home', since the life-world of the C20th has become the world proposed by Heraclitus as its opposite, the anticthonic 'counter earth'. These images are displayed earlier in the book, but with the concrete example of the Kirghiz people, the destruction of earth resides precisely in that loss of collective narrative which can explain what 'native soil' actually means. Thus the poem proceeds as a mangled bulletin, intercutting 'news from the Tarim Basin' with domestic trivia from the home front.

> And at that the fringes wither
> With tight credal echoes, bringing fear into the homely
> Recital. Swear at the leather by the knee-joint
> Shouts Jerome, crumbs ready as a favoured bribe.

The epic tales (Albert Lord's 'return songs') of the Kirghizians now survive in only mangled form, the rubble of medieval and later Soviet purgations and enforced migrations. In the wasteland aftermath of Thomas Pynchon's post-war reconstruction zone, the 'Kirghiz light' is an emblem of visionary absence, everything that cannot any longer be viewed or comprehended within the constraints of contemporary political domination, as the landscape is cleared for its reconstituted inheritors, IG Farben and ICI.[1]

If it weren't for the same quotation of 'credal echoes' you would be forgiven for doubting that Nolan and I had read the same poem. If you must choose which reading to credit, better stick with Nolan, who knows more about Prynne than I do. Those who wish to argue whether 'the "Kirghiz light" is an emblem of visionary absence' are free to do so; I see no grounds for it in the poem, nor do I approve of a distant land and people being used as an emblem for anything. But my main worry with the entire enterprise is the following.

---

[1] Kevin Nolan, 'Capital Calves: Undertaking an Overview' *Jacket* 24, November 2003.

In the 19th century, when the cuneiform languages were being deciphered, some skepticism was voiced as to the likelihood of scholars ever managing to concur on the meaning of a dead text in a forgotten script. Doubts were dispelled in 1857 when the Royal Asiatic Society asked four experts to translate from the Akkadian the transcription of a newly-excavated tablet; the translations tallied.[1] Imagine the same experiment being repeated with a newly-written poem by J.H. Prynne; it wouldn't work. This poetry is not difficult, it is obscure. Read it musically, glean what comes to the surface, move on.

But this lambency wouldn't satisfy Prynne, who has this to say of some contemporary poetic practice:

> ... a switch of semantic field may seem locally disruptive in the most extreme manner; but then the reader may observe some later recurrence of the switched field that sets up a trace or thread, sometimes obliquely or many lines later. This may be not meaning determining its pattern of expression, so much as pattern and pattern-violation generating their own tendencies of meaning—or perhaps we should call this 'meaning', in some second-order sense. I don't think this is equivalent to post-modernist playfulness, where meaning is allowed to skim across a surface in a deliberately arbitrary way, because the use of difficulty as a method of poetic thought is different both in intention and effect from difficulty as a playground or a funfair.[2]

That confidence and earnestness in such a poet and scholar give pause, but much of his poetry does *not* convey decidable meaning – with or without inverted commas – and difficulty is *not* a method. Prynne's work indeed is not a funfair; in terms of tourism and entertainment it more resembles some mysterious ruins, ruins that no two archaeologists will ever agree on, and that for most of us will remain exercises in the enigmatic picturesque. That T'ang poetry should present difficulties is a function of the passage of time; though they deliberately stripped away connectives, thus amplifying the ambiguities, the T'ang poets did so in a context that

---

[1] Jean Bottéro, *Mésopotamie: L'écriture, la raison et les dieux* (Paris, Gallimard, 1987), p. 59.
[2] *Difficulties in the Translation of 'Difficult' Poems.*

was shared by many, and which has been largely and lovingly preserved over time. For a body of work to attain a much greater level of obscurity within the lifetime of its author, even while the author protests that it *does* convey meaning, is a strange state of affairs indeed.

Last attempt

In the same essay, Prynne raises the stakes to a level where most readers would fold:

> ...often difficult language in poems accompanies difficult thought, so that the difficulty of language is part of the whole structure and activity of poetic composition. Shakespeare's *Sonnets* are certainly of this kind; and I have to admit that many of my own poems are like this, with the result that I do not have a wide readership... [1]

I don't accept the comparison of Prynne's poetry with Shakespeare's sonnets, since the latter do convey thoughts that can, for the most part, be understood and paraphrased. Prynne's poetry from 1970 onwards doesn't convey difficult thinking: it makes thinking difficult. It does so much in the same way as the abstract expressionists thwarted representation, and perhaps with a similar purpose. I notice belatedly that I took to the Kirghiz Disasters immediately because it presents what can be seen as reassuring though beguiling unities of time, place and action. More often, the only Prynnic unity of place is the book, while rhythm and style replace time and action.

In discussing a painting, there is nothing wrong with looking into the properties of the paints – Prussian blue, for example, tends to corrode canvas – but paintings aren't made in order to demonstrate

---

[1] J.H. Prynne, 'Difficulties in the Translation of "Difficult" Poems'. http://www.cambridgeliteraryreview.org/wp-content/uploads/PrynneCLR3.pdf.

that. Prynne's poems, similarly, aren't made in order to showcase ideas. But because of his exceptionally rich palette, too many readers get distracted by the bright colours. To demonstrate my point about how his poems operate I'd like to finish by considering *Word Order*, parts of which are the simplest of line drawings. Before that, let's whizz through the works, to set *Word Order* in context.

The poetry of the sixties is various, approachable. I'd have retitled *Kitchen Poems* as Kitchen Sermons; *The White Stones* has a big range, and I can't help but like a poet who writes a 'Charm Against Too Many Apples': '... the ransom is never worth it and / we never get it anyway. No one can eat so / many apples, or remember so much ice' (*Poems* 2005, p. 68). There is a clutch of poems from 'One Way at a Time' onwards that look like journal entries cut into lines: they could hardly be clearer. The two footnoted poems 'Aristeas, in Seven Years' (p.90) and 'The Glacial Question, Unsolved (p.65) are indeed reminiscent of Olson. 'Thoughts on the Esterhazy Court Uniform' (p.99), on the other hand, might have done us the courtesy of giving us a hint such as 'Haendel'. This kind of knowing silence is unfortunate and it may have led his faithful readers to look, in the later work, for subtexts that would similarly provide keys to the mysteries – but subtexts to the later works are not so much keys as distractions.

For that later work – and I am generalizing about three-quarters of Prynne's output – the reader is better guided by the shape of the oeuvre, its presentation in small books, each of which takes a different approach. There is greater tonal variation *between* than *within* books, precisely because each one explores the implications of a different mode, a different *rag*. There are exceptions such as *News of Warring Clans* (1977), which does present a species of narrative and the range of tone that goes with story-telling. Often enough, in other collections, I don't know what's going on, and sometimes (eg with 'The *Time Plant Manifold* Transcripts') I wish I didn't; too frequently I am counting the pages to the end; the most interesting part of the *Kazoo Dreamboats*, for me, is the bibliography. Prynne's poetry, like the verse of Denis Roche, is a manipulative body of work, but it has greater scope and range. Its restless intelligence comes through not in notion or narrative, but in rhythm.

The native mode of *Pearls That Were* is stated in the first stanza:

On the blush cheek making, to one
making to the one, a stealing
tear, of blushing as every age
betrays the sight, alone.

The commas, more than anything, stroke this sequence along, counterpointed by the line breaks. The gentle register – set and maintained with 'blush' – is comforted with half rhymes that become rhymes as the sequence continues. It all glides on a stream of present participles, moving from warm to cold and unsettling, then returning to quietly triumphant. In outline it is not dissimilar to the Pushkin lyric examined in 'Seven Rhymes'. This is not a typical book of Prynne's, but it is typical in its unity. I should admit that, remembering Prynne's recognition of Douglas Oliver and Barry MacSweeney, I couldn't help looking for an elegiac subtext since both of them reworked the Middle English *Pearl* – but there was none. Both poets died in 2000, the year *after* the collection was published.

Word Order (1989). Take just two short parts of this sequence. Page 367:

> They do not want
> It is natural
> They do not want to go
>
> To go out is natural
> They do not want to go out
> Want is natural
>
> It is natural to want
> To want to go out at all
> War is natural
>
>
> They are underneath

p. 369:

> For the attraction
> Take away her long wait
> You must pay up
>
> Sooner you must wait
> She must pay for
> You must take away
>
> Her long awaited
> Sooner you must
> Her attraction must
>
>
> Better go now

The form is a variant of Gael Turnbull's 'spaces', with the last line at a distance, and at a meaningful angle, from the rest. We find musical repetitions and logical variations, the first not very subtle with its switch from 'want' to 'war'. The second piece works much better – terribly sinister in the way it draws the reader into something like complicity in leaving the woman to her fate.

The final point I wish to make about reading Prynne is just as simple. If you proceed from this pared-down *Word Order* to one of the more baroque or florid collections such as *Her Weasels Wild Returning* (1994), you should find it easier to catch the drift. Focus on the text, don't worry about the subtext or gnomic epigraphs which – as we know from some of the spadework done in *A Manner of Utterance* – can be fairly silly. Not everything works, and not every reader will catch what does succeed. It is abstract, it changes and it does give pleasure – not in the way that Wallace Stevens envisaged, but after the manner of American painters who came into their own not long after he wrote his *Notes Towards a Supreme Fiction*.

Geoffrey Hill, the Hanging Judge

In April 1919 Eliot wrote the following to a former teacher of his at Harvard:

> There are only two ways in which a writer can become important
> – to write a great deal, and have his writings appear everywhere,
> or to write very little. It is a question of temperament. I write
> very little and I should not become more powerful by increasing
> my output. My reputation in London is built upon one small
> volume of verse, and is kept up by printing two or three more
> poems in a year. The only thing that matters is that these should
> be perfect in their kind, so that each should be an event.

Quoting this in an article published in *Agenda*, Geoffrey Hill sets
out the extenuating circumstances for Eliot's frigid ambition, and
proceeds, 'however, I find that the letter places a remarkably heavy
stress on the particulars of career-making. Eliot's self-evaluation is
in terms of a calculating idealism; the effect is gratingly
oxymoronic, "important", "powerful", "reputation", "event"; the
commitment suggested by "perfect in their kind" is abraded in the
surrounding context'. ('Surrounding context'? Surely that's a
tautology, Mr Hill.)

But as Geoffrey Hill demonstrates in the same essay, the Ez and
Possum reputation game can even be played solo. Taking two
words from Shakespeare's Antony and Cleopatra ('ah, soldier'),
Hill says Christopher Ricks showed unparalleled acuity in saying
Eliot was a genius if only in pointing out that Shakespeare was a
genius for adding those two words to his source text. (Got that?
Good.) Ricks, though, was not quite up to the mark in approving of

217

Eliot's recourse to cliché in Four Quartets. Who does that leave on the rostrum? I make it Bill and Hill.

The article is entitled 'Dividing Legacies'. It follows extracts from Hill's 'Psalms of Assize'. Then there was 'Did Péguy kill Jaurès?' His focus is not poetic but forensic. The man missed a fine career as a hanging judge. He is a good poet; if he seems to evince the 'pleasure in varying the accepted postures of judicial death' which he finds in one of his subjects, that's his affair. But he has this habit of putting good poems in the dead mouths of great poets and others: Boethius, Campanella, Bonhoeffer; when the torturer has finished with them Hill takes over. There are plenty of examples, but to me the most galling and inept is the one on Aleksandr Blok (what are all those Roman gods doing there?). Here is S.J. Ellis 'On Geoffrey Hill's Decade of Reticence' (*PN Review* 98, 51-2).

> Intermittently, Hill mimics Blok:
>
> > into the rain's
> > horizons, peacock-dyed
> > tail-feathers of storm,
> > so it goes on.
>
> 'So it goes on': the wry aside comments upon the heightened rhetoric of dazzling vagueness in Blok's poetic vocabulary.

Ignorance in praise of arrogance! Is no cadaver safe from Hill's ventriloquy? None. Not even if, like Blok in later years, you try to live 'stiller than water, lower than grass'. It might be objected that I should be taking issue not with Hill but with his less critical critics (only a true fan could see the fact that Hill wasn't writing as something to write about), but a real poet does in the long run set the tone of the criticism; unlike Hill's own chosen subjects, he is still in a position to object to what is said about him. Besides, what does Hill do to Blok? He begins his poem with an epigraph that makes Blok appear a pretentious fool. It's a quote from Volokhova, the subject of a number of Blok's poems 'Joyfully I accept this strange book, joyfully and with fear – in it there is so much beauty, poetry, death. I await the accomplishment of your task'. She was an actress and she said what she thought she was supposed to say, sometimes with fine results: 'Having been endowed by nature with a tragic style of beauty I had too much good taste to cultivate a cheerful personality'.[1] Blok did learn to speak for Russia, in a way that would move almost anyone; Hill tries hard to speak for his own country, but I don't believe he has it in him.

You may have gathered by this stage that what prompted me to this attack was Hill's apparent condescension to Aleksandr Blok. To put it bluntly, no poet alive is big enough to look down on Blok. And gey few of the deid. It is only after my outburst, though, that I see that my two complaints about Hill are related, and realize that there is no point in looking farther into his poetry, because the crux of his practice is a turning away from the essential – in himself and in his subjects. A writer's obsession with martyrdom is an obsession with reputation – ultimately his or her own reputation – and this focus on accident fudges the poetry.

Boethius is important not because of his execution (on which Hill lingers 'Iron buckles gagged; flesh leaked rennet over them; the men stooped, disentangled the body' ('Mercian Hymns', XVIII) but because of the *Consolations of Philosophy*. Campanella's name remains with us not because he survived torture in the Inquisition jails for many years but because of his poems, and because of *The City of the Sun* – which, by the way, shows Campanella's authoritarian nature. I wouldn't have wanted to land up in one of *his* jails. There's no inkling of that in Hill's account. Hill repeatedly invokes the argument of blood – that because blood has been shed over it, the matter is important. Would he ever have written about Robert Desnos if Desnos hadn't died in a Nazi camp? I doubt it. But in Celan, in Mandelshtam, in Desnos, the death is not the central fact: the poems are.

---

[1] Avril Pyman, *The Life of Alexander Blok* (OUP 1979), I, 266

The Woden Dog Fan Club Presents: Christopher Middleton

False starts, and more than one – but that's ambition: to beat the sound of the starting pistol. 'It is … the task of moving minds, by weaving tissues of linguistic sound, toward a restitution of the lost flesh of God, at least toward a re-membering of his forgotten flesh'.[1] High church gives way to high modernism (rather as Hugh MacDiarmid's Knox on the head resulted in Marx on the head); 'ambition' doesn't quite catch it: Dante was more modest in his aims. Does Middleton reach his goal? I wouldn't know, though I see how the ultimate hopes aroused and disappointed by religion can be carried into the realm of art by the refugee.

And here is the second difficulty in Middleton: he wrenches tradition almost out of its socket. Is he an English poet? Yes, but with a German graft (though it seems his Anatolian connection has nothing to do with the Baghdad to Berlin railroad). Here already I am out on a limb, because I don't know German. Worse: since I'd always reckoned I'd get around to learning the language one day, I haven't even read much German literature in translation. But I'm going ahead because there is a danger that the critical hush around Middleton's work will further deepen: the nearest we have to a study of his work is a festschrift in the *Chicago Review*,[2] and even that talks too much about one essay and one poem. Besides, Middleton himself once risked a literary analysis of a Chinese

---

[1] Christopher Middleton, 'Ideas about Voice in Poetry', in *Jackdaw Jiving* (Manchesteter, Carcanet, 1998), p. 96.
[2] 51: 1/2, Spring 2005, 7-137.

poem in translation, when he really ought to have conferred first with a Chinese scholar.[1]

But there is something for everyone in this poet. I would like to give newcomers to his work a few points of reference, one of many possible approaches to his twenty-odd books of poetry spanning sixty-four years, several books of prose and many, many translations, some of which are major bridges into German literature.

The bibliographies have *Torse 3* as his first book of poems, but the copy I obtained still had its dust-jacket, which said 'He has published two earlier books of verse in Great Britain'. *Poems* was published in 1943 and *Nocturne in Eden* in 1945, both by Fortune Press in London. Another, it is rumoured, was published samizdat at Merton College Oxford, which I leave to the bibliomaniacs. Middleton clearly wants them forgotten, so I won't dwell long on them. The first is the work of a talented teenager, suspended somewhere between John Donne and Rimbaud, reworking classical and Christian themes, and featuring conceits of the kind you might find in the Pléiade. The War is far away. The second book is much stronger and stranger, and the War comes into the reckoning. Although that book contains a poem called 'Belshazzar's Feast', Middleton had not yet connected with Benjamin Fondane.[2] He writes, 'Actually I started with Shestov at Oxford (c.1951?), and at that time did read in *Horizon* D. Gascoyne's essay, which put me on to Fondane,[3] whose books were so hard to find, and unsettling yet reiterative. (I read the most *errant* stuff on Rimbaud in those days, for an essay recited at a tutorial.)'[4]

A short aside. In music, it's no surprise when a composer turns out to be hugely influenced by Bach – even such wild men as Conlon Nancarrow. But I'm constantly surprised when Lev Shestov turns

---

[1] Christopher Middleton, 'Pai Ch'iu's Arm Chair', in *The Pursuit of the Kingfisher* (Carcanet, 1983), 51-54.
[2] See Benjamin Fondane, *Le festin de Balthasar* (Paris, Arcane 17, 1985).
[3] See e.g. Benjamin Fondane, *Rimbaud le Voyou* (Paris, Plasma, 1979).
[4] Christopher Middleton, letter to PMcC, 10 December 2006.

up among poets; it's as though this philosopher, who hardly features in the annals of philosophy, were preserved in the work of poets, one of whom (Fondane) abandoned poetry to follow him. MacDiarmid, Brodsky, Bonnefoy, Middleton – people who wanted out.

Middleton wanted out of England, and Germany was the way.[1] This is, perhaps, the moment to probe that dearth of critical response in the UK. It is not so much the fact of exile as the company he chose. I'd like to set aside Hermann Hesse, the subject of his doctorate[2], as another of the false starts. The three wise men of his Germanic pantheon, all of whom he translated, are Friedrich Hölderlin, Friedrich Nietzsche and Robert Walser. All of them went mad in their prime and were effectively re-absorbed by their mothers and sisters. In Walser's case at least this was a benign process; in Nietzsche's there was a fairly successful attempt to suborn his work also; in Hölderlin's I have the impression that his mother wanted control of his inheritance, wanted him good and mad. Middleton:

The Lime Tree

Thank you for giving birth to me in the first place,
Thank you for delivering me from the dark,

You whose round arms I stroked with feeling
Made presence atmosphere and contact known.

And I wanted not that Englishness;
I wanted deliverance from you so soon,

From the sticky stuff you weltered in,
Leaf, branch, and bole in your shade they dispensed

---

[1] For the Shestov connection, and for reminiscence on Middleton's RAF service in WWII, see *Palavers & A Nocturnal Journal*, (Exeter, Shearsman Books, 2004), most of which is CM in conversation with Marius Kociejowski.
[2] See also parts of his *Bolshevism in Art* (Manchester, Carcanet, 1978).

The glue, the fragrant glue, but your blossoms,
Lady, they did provide the pleasure of tea.[1]

The 31 couplets of that poem show the speaker setting aside the irony and distance with which he had fought free of that familiar glue. It was a process that put decades and oceans between himself and the motherland. Middleton (unlike Heaney) is not much given to reminiscing on childhood, or to sounding off about England in the manner of Geoffrey Hill. But by this late stage, though the emblem of the lime tree seems more German than English still, he really is an English poet; the prodigal son has gone home. Time for a fatted calf, or a critical tome at least.

Until the PhD on Middleton and German literature is written, I can only guess at what is essential to a good understanding of his poetry. As follows. Nietzsche is behind several of the authors Middleton reveres, and his view of ancient Greece is filtered through the good professor; in the essay quoted at the start of this piece, he develops a genealogical argument that owes much to Nietzsche and Shestov, about how Western culture lost its way:

> A solitary fisherman, offshore from Halicarnassus in 604 BC, had he attended to the splash and ripple of waves against the hull of his boat, might have thought that some other being was around him, at large, but within earshot, even if that other being authorized his element, water, to speak through a different phonetic system from that of the fisherman's Carian.

> The manifold voices of the ancient cosmos, subhuman or superhuman voices, might also have engendered in the fisherman's inquiring mind the tremendous thought: 'They alone speak truly who, having learned and understood them, utter the voices of the cosmos'. Instead of accommodating that thought, and as they became Western and aggressive in their ways, peoples of the north-eastern Mediterranean entrusted their fate to

---

[1] *The Word Pavilion and Selected Poems* (The Sheep Meadow Press, 2001; also Carcanet), p. 352.

another thought: 'They alone shall possess the earth who live from the powers of the cosmos.'[1]

Hence, I would have thought, Middleton's focus on Dada, whose Nietzschean intellectual was Hugo Ball: 'The will to image. Morality detaches itself from convention and works toward one end: to hone the sense of measure and weight'.[2] For Middleton, Dada went off in several directions, one of them political – because a surprising thing about this poet, who can come over as an aesthete, is just how important the political context is to every author he writes about: discussing Hölderlin's poems to Diotima, he does not neglect the political maelstrom that relationship passed through; and he roots Dada firmly in the even more violent politics of its time and place. I do not doubt that he could describe in some detail the transition from the former upheaval to the latter. It must have brought Middleton joy to have the venerable Hans Arp open and close his *German Writing Today*[3], enfolding the mid-century in his benign embrace. Dada led on to OULIPO, and to Middleton's *Pataxanadu*.[4]

Hugo Ball had become disenchanted with Dada as early as 1917. As Middleton puts it,

> Dada had asserted itself precisely as a voice and not as an echo, not as a reflex action of social chaos, but as an initiatory and concrete utterance of the autonomous logic of imagination. Dada was an attempt to reinterpret those reserves of mind which constitutes all art and literature, no longer now through traditional canons, but in spontaneous lyrical terms and by the game with chance. Yet it had come to seem like little more than an exclusive and hubristic form of autotherapy.[5]

---

[1] *Jackdaw Jiving*, p. 89.
[2] Quoted in *Jackdaw Jiving*, p. 1.
[3] ed. Middleton, (Harmondsworth, Penguin, 1967).
[4] (Carcanet, 1977).
[5] 'Dada versus Expressionism', in *Bolshevism in Art* (Carcanet, 1978).

In an essay of 1961, 'The Art of Unreason',[1] Middleton brought Ball's analysis to bear on English writing of the previous decade, asking 'Do critics now seek to bury the energies of revolt underlying past pioneering movements by fitting them into their unexamined schemes of dread?' The stakes, as he saw it, were high: 'to recover the spontaneity of the individual self not only for art's sake but also for the sake of human survival'. He concludes:

> Dada... showed how ... unreason is only a start. The Dada experiment shows too, however, that 'intelligibility' also is only a start: that 'intelligibility' bears only a contingent relation to a poem's poetic sense and to a painting's painterly sense. In poetry especially Dada tells. Current versions of the experiment, in some of the *New Departures* poems and displays, and in those of some Beats, fail simply because the exponents have talent not as poets at all but only as impotent puppets of the systems which they excoriate, and as victims of the temptation to create without toil.

These are hard words, against which Middleton would expect us to measure his own efforts. In that great span of work there are many pieces I don't understand; in Middleton's own readings of the work of others I don't always see where he is coming from; on occasion I think he gets a detail wrong: translating 'Kiefer' as 'jawbone' as well as 'pine' in Günter Eich's 'Ryoanji'[2]. (Kiefer can mean either jawbone or pine; spelling out both in the translation foregrounds a charnel-house image that might have been only an echo in the German. I'm not suggesting that he falls into the translator's trap of over-specifying, but rather that he couldn't resist a word he has used more than once in his own poems). Still, his assessment of the terrible strengths and weaknesses of Paul Celan convinces me more than anything else I have read about Celan and the industry that has grown around him.[3] Also, the fact that this great translator of German literature never once quotes Walter Benjamin's famous essay on the art of translation, extends his credit with me further than I could say.

---

[1] in *Bolshevism in Art*, pp. 78-86.

[2] *Jackdaw Jiving*, pp. 114-5.

[3] CM, 'On a translation of Paul Celan's *Atemwende*', in *Jackdaw Jiving*.

A long pause as I consider what I could usefully write about his poetry, or indeed about anyone else's. Most of the living poets I read are people I know or have corresponded with, which strikes me as suspect. The industry, on the other hand, is pushing too many two-book bards on five-book contracts that have to be padded out with second-hand translations.

I'm tempted to compare him, then, with two famous poets I've had almost no dealings with: Murray and Muldoon, the spaniel and the fox – Middleton figuring as a superior sort of feral feline. Murray works hard for praise; Muldoon deserves and gets it; Middleton is much more inward, but in the end, he can't help being a little perplexed at the silence around his work.

The most blatant (though hardly the most important) difference among the three of them, is their political situation.

Murray can probably be credited with publicly establishing the place of poetry in his country as a civic, political and spiritual practice. That is a huge achievement, which depends essentially on the sheer, patent quality of his writing, a poetry that seems intent on repeating in verse the colonization of the Fatal Shore: the blank page as *terra nullius*. The corollary to the poet's political power is a certain contamination, something that Aleksandr Blok saw as a necessary evil, the kind of leaven by which a poem might survive. Murray seems to be building credit with metaphor and squandering it on assertion, as though the reader were being invited to assent to the proposition that, if the simile is accurate, then the adjacent dogma or opinion will be correct. When Brodsky, in one of his mad tributes, said of Murray 'he is, quite simply, the one by whom the language lives', Murray didn't quite manage to repudiate it: for whose greater glory is this? And where is his old Vernacular Republic? To sup with the devil…

I have known only two Ulster intellectuals of Muldoon's age; both sought (unsuccessfully) to protect themselves from the politics of their adolescence with outrageously corrosive wit. 'The More a

Man Has the More a Man Wants'[1] seems to stem from the same root. And yet, in that narrative whose smithereens the reader can't quite reassemble, there is no glory, or glory in the slaughter. Since those days, Muldoon has been changed from a poet who could speak with Murray's political freedom to one who can speak with Murray's political power. His poetry is well-connected one way and another, which brings its own restrictions.

Middleton's work has not gone unrecognised, especially in Germany, but it is probably fair to say that he has no more political power than the average citizen. Which brings us to another implication of Blok's observation: if a corpus of poetry has no political purchase at all, can it survive? It might in the long run, if it acquires some kind of patina. In the long run, contemporary references are likely to be eroded. As though to guard against such loss, Middleton's poetry seems to have very little in the way of topical reference, though plenty of allusions to other times and other arts. The civic sense that brings him to tackle certain current problems is tempered by the tact that makes him a poet, not a preacher or columnist. By coincidence, I first heard a recording of Middleton's voice within twenty minutes of hearing the summing up for the prosecution in one of the Nuremberg war trials. The coincidence is that the poem he read, 'The Digging'[2], was about mass executions. It ends 'I should return with my spade to simple tombs'. With that, I'll return to the perhaps simpler matter of where Middleton's writing seems to spring from, as opposed to that of Murray or Muldoon.

While Murray invests his senses in the natural world, possessing a strangler fig or a snake with his reverse-engineered shamanism, Middleton confronts a responsibility to other creatures that is often resolved in death – even when he is considering a greenfly on a train window. 'Coral Snake' is the classic example, but his work is peppered with such confrontations, from *Torse 3* onwards (not his first two volumes, which were too bookish for nature to get a look

---

[1] From *Quoof* (1983), in *Poems 1968-1998* (London, Faber, 2001), pp. 127-147.
[2] http://www.poetryarchive.org/poetryarchive/singlePoet.do?poetId=1003 #.

in). There is a strange contrast between Middleton's anxious encounters with creatures and his serene inhabiting of landscapes, which produces some quite luminous poems in verse and prose.

The natural observation that is the focus of Murray's work is a means to further ends in Muldoon, who has great fun with verse forms. When out of steam, he'll try smacking a few disparate elements together to see what happens, as the physicists do in CERN. It often works. Incidentally, I was sincerely flattered, reading 'The last time I saw Chris' in *Horse Latitudes*[1] to see he had read the copy of *Tantris*[2] that I gave him, or at least the homonym sestina it opens with. Muldoon is near unique in having managed the transition from child prodigy to master of his art while producing the goods with such consistency. Where it all comes from is his business; but like the work of the late Franco Fortini, it seems to be heading in an increasingly elegiac direction.

You cannot translate verse without acquiring mastery of traditional forms, yet Middleton's centre of attention is not there. Inward and shy though he is in his work, his great concern is always the other: the other self that emerges in dreams (which he takes very seriously), the other presence or absence he finds in beast or ghost or other people's rooms or countries; the powerful erotic charge of foreign languages. Middleton's singular contribution to form in English poetry is short prose, which has flourished in many a language, but not in English, not till now.

This brings us back to Robert Walser. Middleton links him with Dada and, by antonomasia, with Nietzsche, quoting Max Brod: 'After Nietzsche, Walser had to come'.[3] Brod's friend Kafka had appreciated Walser's work, and the obsession with vanishing smallness is shared by both. Middleton came across Walser's writing, his infinitesimal script, while teaching at Zurich in 1954; Walser was still living in a Zurich mental asylum at the time

---

[1] (London, Faber, 2006), pp. 92-3.
[2] P.McC., 'Tantris', *Lines Review* 140, pp. 5-36, republished in *Collected Contraptions* (Manchester, Carcanet, 2011).
[3] See Middleton's afternote to his 1965 translation of Robert Walser, *Institute Benjamenta*; also 'The Picture of Nobody' in *Bolshevism in Art*.

though neither writing nor receiving strange visitors: 'I'm not here to write', he said, 'I'm here to be mad'.[1] He died in 1956. I don't share Middleton's enthusiasm for him – I don't trust his humility – so I'll leave it to others to deal with him. Middleton's prose began to impinge on his poetry in *Our Flowers and Nice Bones*[2] (the title is from Kurt Schwitters), and blossomed in *Pataxanadu*[3], which for me is his first great book; it lives up to the beautiful title. It is perhaps odd to claim that such a precocious poet produced his first great book at the age of fifty, especially since it is ninety-nine per cent prose. Read it and see.

Next was *Carminalenia* (1980). Another aside. The cover shows a photo of a Roman coin, described in the poem 'A Small Bronze of Licinius I' – presumably from the collection Middleton began at a Cambridge market in his school years. There is a fairly poignant contrast between the survival of the Roman coin and the decrepitude of this ageing paperback, printed on what looks like Kremlin-issue toilet paper. A back-handed compliment to Carcanet for sticking by this poet through thick and thin. The early 80s, judging by the production values, were thin. But Middleton's poetry and prose are available partly because Carcanet has backed him for more than 30 years.

The opening poem of *Carminalenia*, 'Anasphere: le torse antique', takes us into open waters. The epigraph is in Japanese, from a 12th century text, and parts 3 and 4 draw on ancient Chinese shamanic motifs, according to the footnote. The endnote makes me feel like I need another note – or none at all. I don't know what's going on. By this stage, I trust him, but I cannot follow this. One odd consolation is the *LRB* review of Muldoon's *The End of the Poem* (a rather high-falutin, Heanic title, I note with disappointment), where single words are taken by Muldoon as subtle references to that same word as used by Wordsworth in a certain poem.

---

[1] Carl Seelig, *Wanderungen mit Robert Walser* (1957), quoted by CM in his afterword to the translation of *Institute Benjamenta* (London, Serpent's Tail, 1995), p. 144.
[2] (London, Fulcrum Press, 1969).
[3] (Manchester, Carcanet, 1977).

Reference, ultimately, is personal, whether you stick to a trad canon or range as far as you can. We're on our own.

Now comes the first of the collections or recollections that Carcanet and the Sheep Meadow Press perform: *111 Poems* (1983). It contains the 'Old Water Jar' that begins *Two Horse Wagon Going By* (1986), the first of Middleton's books that I read as it appeared. So let's say it's the first of his poems I noticed, and one that he clearly wants to keep.

> *Old Water Jar*
>
> Like one of the old ideas
> It won't hold water any more
> But it is round in the belly
> And has strong bladed
> Shoulders like a good woman
> Elegant even the curves
> Run down from the mouth
> In a long sweet wave
> You can't help liking it so
> Simply for the way
> It stands there

Another incidental about Middleton poems: some of them end with full stops, others don't. This one doesn't. And it really really is not correct in a political sense at all: 'strong bladed shoulders like a good woman', the gift horse an implicit term in the comparison of jar and woman. The auction block. And yet. For years I misread the shoulder blades as collar bones, transferring my affection from that jar to one particular woman, the delicate yoke of her clavicles. There is a complex of attitudes and emotions in that poem that I will defend from obtuse attack, firstly by quoting part 3 of the 'Far-from-home Poem'[1]:

> It calls with the buzzard
> Seen above oaks and circling
> As you lie in a hammock naked

---

[1] *111 Poems*, p. 175.

It calls with the bodies of things
A little statue a Roman lamp a waterpot
You gathered up for they outlive you

The male owner is suddenly what he is – mortal, a steward of whatever he owns or owns up to. This comes up again in Middleton's attitudes to women. Perhaps this is the time to consider them. But briefly. Telling or not, the three pieces that come to mind are prose. One concerns a little girl, one a young woman, and one an old man, as observed by a housewife. The first and third are in Turkey, the second, though titled Erato, is probably not Greek. It is the story of a real woman; bits of the story surface elsewhere in his work – 'Once I saw only one eye flash silver blue with a sideways glance, after we had made love and come together. Goddesses have been made out of that look'.[1] As any real woman would, 'She attacked me hammer and tongs for seven days and nights, stripping me, she thought, of every fantasy I might have had about her, the goddess and that stuff'. What does Middleton call the piece? – 'An Allegory of Erato'. Which strikes me as not, essentially, very clever: a regression to his first two books, where literature blocked out life. Perhaps I'm missing something. The piece on the little girl, from *The Balcony Tree* (1992) is part 3 of 'From Earth Myriad Robed' – one of several beautiful pieces on Anatolia, a couple of them very funny. This one though is mysterious. He describes Elif, and we are three paragraphs in before we realise she is a child. 'The throne she sat in was of wood and canvas': throne? We're deifying again. Then she is dancing, when not serving beers to customers.

> I had not made any sign to her, but now she stood near. She spoke, at first with a little smile, in surges, at times in leafy whispers, now and then with cries, low but sharp, apparently in a gibberish she was inventing, but always as if it was a great adventure to speak. Some phrases I heard as Greek, others as Turkish. Several sounds I must have misheard, glossing them as English, but her voice drew them up, I thought, while she sang

---

[1] 'An Elegy of Erato', in *The Pursuit of the Kingfisher*, p. 183.

them out, from an origin as indistinct as Hurrian. As she spoke, she pointed a finger, this way and that.[1]

Hurrian?

> In 1887 a cache of clay tablets, ancient correspondence between Egyptian kings and Middle East potentates, was unearthed in Egypt. All were written in cuneiform, and all but three of the several hundred tablets were in Akkadian, a Semitic language used at that time as an international diplomatic language in the region. One letter was in Hurrian, an extinct language of unknown affiliation spoken around 1400 BC in what is today southern Turkey. The final two letters were in an unknown language.[2]

There follows a page or so in the gibberish he mentioned. I tried it out on a Turkish friend whose mother is a Ladino speaker, but she nodded off in the middle of it. (A much more successful attempt at evoking the mystery of exotic languages is found in 'The Old Tour Guide – His Interpreter'[3], which is filtered through the interpreter's English.)[4] The section ends with a nod to Walter Benjamin's Angel of History:

> More now than purely thoughtful she came back, just once, she came back and chose to give me her hands. I would have heaped them with apples, but none grow there. I would have given her a flock of silky black tinkling goats, a box of stories and sketchbooks and pencils, rolls of embroidery, bushels of wheat, her school fees, an orchard I would have given her, a family of ponies in it, but, as it is, I take her suffering with me, and stupidly I tell her 'Ya no hay remedio,' for a wind in reverse, enormous cyclone, pulls her backwards into the future, pretty soon its teeth will have torn her wings off. Hearing behind her the howl of that wind, Elif has become an outline against a rose trellis, a figure unwinking, mantled enthroned, in a faraway

---

[1] p. 87.
[2] Merritt Ruhlen, *A Guide to the World's Languages;* Volume 1: Classification (London, Edward Arnold, 1991), p. 55.
[3] *Intimate Chronicles* (Manchester, Carcanet, 1996), 30-31.
[4] This poem is discussed by various authors in the *Chicago Review* festschrift.

tomb frieze, and now I'm gone, the dust is nowhere, Elif nowhere, stretching her arms out. The dust, with her long gaze she fathomed it.[1]

The third piece, 'The Gaze of the Turkish Mona Lisa' is from *Crypto-Topographia* (2002), where Middleton allows the tables to be turned, and reflects on this Anatolian housewife, out for a simple meal with her family, watching the old foreigner at the next table. It's a rich five-pager that changes every time I read it. The 'moralitas' finally gets him clear of the deification routine, and the last sentence, in its beautiful panning shot, reminds me of the disarmingly humble envoi to the Second Book of Maccabees:

> Old misery festers, old fear persists, and difference animates an increasingly nervous few. Yet from the gladness we learn not to mistake myth for contingency, and not to mark out, as Adversary or Angel, any other kind of unquelled ego who happens also to be passing by.
>
> These, at least, were my afterthoughts in the night bus travelling south to the sea.[2]

That's almost it: science and serious critical endeavour can do justice to all the rest, except for Woden Dog. It wasn't until I read *Genji* that the question of which character in literature I would like to be even occurred to me, and Genji was the answer. Similary, I've never been tempted to start a fan club for any character until I came across Woden Dog.

> Wot doth woden dog
> Por dog drageth plow
>
> Thing odd dog not
> Much good plow drager
>
> But por dog drageth
> All same plow
>
> More come jellifish

---

[1] p. 89.
[2] p. 94.

>   Sting him woden dog
>   Jellifish in air now
>   Other odd thing (…)

'Other odd thing'? You bet.

All the greatest poems in world literature are twelve pages long, and this is one of them. You need to see it in its full glory, in the pamphlet issued by the Burning Deck Press, if I haven't bought them all. Once you've read it a few times, look at 'Third Generation', in *The Lonely Suppers of W.V. Balloon*. What else can I say? Read this:

Christopher Middleton, *Collected Poems* (Carcanet, 2008), 732pp

At last! The weather clears and you see the whole range at once as it stretches from Anatolia through Provence to Old Mexico, with the same goats browsing at either end and a suspicion that, if he had headed East instead of West, Middleton would have come to the same place, crossing the ancient land bridge with the help of some shaman.

Getting there and away: if you have only a short time in the area you might start around page 100 and compile a personal playlist that would probably have a strong geographical stamp (although, if you are fond of animals, there are more cats and owls here than in Harry Potter). You might notice a progression from the rather easy elegiac:

>   .. It bears comparison
>   with a bunch of grapes on a plate on the table
>   in a whitewashed room among wrinkled olive boughs
>   where the sun beats, and it is not yet time
>   to be gone from that place. (p. 11)

to the here and now

>   This peak infuriating the winds
>   this valley fluting down the foothills
>   these crabby oaks and soon apple trees and blue grapes

to a place where time stops on the moment, often with a lightness and laughter not usually associated with lyric balance – 'Hotel Asia Minor' being one example. And on from there to festive treatment of what, in lesser hands, would have been an elegiac theme (The Counter-Missionary, p. 546).

You could compile a portrait gallery – for this man knows how to listen to people; try 'A Portrait of JLM', (p. 323); 'Party Night at the Yellow Rose' (p. 528) 'Felo de se' (p. 716), and 'Old Woman at the County Dump' (p. 161):

> Sitting in her cracked hutch,
> beneath trees, hidden from the road,
> she is the guardian of a torrent
> of burst mattresses, rust and rubber,
> bodiless lids of objects without present function…
>
> At night, I imagine,
> stuck to her rocking chair, she dreams,
> dreams of being guarded by the garbage.
> A block of rusty bedsprings at her door,
> plucked by rat claws, gives off
> intermittent echoes of an old serenade.
> With all its worms a portly wardrobe,
> her protector.

That diffident 'I imagine' is one thing that sets Middleton apart.

You might prefer to compile a book of dreams, from Victoriana (p. 106) to Recovering Dream (p. 524), but this is where you would run into difficulty, for difficulty there is, and it begins in a big way with the animist tack adopted in the third book collected here; Middleton never mentions Jerome Rothenberg's *Technicians of the Sacred*, but it might be helpful, for the difficulties in this poetry are not in its references, recondite though they can be, but in approach. I'd like to consider that approach, not in order to solve the difficulties (that's your job, and explication won't help), but in order to say why this work really is worth tackling, if you have more than a few days to spare.

> *As for what*
> *I wrote – thumb through it on*
> *Weekdays, and skip, if you will, the rotten bits.*
> (p. 257)

Poetry can be leveraged far beyond its worth – by poets themselves, before it even gets to market. The obvious mechanisms include allusion, woodwork and alienation. The deployment of classical allusion these days has three main effects: it ennobles the utterance, it keeps teachers and students busy, and it provides spin-offs in the re-translation and re-publication of classical texts – all harmless enough, if rather ingrown. Next is woodwork. Until the 20th century, this was a matter of turning one's hand to certain poetic forms, such as the sonnet or the heroic couplet. These days, it's a matter of theme rather than form. The author hits on a promising subject and works it up: 'Famous name in unusual location' is typical – Dostoevsky in Glasgow, or whatever. Another standard is the soliloquy by a name from the past, where the trick is to keep it recognizable but make it slightly surprising (Middleton's only conventional example is 'Paris' (p. 420)). A variation on this category is the soliloquy by an animal or a thing. These are parlour games that pad out many a collection but rarely amount to poetry. Last is alienation, often through micromanagement of foreign bodies – usually scientific or technical texts – to evoke some kind of emotional response, almost an immune response. Their value is in nudging readers out of certain tramlines of thought. But that would seem to be as far as they go. All in all, great bonuses are being leveraged out of an exiguous capital base.

What alternative does Middleton offer? Enjoyment of 'The Word Pavilion' (p. 546) is certainly enhanced by awareness of earlier texts: the Cavafy poem 'The God Abandons Anthony', Anthony and Cleopatra IV, iii and probably Plutarch, so his work is not devoid of literary allusion. He does refer to Greek gods, though not as ennobling or enabling precedents: he tries to get beyond their names, to how they must have reeked and frightened long ago. His footnotes tend to be matters of historical curiosity rather than essential to appreciation of the work, because his poems do not harp back. As to arts and crafts, Middleton rarely espouses traditional forms or conventional development of themes – indeed he is often referred to as an experimental poet, which is not quite the point; it's more that, as Morton Feldman would have put it, he doesn't let a set form do the listening for him. The essence is that he listens, and you can feel this listening intensify over the decades, to an astounding pitch. In the early mid period he seems puzzled himself by what he hears

> as a more or less literate person
> Who writes down things that have
> Some connection with the English language,
>
> What should I do with a wild horse
> Suddenly presenting itself to my thoughts
> In Berlin this winter morning?   (p. 251)

There is a similar bemusement at the phrase 'Rilke's Feet', which triggered a longish poem. On occasion, Middleton dramatizes the process: the first line of the Halicarnassian Ghost Dialogue" (p. 302) could be applied to himself: 'What can the old fool have been looking for?'

> …Spinnakers
> Of oddity, majestic
> The ripple of ideas, these, our thread,
> Irreducible amalgam of our discourse,
> He combed from the gabble of old salts,
> Horsemen, crones, bandits.
>
>   Listen, was it
> His feeling that any heap
> Of rags, palpitating on a roadside,
> By a tethered goat, or roping hay
> Into a sack, has something to speak of…?

The whole matter of puzzling over a numinous phrase is dramatized again in 'The Old Tour Guide – His Interpreter' (p.

435), but it recurs without drama, lyrically, in very many of the poems he writes. Increasingly, the process resembles not composition but the attempt to recall a forgotten name – a comparison he makes himself in 'Language Learning' (p. 549). The intensity, and the uncertainty, seem to increase with time, till in the last third of the book hardly a poem lacks a question mark (though many questions are unmarked), and many poems seem to consist of nothing else. Nothing but the bright world and its creatures.

The Little Wild Goose Pagoda

'He arrived at the frontier gates of death carrying the melons on his head.'
I tried to put it back on the shelf and leave it but I really couldn't not buy that: *Monkey* by Wu Ch'eng-ên, translated by Arthur Waley (London, 1942), 3rd impression 1943, 'BOOK PRODUCTION WAR STANDARD ECONOMY', £2.50 from Voltaire and Rousseau.

I liked those wartime editions partly because I could afford them, partly for the poignancy of people reading in the blackout. I've never bought a book because it was a first edition or because it was a beautiful object. Blame the Vatican and the Kremlin. The book is the wrapping; the Word's the thing. In the USSR the handsomely bound efforts were Brezhnev, Leonid, opera omnia. Anything worthwhile circulated in the barter system on the usual cheap paper. My Gaelic books got me a set of Blok's poems and a cruel hangover.

But some things just weren't available: Shestov, for instance. Even in the year the Soviets were publishing Mandelshtam, Lev Isaakovich was invisible, in the central libraries but not in the catalogues. I know he was there because I saw a young librarian reading him in a café near the Academy of Sciences Library: she'd taken it from the secret stacks. Does this sound like The Name of the Rose? It should, because printing does not guarantee survival. Nor does the writing. A work's survival depends entirely on the individual reader. And as for the bookshelf – the more important a book becomes the more you realise you don't own it at all: you're looking after it.

The Soviets were afraid of books: afraid of letting them in, afraid of letting them out. It took time to get permission to leave with books I'd brought with me to Leningrad, and a big official stamp was put on the last printed page of Morgan's translations of Mayakovsky; same for Dante's *Inferno*, whose last canto now ends with an exit visa from the Soviet Ministry of Culture.

If heaven is a bookshelf, hell is a book. Choose carefully. You might find yourself in *Russia's War* by Richard Overy, in Malcolm Caldwell's South-East Asia. You might find yourself selling them all for bread, your pension not worth tuppence. Which is still better than living on the street in Manila.

Bookish fears of the well-to-do become encysted and transfigured on the right side of the law: to break the law is wrong but to gain from it is surely sinful. Solution? Posit something infinitely worse than hell on earth to paralyse the conscience. My bookshelf is blessed with a

HAND BOOK OF
CHINESE BUDDHISM
BEING
SANSKRIT-CHINESE
DICTIONARY
WITH
VOCABULARIES OF BUDDHIST TERMS
in Pali, Singhalese, Siamese, Burmese,
Tibetan, Mongolian and Japanese
ERNEST J. EITEL
SECOND EDITION
REVISED AND ENLARGED

prefaced in Hongkong, March 1888, reprinted Madras 1992. I use a lot of odd dictionaries, some of which, if you were to sling them in a pond, would mushroom into so many second-hand bookshops, the proprietor hunched over a calor gas stove in the corner, perishing from black lung, and a plastic sheet under the leaky roof bellying with bathfuls of rainwater, an accident waiting to happen; a dozen hapless browsers immortalized in papier-mâché while consulting:

1. L. Levitchi, *Dictionar Romîn-Englez* (Bucharest, 1960): 'joian *s.m.* name given to an ox born on a Thursday'; 2. *Brewer's Dictionary of Phrase and Fable*: 'God bless the Duke of Argyll': a phrase supposed to have been used by Scottish Highlanders when they scratched themselves; 3. *Dorland's Medical Dictionary*, 24th ed.: 'NOTE - an infusion flows in by gravity, an injection is forced in by a syringe, an instillation is dropped in, an insufflation is blown in and an infection slips in unnoticed'; and 4. a dictionary of Russian prison camp slang which, for empty prattle, gives the elaborate 'discussing the effects of lunar rays on herpes in the hereafter'.

Eitel, though, is in a class of his own. His entry for 'Nâraka' has to be seen in its enormity:

> NÂRAKA (Pâli. Miraya. Siam. Narok. Burm. Niria. Tib. Myalba. Mong. Tamu)... explained by ... (nara)...(ka), lit. men's wickedness, or by ... lit. unenjoyable, or by ... lit. instruments of torture; or .. .(Niraya) explained by ... lit. prison under the earth, or by ... lit. the prefecture of darkness. General term for the various divisions of hell. (1.) The hot hells (...), 8 of which (see Samdjiva, Kâlasûtra, Samghata, Râurava, Mahârâurava, Tapana, Tratâpana, and Avîtchi) are situated underneath Djambudvîpa in tiers, beginning at a depth of 11,900 yôdjanas, and reach to a depth of 40,000 yôdjanas; but as each of these hells has 4 gates and outside each gate 4 antechamber-hells, there are altogether 136 hot hells. (2.) The cold hells (...), 8 in number (see Arbuda, Nirarbuda, Atata, Hahava, Ahaha, Utpala, Padma and Pundarîka), situated underneath the 2 Tchakravâlas and ranging shaft-like one beneath the other, but so that this shaft is gradually widening down to the 4th hell and then narrowing again, the first and last hells having the shortest and the 4th hell the longest diameter. (3.) The dark hells, 8 in number, situated between the 2 Tchakravâlas; also called vivifying hells (...), because any being, dying in the first of these hells, is at once reborn in the 2nd, and so forth, life lasting 500 years in each of these hells. (4.) The cold Lôkântarika hells (... lit. hells on the edge sc. of the universe), 10 in number, but each having 100 millions of smaller hells attached, all being situated outside of the Tchakravâlas. (4.) The 84,000 small Lôkântarika hells (... lit. small hells on the edge), divided into 3 classes, as situated on mountains, or on water, or in deserts. Each universe has the

same number of hells, distributed so that the northern continent contains no hell at all, the two continents E. and W. of the Mêru have only the small Lôkântarika hells, and all the other hells are situated under the southern continent (Djambudvîpa). There are different torments in the different hells; the length of life also differs in each class of hells; *but the distinctions made are too fanciful to be worth enumerating.*

My italics. It goes on, though, and ends with a special hell for females '(... lit. placenta tank), consisting of an immense pool of blood. From this hell, it is said, no release is possible'...

Clearly, the former S.U. is the cold hells, the former Zaire the hot and Nâraka itself is governed from Bretton Woods. Back to the bookshelf. What is it with books? Why are most of them novels and biographies and cookery? Do people really have to be spoonfed? It's true that a novel can take my mind off squabbles with other bureaucrats, but in almost everything I read I find myself checking how many pages are left till I'm done with it. The last big exception to that was Nicolas Bouvier, *l'Usage du monde*[1] and it was, of all things, a travel book. Most travel books seem designed to endorse the reader's prejudice or laziness. This one had me champing at the bit, wanting to take off now for the East. The author's father was head of the Geneva Public and University Library, whose utmost stacks and incunabulae – Scottish universities take note – are available to the reading public of the city. It's where I borrowed a copy of Athanasius Kircher's China, when I got back from Xi'an – city of the T'ang poets, who knew that government and the law existed to make room for music and verse. In the 'Forest of Steles', where the classics and historical documents are engraved in stone, I got a calque of a poem:

> Moon down, crows up, sky of frost
> River trees, fishing lamps, weary mind,
> Past the town, Cold Mountain Temple
> Midnight bells the traveller's skiff

---

[1] Droz, 1963; reissued by Payot, 1992 (in English - *The Way of the World*, translated by Robyn Marsack).

The collection also displayed a document in Chinese and Syriac about a Nestorian Christian church established there in 631AD. Kircher devotes much of his book to it. Islam came later – and has stayed. But in that year of 631, a monk was heading west out of the T'ang dominions, along the Silk Road and round to the Ganges. In 645 he brought back the Buddhist scriptures, and the Little Wild Goose Pagoda – still standing – was built for their protection and study. His journey became the stuff of legends, which were set down in the Ming dynasty as 'The Journey to the West', of which *Monkey* is an episode. I'd just got round to reading it.

The Little Grey Book

There is a revealing book on *Charles de Foucauld: Explorateur du Maroc, Ermite du Sahara*, by René Bazin of the Académie Française (Paris, 1924). Foucauld, a former soldier and not so much explorer as government spy, founded a particularly ascetic religious order that didn't acquire any full-time members until after his death. He was killed by Bedouins allied to the Germans, in Tamanrasset in 1916. His monastery at the time had become something of an arsenal. In 1914, he had written

> ... I hope that from the great evil of war a great good will emerge for souls – good in France where that vision of death will inspire sombre thoughts, and where the accomplishment of duty in the greatest sacrifices will uplift and purify souls, bringing them closer to Him who is Good incarnate, making them more able to perceive the truth and to live by its dictates; good for our allies who, in coming closer to us, come closer to Catholicism, and whose souls, like ours, are purified by the sacrifice... (p. 431)

Foucauld was a monstrously impressive man, in the tradition that runs from Joan of Arc almost to Simone Weil, an avatar of that chilling French strain of Catholicism. But the secular version of such thinking is, if anything, even more macabre. Mallarmé was able to regard anarchist bombings as aesthetic statements. And look at 'An Exultation', written by William Carlos Williams in summer 1941:

> England, confess your sins! toward the poor,
> upon the body of my grandmother. Let the agents
> of destruction purify you with bombs, cleanse

you of the profits of your iniquities to the last
agony of relinquishment.
She didn't lie! Neither shall you, if
day by day you learn through abnegation
as she did, to send up thanks to those who
rain fire upon you.
Thanks! thanks to a just and kind heaven
for this light that comes as a blasting fire
destroying the rottenness of your slums as well
as your most noble and historic edifices, never
to be replaced!
If! You will survive if – you accept it with
thanks when, like her, excoriated by devils
you will have preserved in the end, as she did,
a purity – to be that never as yet known
leader and regenerator of nations, even of those
rotten to the core, who by a sovereignty
they cannot comprehend
have worked this cleansing mystery upon you.[1]

Sixty years and some months later, that exultation acquired a certain resonance. Poets, accustomed to pushing words around, can make vicious politicians. Politicians don't tend to shine as poets. Whereas it is usually reasonable to encourage the cobbler to stick to his last and Jowett to his legislation, we are now at a stage where poets need support and politicians – especially the men of vision – should be encouraged strongly to resort to verse.

I propose a Little Grey Book of politician poets, from Mao Ze Dong to Hitler – he must have dabbled in verse – to Radovan Karadzic, 'the warrior poet', of the *Times*, and on to our day. The big names would sell it and the little grey men of letters in parliament would swell its ranks. Since the goal is not to make money from the anthology but to protect civil society, it would be much better, much much better, to catch these men and women after they have started writing verse but before they hear the call to public service. The ideal would be to fund poetry magazines not

---

[1] *Collected Poems*, ed. C. MacGowan, New Directions, New York, 1988), vol II, p. 42.

just through the Arts Council but on a massive scale, through the Home Office and perhaps the Ministry of Defence – though the ultimate source of funding need not be publicized. There would be thousands of magazines and spin-off slim tomes throughout the United Kingdom, and indeed elsewhere in the world. In that way, they would damage nothing more than a few trees in Norway and, when it all migrated to the web – not even trees. All the bad vibes would go into bad verse, and none of those rotten bards would ever order the destruction of defenceless civilians.

At the same time we must nurture real art so it can nurture us. Might we learn from the mistakes of the past? I once pulled from my shelves all the books that had been written by people in prison or exile. There were roughly 50 exile and 20 prison books, out of maybe 2000, a third of which would have been dictionaries, reference works and picture books. That means 70 out of 1400, or 5% of the literature. Which seemed rather a lot, even by American or Chinese standards of incarceration. It may be that my collection of books was simply biased: I do have a penchant for writers who try to embrace all and everything, and imprisonment and exile will tend to push writers in that direction. Having no control over the present, they appeal to past and future; being out of their political mainstream they get an overview of the sense it's taking. Then again, since I've mentioned the subject to friends I've found gaps: Cervantes and Genet, Sade. There's an astounding sequence of Italian prison writers – Boethius, Polo, Machiavelli, Bruno, Campanella, Casanova, Pellico (not so great, I'm told), Gramsci and Primo Levi.

Perhaps I've got the cart before the horse. I say prison and exile pushes them to take an overview; it may be that their attempt to show the big picture was what got them into trouble. There are a number of strategies taken by writers in exile.

1.   Tristia: the writer harks back obsessively to his native land. Ovid, followed deliberately by du Bellay, then Mandelshtam, Graham, Joyce, Blixen (inverted), Kundera, the later Solzhenitsyn and Brodsky (who transferred his nostalgia to Venice, the Leningrad of the south, the nearest Byzantine place).

2. The Divine Comedy: The writer strives to encompass the place of exile and the native land; John Knox did this, and Marx, and Herzen. Alasdair MacIntyre. Rather a grim bunch, there.

3. Conrad: the writer goes native like Mistah Kurtz, like Eliot, Beckett, maybe Wittgenstein.

4. Shestov: The exile is or becomes existential: Buber, Fondane, Husserl; all Jewish, all following the great book of exile, one way or another.

5. Don Juan: write your memoirs. Stevenson, John Muir, Cendrars.

Strategies in prison are similar, though the balance is different:

1. Marco Polo, Ezra Pound, Cervantes.

2. Machiavelli, Bruno, Campanella, Gramsci, Urquhart, Solzhenitsyn (*The First Circle*), Havel.

3. Villon, Genet, George Jackson, Jimmy Boyle.

4. Bonhoeffer, Boethius, James I, Thomas More.

5. Most of them: Verlaine, Wilde, cummings, Garioch, Primo Levi, Dostoevsky, Soyinka, Lowell (a few poets here, perhaps thriving on the strict forms imposed on them).

A dozen of those people gave their lives magnificently or reluctantly; more than a dozen others risked that end; there were some whose fault was criminal, others whose fault was poverty. One theorized revolution, two foisted it on their compatriots (one or two of the martyrs might have done worse, given the chance). Some were refugees, but most did manage to live and work and even to make a living name for themselves outside the prison walls, in other countries. How might that proportion be increased?

There is no evidence that the survivors tended to thrive more in one place or political régime than in another; they were intellectuals, writers with a product that sells or a patron that pays, academics, theologians, diplomats. It was Europe that killed most and Europe that kept most. Did Marx read Sade? Lenin read Marx; Blok saw the writing on the wall.

When good writers are sustained and the market is flooded with post-political mediocrity, readers will be safe to read. But how are they to locate the good stuff? There is a way. But meanwhile, to keep the murder out of politics and writers out of trouble, there is no safer bet than that Little Grey Book. Subscribe now.

ЛЕНИНГРАД

Having diverted dangerous men and women from politics into poetry, how can we discern what is of value in the resultant morass of published verse? Live performance can guide us towards what merits careful reading, and yet if we don't know the performer's work beforehand we can easily miss such merits.

A codger in the front row of auditorium B111 at Geneva University was fidgeting with an iPad when he wasn't drinking from a bottle that he kept in a paper poke under the desk. I was trying to recall the Russian for mustard, since the anapaests of the lady at the lectern weren't cutting any, though they kept pouring out, even between poems.

This was after work one Thursday, the first evening reading in a three-day conference organised by Professor Jean-Philippe Jaccard on Leningrad poetry in the 70s and 80s, and this first reader had begun by recalling the atmosphere in the libraries and lecture theatres of Leningrad University at the time, and all the remarkable people she had rubbed shoulders with. The poet mentioned an authority on Aleksandr Blok quoted elsewhere in this book, and another utterly remarkable academic – who had been my wife's supervisor, and who had seemed to us a rather mean-spirited hack. But then the poet at the lectern was like that. Everyone she recalled was utterly remarkable, dazzling or divine. Perhaps she had erased the dark side and retained only the good, only the good people from that shabby demesne (though the word 'nauseous' recurred in her reading).

When she stopped, one of the younger generation got up to introduce the next reader. There were so many portentous pauses and dark glances in his introduction that I took out my mobile, hoping to find more entertaining fare among office emails. The next poet, he was saying, was not simply a Russian phenomenon, but a poet of global significance, to whom the younger poet had dedicated more than one of his own works.

The man in the front row set aside his paper bag and went to the podium. He introduced and started to read several poems, but had forgotten how to turn the page on his iPad, so we didn't actually hear the end of any of them. When I lived in Leningrad in 1980-81 some people still talked about Brodsky as though he had just left the room, but the only person who was introduced to me as a poet was so drunk at the time that he moved around on his hands and knees. It might have been the same man.

Before the fall of that empire it was difficult to gauge the value of any living writer, such were the political pressures on them and on their readership. In Paris *Russkaja Mysl'/La Pensée Russe* boasted the intellectual level of a provincial newspaper, and offices fit for an embassy. Authors who might not otherwise have been noticed found themselves published and reviewed in grand style. Even an indisputable great such as Brodsky could not be seen straight. One passionate and erudite admirer of his assured me that Brodsky was capable of expressing the profoundest of thoughts in the lightest of language; I found him capable of quite the reverse.

But who was I to opine? How could any Westerner understand what Soviet dissidents had suffered? The answer to the second question was – none could. But the second question really isn't relevant to the first. Plenty of people suffer and don't produce great poetry; scandalous as it seems, some great poetry has been produced without evidence of much suffering. Take away the shield of dissent, knock down the Berlin Wall and what's left to the man at the podium? Poetry as a hobby for drunks.

And yet when I checked his name that night on the net I found warm words from Western poets, visiting professorships in American colleges – the kind of treatment Seamus Heaney had in the 1970s. It's very likely that I had got both readers on a bad night, in a bad light.

The next night's reading was in B106; the last person I'd heard read there was Derek Walcott. This poet briefly introduced himself as someone who had first been published around 1955 then 'to put it mildly' roundly criticized in the Soviet press. His first book of poems didn't emerge for another two or three decades. He had a microphone clipped to his shirt, just under a beard that should be advertised on E-Bay as a semantic baffle, while the loudspeakers high on the wall smeared the old Saussure. I resigned myself to studying the rhythm and intonation, which were varied, reassuring, a less emphatic and rhetorical descendant of the singing declamation you can hear in recordings from Mandelshtam through Brodsky and onwards. The end of an era. I didn't catch his name.

The second reader was another Leningrader of the 70s. He clumped up to the dais, sat down and said 'I am going to read a poem'. The word was 'poema' which means 'long poem' in Russian, and it was.

Here (as I recall) is how it was structured:

> Detailed weather report for the morning of a specific day in Leningrad in winter 1941.
>
> Liturgical calendar for the same day (feast day of which saint, details of what diet was permitted on which days of the week in Advent)
>
> Details of ration coupons (200g flour, 100g meat... subject to availability)
>
> Then a number of parts beginning "And I / you / she / he / you (plural) / they / we said...
>
> And I said I will have a pantry. In one place there will be beef; in another place, pork..
>
> And you said (I don't recall what this conveyed)
>
> And she said 'They're stuffing their faces again!' or 'I can't go to sleep for fear they'll steal my ration book!'

And he said (description of the physiological consequences of slow starvation)

And you (plural) said (lyrical interlude)

And they said (a detailed bulletin from the government about the latest victories of the Red Army)

And we sang at matins (a sung excerpt from the Orthodox service).

Each part had this form, and there were about seven parts to it that conveyed the boredom and desperate obsessions, and also the inept humour of the Siege of Leningrad. The poem went on for ages. Remember that the previous reader had introduced himself as someone who had first been published in the USSR not so long after the end of that war, in which the Siege of Leningrad was one of the cornerstones of Soviet history – not only in official circles, but in the hearts of Leningraders for as long as the city bore that name. It was *not* funny. At around the half-way point I began to wonder how he could satisfactorily conclude the piece – surely not with another snatch from an Orthodox hymn? It turns out that he did have a solution, which I won't give away.

In avant-garde performance, if members of the audience aren't walking out within ten minutes, the artists clearly aren't trying hard enough. Here at last was something that went beyond the temulent comfort zone of the old Leningraders. They were fidgeting in their seats, and the final applause was barely sufficient to see him off the dais. Sergei Zavjalov is his name, and I returned the next morning to hear him set the 70s poets of Leningrad in context, which he did dispassionately, beginning with the change in national historical perspective in his generation of poets, noting the Russian underground poets' incomprehension of Western politics and culture at the time – everything from free verse to the My Lai massacre. He dealt lightly with the vicious literary politics of those years, and started to relate those struggles to what has happened since, but he ran out of time, and was obliged to give the floor to the lady who read on Thursday evening. She listed dozens of utterly remarkable contemporary poets, and mentioned a collection of one hundred 19th-century women poets, who all dwelt in the shadow of Pushkin.

I had gone to the conference as much to catch up with new poetry as to hear about the old schools of Leningrad, and had come away with a name to investigate, and the impression that the binary opposition of Soviet to Russian poetry had shifted towards the ternary divide (communitarian, individualistic and avant garde) that is perhaps more typical of contemporary poetry elsewhere. The first reader evinced the memorial function of verse, which brings the living and the dead into community; the classic expression of this strategy in Russian modernism is Akhmatova's *Requiem*. The younger, second poet seems to follow the Russian version of T.S. Eliot's business model, while Zavjalov is looking to renew the resources of poetry.

The Eliot career strategy might be blagged as a poetic lineage: Eliot through Auden to Brodsky; Brodsky through the man with the iPad to the younger poet. Indeed we could stretch the perspective back a lot further, by considering Brodsky's wonderful elegy on John Donne, and noting the contribution that Donne's poetry made to his own career. But art has to feed off the artist more than vice versa. Ambition for the poet rather than for the poetry sets emulation above direct attention, missing the point.

An astonishing illumination of this second strategy was provided a week later by Ilya Kamensky, at a translation workshop in Vevey, where he shared the podium with Nora Gomringer and Vincent Barras. Kamensky writes in English and in Russian. When he started to read aloud, I was knocked sideways by his rather vicious parody of the old style of chanting delivery. It took me the best part of a minute to ascertain that he was declaiming in English, not Russian, and a further five to conclude that the parody was not meant to be malicious. It turns out that Kamensky is clinically deaf, and has been since the age of four (this is stated in the note to the first poem in his book *Dancing in Odessa*). In that slim volume there are poems dedicated to Brodsky and to Tsvetaeva, plus a piece called 'Paul Celan', an efficient pastiche of Celan's imagery. So what?

In the Soviet Union, the pressures on poets were deadly. The strict verse forms they favoured were methods of self-defence, each completed poem an axiom, something settled for the future. Something that could be committed to memory and torn up. The personal lineage they established and claimed was a further means of protection – as had been clear ever since Stalin phoned Pasternak to ask whether Mandelshtam was really that good a poet. When Anna Akhmatova conferred her aegis on Joseph Brodsky, it was surely a bigger deal for him than the Nobel Prize. It must have been more like the designation of the Dalai Lama, exposing him to the rancour of the Soviets and the protection of the West.

Ilya Kamensky is an exceptional poet who manages to produce serious work that – most unusually – can be understood at one reading, and this is because his poems resemble nothing so much as early Chagall (a man running for a tram, his pockets full of tomatoes; Aunt Rosa dancing, wearing nothing but galoshes; a poet's ghost dressed in a sail). They do not have the formal tightness of Tsvetaeva or Brodsky, because Kamensky's words do not have to close ranks as theirs did. To claim their lineage and to bracket Brodsky with Celan seems a failure of tact that fits with the discordant noise of his reading. It's to be hoped that, unlike Chagall, he doesn't spend the next half century imitating his early inspiration. Though even that would be no small achievement.

Back to the third strategy of modern poetry, the avant garde. The man presenting Sergej Zavjalov said that the latest stage of his work was more prose than poetry. Zavjalov pointedly presented it as 'a long poem'. It is a poem: in its use of repetition, refrain and the management of contrasting tonal material in a rigid framework it couldn't be called anything else. The full quotation of the tiny details of ration cards alongside the lists of captured ordnance and annihilated battalions weirdly equates the two in the dazed mind of the narrator. It's not something that could be done with the tools available to lyric poets. The poem's structure is wide open to the reader (much more welcoming than Prynne's work, for example), but challenging enough to madden traditionalists, as his Geneva reading showed.

The memorial function of poetry is needed, and the narcissistic character of the art is irrepressible, but it was the renewal of experiment, in a way that clearly connects with the history of Leningrad and of its surviving arts, which told me that its poets have not lost their voice with its name.

Part IV

Language, Politics, Policy at the Millennium

> *Let forrain nations of their language boast,*
> *What fine varietie each tongue affords:*
> *I like our language, as our men and coast:*
> *Who cannot dresse it well, want wit, not words.*[1]

The palaeoanthropologist can take us back a few million years, while moral philosophers try to gauge the welfare of 'tens of billions' in generations yet unborn. As we turn to transactions among languages, with translation as a central function of human communication, it's worth deploying some more precise but very large numbers, numbers of people – partly to put this particular language in its place but also because translation, these days, is increasingly a numbers game.

Even though this language has been sounding off for a millennium, even if it is an official vehicle in a third of today's States, what though it's true (and will be true for another century) that more people are alive now than have ever lived in the past, most of us never did and never will understand a word of it.

So consider the following wide-angle shot of the linguasphere in the year of grace two thousand, the year in which this great medium, our international chewing gum, may well have reached its apogee. And weigh the advantages it confers on those who are born to it.

---

[1] George Herbert (1593-1633), 'The Sonne'.

International Languages

Where languages are in contact they are also in conflict.[1] Their users communicate, and they contend for power. Consider the advantages enjoyed by native speakers of the major international language today:

> (1) They need not spend time and energy learning a foreign language (though if they do, they learn the language of their choice).

> (2) ...they are, as a rule, linguistically superior in the international language to non-native speakers: . . . they can express their ideas more precisely, more correctly as to grammar, more elegantly, and more fluently; their discourse will therefore often be more convincing . . . in diplomatic or business negotiations, or in discussions between scholars or scientists, especially when they take place in front of an audience.

> (3) Still other advantages . . . arise from the fact that an international language, particularly if it serves various functions, tends to be brought up to date constantly. Here, members of the international language community have better access to the current terminology than do members of other language communities. Modern terminology, in particular technical terminology, is often taken over in its original, untranslated form by the non-international language, thus – among other things – increasing the gap between experts and lay people in the non-international language communities.[2]

The result, when learners deal with native speakers, can be like pitting a village eleven against a world-famous football team that

---

[1] Peter Hans Nelde, Language Conflict, in *The Handbook of Sociolinguistics*, ed. F. Coulmas (Oxford, 1977), 285-300, 292: 'The statement that there can be no language contact without language conflict ("Nielde's Law" – K. de Bot in his GAL (Gesellschaft für angewandte Linguistik) presentation in Göttingen on January 10, 1989) – may appear exaggerated, but there is in the realm of the European languages at present no imaginable contact situation which cannot also be described as language conflict.' Pioneering studies of the subject were made in Norway and in Switzerland.

[2] 'International Languages', in *The Encyclopedia of Language and Linguistics*, ed. Asher and Simpson (Oxford, 1994), p. 1729.

can buy in the players it wants: there may be a referee to ensure that the rules are observed, but the contest is not fair. But is this a matter of fairness or a matter of fact? In international business, the dealer who takes advantage of being born to an international language is doing his or her duty to shareholders in pressing home the advantage. Many countries would use the ubiquitous stakeholder metaphor to justify similar behaviour on behalf of their citizens.

Commercial, linguistic and territorial dominance are matters of culture, history and the spoils of war. After the Second World War the victors divided the spoils among five major languages in the United Nations. Of the other major languages of the world, German and Japanese were excluded as languages of the defeated powers, as of course were the likes of Bengali and Hindi, which had no political power to speak of. Arabic imposed itself in the 1970s.[1] The arrangements entailed systematic use of simultaneous interpretation, which had been pioneered by the International Labour Office in the 1920s.[2]

At present, about half of the world's population would understand one of the official languages of the United Nations[3] – and that is partly because there is a continuing adjustment to international languages. Thousands of natural languages are channelled into hundreds of national languages, then into a score of international languages and then the official languages of the United Nations.[4] Highly educated Hindi and Bengali speakers, for example, bridge to English, which many Japanese speakers have learned also. The United Nations system has handled this volatile issue with remarkable grace.

The situation is accepted by the UN agencies also, but two things point to problems at meetings below the level of general assembly

---

[1] The languages mentioned are all in the top twenty in terms of numbers of first language speakers. See table 1, 'First language speakers'.
[2] See next chapter.
[3] See table 2, 'First + second/alternate language speakers'.
[4] Table 4 shows how many states recognize which international languages.

or conference: (1) even when eight international languages are used (because German and Portuguese are included by some agencies), half of the world's population is left out, and (2) English is overshadowing the other international languages.

The increasing predominance of English is an advantage and a danger. An advantage in that it has become the language of finance, economics, statistics and computing. It's a digital language. Anyone who wants to advance in those areas must acquire it along with Excel and Access. It is now the leading language of science and technology (although others such as Japanese, German, Russian and French continue to function). In the social sciences and the humanities it is one of the great languages. However, over 80% of the world's population knows no English at all. A further 10% has learned it, and copes with the disadvantages adverted to above.[1]

In an international organization that has a technical vocation the problem is, of course, compounded by technical language. It has been known since the break-up of Latin that professional dialects can be as distinct as geographical ones.[2] The specialised vocabulary and usage of the medical profession marks out its intellectual territory. Social scientists and economists have their own international dialects. The specialized agencies operate where certain professional and national languages intersect. The number of people who can function in that intersection is small.

In an international organization experts must be able to express themselves in one of the languages used in the secretariat. Even if there are no official working languages, it is not unreasonable for experts from sub-Saharan Africa or from the Indian subcontinent, people with several national languages plus one international language, to expect interpretation at a meeting conducted mostly in another international language; failing that, they should be entitled to use the Danish gambit (see below), and insist that the anglophones express themselves in French and vice versa. In order

---

[1] See tables 'Native speakers' and 'First + second/alternate language speakers'.
[2] See Dante Alighieri, *De vulgari eloquentia* (1304-05).

to avoid such a quandary, anglophone organisers of the meeting might be tempted to obviate the problem by inviting only English speakers. In certain fields (such as economics and statistics) this would do little harm; it might well expedite matters. In others it would compromise the accuracy and indeed the legitimacy of the conclusions: a conference on women's health, on poverty, ethics, minority or community health, would be severely hampered if discussion were restricted to any one language. Without the major international languages communication within the UN agencies would not be possible.

Community / Identity

In 1999 the European Union had eleven official languages and three 'vehicular languages'. The financial cost of language arrangements is great, although the political cost of neglecting such arrangements can exceed it.[1] In the 1970s, the Danes proposed reducing the number of European Community languages to two: English and French.[2] Paris and London were full of glee until they realised that the proposal was conditional on the British using French and the French using English when they took the floor. Had they been able to look into the future, the French and British might well have bitten the bullet and accepted, since the cost of training their civil servants and diplomats in one foreign language would have been less than the cost of present arrangements in Brussels. A level playing field would have been guaranteed. Or would it? Because the principal beneficiaries of the Danish gambit would have been the Danes themselves. While they are not major world languages in demographic terms, all the Nordic languages are in the top ten as regards per capita GNP.[3] A portion of that wealth has been invested in excellent foreign

---

[1] See, for example, *Repubblica*, Sunday 5 September 1999, on the meeting in Finland where the Italian and Spanish prime ministers, in protest at the German insistence on German interpretation in the meeting, took the floor in Italian and Spanish instead of French or English, as had been the custom at informal meetings.

[2] Nelde, *op.cit.*, p. 294.

[3] J.A. Laponce, *op. cit.*, p. 82, table 16, 'Languages ranked by wealth'.

language instruction, with the result that the Danes have unrivalled skills in their international second language, plus a language of their own that fulfils the inestimable and often underestimated role of identification (more on this below).

Compare this to countries such as the Philippines[1] and Cameroon[2], both of which are heavily involved with international second languages: English, and formerly Spanish, in the case of the Philippines; French and English (and formerly German) in the case of Cameroon. The educational authorities face a dilemma from the outset: should they teach children to read a local language first, then the international, or vice versa? Both together? In the Philippines primary education is free of charge, but since uniforms and schoolbooks are not provided, many children cannot afford to go, or will quickly drop out if they do not feel they are progressing. If they persist and become literate only in the international language, their sense of identity may be compromised. Knowing who you are and where you are from is not only a matter of being able to say things to your friends without being understood by foreigners, useful though that can be at times. There are two main functions to speech: communication and identification. One function conveys messages and the other shows where the messages come from. One makes bridges and the other draws borders, often between two people who are trying to talk to each other. Both are vital.

The importance of identity was always apparent – if only negatively – to those in power. The Gaelic language was outlawed in 18th century Britain after an uprising. Linguistic repression since has become more subtle and much more effective. The native languages of the underprivileged have been allowed to die out,[3] and literacy in the major languages that they are compelled to

---

[1] Bonifacio P. Sibayan, 'The Filipino People and English', in *Scientific and Humanistic Dimensions of Language*, ed. by K.R. Jankowsky (John Benjamins, 1985), pp. 580-593.
[2] Emmanuel N. Chia, 'Second Language Teaching and Learning in Cameroon Today and Tomorrow', in Jankowsky *op.cit.*, pp. 539-549.
[3] See Ken Hale, 'Endangered Languages', *Language*, vol. 68, no.1 (1992), 1-42.

adopt is, at times, not encouraged beyond a certain point. It is not unknown for migrants to be helped to functional literacy but no further in their new country, so that they can perform only menial jobs.[1] And the huge discrepancy between female and male literacy in certain major languages indicates the reluctance of the authorities to let women develop historical awareness of who and what they are.[2]

History is written by the winners, but it is understood by the losers. People from poor countries educated in an international language who make the long and difficult journey home to their own identity and community are the only ones who can properly communicate the state of their own country to the world. Part of the difficulty is that mastery of an international language can be the badge of a national elite, something that cuts the masters off from their own people. Unless careful attention is paid to what emerges from less powerful language communities, the smaller languages will be starved of value (such as poetry) that the big languages will be unable to digest. A language that excludes women from literacy maims itself. An education system that morphs from a public good to a commodity willfully excludes most of its talented people (and that can be done quite effectively, these days, without imprisonment or exile). Of course its controllers can survive as a limited company, and can continue to bring a certain number of outsiders into its gated community, but its chances of avoiding catastrophe or producing wonders are drastically diminished.

[1] Alastair Pennycook, 'English in the world / The world in English', in James W. Tollefson, *Power and Inequality in Language Education* (Cambridge U.P., 1995), pp34-58, p. 41.
[2] See table, 'Literacy by language'.

Table 1: Top 20 Languages by Population, first language speakers only (millions)[1]

Language Name	Primary Country	Population
Chinese, Mandarin	China	885
Spanish	Spain	332
English	United Kingdom	322
Bengali	Bangladesh	189
Hindi	India	182
Portuguese	Portugal	170
Russian	Russia	170
Japanese	Japan	125
German, standard	Germany	98
Chinese, Wu	China	77
Javanese	Indonesia/Java/Bali	76
Korean	Korea	75
French	France	72
Vietnamese	Viet Nam	68
Telugu	India	66
Chinese, Yue	China	66
Marathi	India	64
Tamil	India	63
Turkish	Turkey	59
Urdu	Pakistan	58

---

[1] *Ethnologue: Languages of the World*, February 1999. The population figures refer to first language speakers in all countries.

Table 2(a): First + Second language speakers (millions)[1]

Mandarin	885
English	470
Hindi	418
Spanish	352
Russian	288
Bengali	196
Portuguese	182
Arabic	170
Malay + Indonesian	140
Japanese	125
French	124
German	121

---

[1] *Ethnologue.*

Table 2(b): Spoken languages, estimated totals of primary and alternate voices (millions)[1]

Language	Primary voices only	Primary plus alternate voices
Mandarin Chinese	800	1,000
English	400	1,000
Hindi + Urdu	550	900
Spanish	400	450
Russian	170	320
Arabic	200	250
Bengali	190	250
Portuguese	180	200
Malay + Indonesian	50	160
Japanese	120	130
German	100	125
French	90	125

Dalby explains the difference between 'second' and 'alternate' languages as follows:

> The ... estimates relate not only to the *primary* voices of each language but also to its *alternate* voices. The first of these categories includes all who acquire 'native' or 'native-like' competence in a language, most frequently their 'mother-tongue', whereas the category of alternate voices includes all those whose speaking of the language in question is influenced by their knowledge of one or more other languages, especially their own mother-tongue. These two categories replace the earlier tripartite distinction sometimes made between 'mother-tongue speakers', 'second-language speakers' and 'foreign-

[1] David Dalby, *The Linguasphere Register of the World's Languages and Speech Communities* (Linguasphere Press, Wales, 1999).

language speakers' (where the distinction between 'second' and 'foreign' was based on the political status of a language in a particular country).

Dalby also pairs major languages where there is a good degree of mutual comprehension (hence Hindi + Urdu and Malay + Indonesian, above). Comparison of the two tables shows that, while absolute numbers depend on definition, the resultant order is similar.

Table 3: Literacy by Language

Language	Total adult literacy (%)	Adult literacy in women(%)	Adult literacy in men (%)
Chinese	81.5	72.5	89.9
English	62.1 / 95+	53.1 / 95+	71.5 / 95+
Spanish	92	90.5	93.5
Arabic	60.4	49.9	71.1
Bengali	38.1	26.1	49.4
Hindi	52.1	37.7	65.5
Portuguese	80.6	79	82
Russian	99+	99+	99+
Japanese	95+	95+	95+
German	95+	95+	95+
Korean	98	96.7	99.3
French	53.4 / 95+	46.4 / 95+	64.8 / 95+

These figures were not readily available from UNESCO and United Nations statistics. The notes below explain why. The figures were formed from data on numbers of illiterate people per country (where figures are available) in relation to UN figures for total population aged 15 and over. The most reliable figures are those for a language that coincides closely with a country: Korean, Russian and Chinese. Next come figures for certain groups of countries – Portuguese, Spanish and Arabic – where literacy will be predominantly in the languages named. General literacy for India gives a rough idea for Hindi, though here the approximation is still more gross, in that there are several major literate languages in India that will seriously skew the picture. Vaguest of all are the figures for English and French. UNESCO shows no literacy statistics for the developed countries concerned, and the wealth of local languages in former colonies – especially in Africa, from which the figures above are drawn (to give a developing / developed country contrast) – is such that English and French literacy, even if they could be calculated, would give only a very partial idea of how people there communicate. Extra figures for developed countries are drawn from *The World: A Third World Guide 1995/96*.

Table 4: Countries in which international languages are official/recognised languages[1]

Language	Countries in which official	Countries in which recognised
Arabic	20	3
Chinese	3	1
English	64	6
French	31	6
Spanish	21	1
Russian	8	7
German	8	3
Portuguese	7	
Bengali	2	
Hindi	1	1
Bahasa	3	
Korean	2	1

[1] Source: *L'état du monde, édition 1998* (Paris, La Découverte, 1997).

Table 4 shows countries in which major international languages are *the* or *a* language recognised by government. The criteria are primarily political rather than linguistic, which produces some paradoxes, especially in the 'recognised language' lists. For example, French is recognised in Italy, but Neapolitan/Calabrian – which *Ethnologue* ranks 101st in the world, with over seven million speakers – is not.

And the Next Millennium

What language will speak for the year 3000? English is, like the guitar, an instrument that can afford users a passable level of competence in a short time. Spanish is another such. Chinese is not, but then it has a couple of advantages. Like numerals, its written form is detachable from its pronunciation, which makes for a big geographical and temporal spread. Another – disputable – advantage is that it conveys information with particular speed. This is difficult to prove, but I am persuaded by film credits and analogue watches. The next time you see a Chinese film with English subtitles, try to read them through before they disappear. My impression is that the average Chinese cinema-goer gets the message quicker than this European glossomaniac. As regards watches, remember how digital timepieces were hailed as a great advance on analogue; I mean digital as opposed to analogue, not as opposed to clockwork. Like alphabetical information, digital time is displayed in a combination of discrete signs: four digits and one punctuation mark. Analogue time, though displayed on two hands, really presents its message in a single sign, a single shape. The burden of Chinese characters, like analogue watch dials, is assimilated at once, while alphabetical (and numerical) messages have to be recomposed before they can be understood.

Does this make Chinese the language of the future? No. But given that patent advances such as the digital display can turn out to have deficiencies that make people turn back to older technologies, it is not impossible that the antique, illogical writing system of the Chinese will find new strength in another language family. You could imagine a language that, unlike Vietnamese and Korean that migrated from Chinese characters to analytic alphabets, moved in the opposite sense, into ideographic space. A Latin language, or Turkic or Semitic, whose alphabet was displaced by emoticons, idioticons, logos (logograms, that is, not the Word) and other composite signs. A language that coined facts with ease and made comparative analysis rather difficult. Oligarchs would love it. Artists on the make would compose new epics in their honour.

The two essentials for the future of human communication are – typically of language – contradictory. The language must be able to transmit meaning over unimaginable and unprecedented stretches of historical time, if only to warn our distant descendants not to open the boxes of plutonium waste. At the same time, no single language should silence all the others, because if it did, and if humanity lost the gift of Babel, we would lose with it any ability to enter the imagination of others. Without that paradoxical gift our descendants would not have a hope in hell of understanding the warning signs left by their remote ancestors.

I have no real fear for the gift of Babel, but no idea of how long-term transmission could be achieved – except, perhaps, if the very practice of translation could morph into a meta-language, something analogous to John Anderson's hope for his own discipline: 'philosophy should be systematic, not a comprehensive set of solutions, but a single logic'. If that were to happen, if language itself were to become a monolithic practice capable of transmitting sense over tens of thousands of years, then the faculty of sympathetic imagination and the voice of human identity would probably migrate out of language altogether, perhaps into music. The danger then would be a radical separation of thought from feeling at the highest levels. But perhaps we are there already.

Translator Trattoria

How sick and tired I am of translation, and what a losing battle it is always. Wish I had the courage to wash my hands of it all, I mean leave it to others and try and get on with some work.[1]

One day when I was in Alcaná de Toledo, I saw a boy selling some old papers and portfolios to a silk dealer; now, since I am fond of reading - even old scraps of paper found in the street - I followed my natural inclination and took one of the notebooks the lad was selling; I recognised the script as Arabic. Although I recognised it I could not read it, so I cast about for a baptised and lettered Moor to read it for me; it was not very difficult to find such an interpreter, since even translators of an older and better language were available. Fortune found me one who, when I told him what I was after and put the book in his hands, opened it in the middle and, after reading a few lines, began to laugh. I asked him what the joke was, and he said it was a note written in the margin. I asked him to tell me what it was, and he, still laughing, said:

- As I said, in the margin it says: 'This Dulcinea del Toboso, who is so frequently mentioned in this story, is said to have salted pork better than any other woman in La Mancha'.

When I heard the name 'Dulcinea del Toboso' I was astonished and amazed, realizing that those notebooks contained the story of Don Quixote. I therefore urged him to read the beginning and he, immediately turning the Arabic into Castilian Spanish, told me that it said: **The History of Don Quixote of La Mancha, written by Sidi Hamete Benengeli, Arab Historian**. Great

---

[1] Samuel Beckett, quoted from James Knowlson, *Damned to Fame: The Life of Samuel Beckett* (London, 1966), p. 438.

273

presence of mind was required to conceal my satisfaction when the title of the book reached my ears; racing to the silk dealer's I bought all the papers and portfolios from the boy for half a real (i.e. one eighth of a peseta); had he had the wit to see how much I wanted them, he could have got more than six reales out of the deal. I then took the Moorish convert to the cloister of the cathedral and asked him to translate into Castilian everything concerning Don Quixote, omitting nothing and adding nothing, for the price that he would name. He settled for two arrobas of raisins and three bushels of wheat, promising a faithful and prompt translation; however, to simplify matters, and so as not to let slip such a bargain, I brought him to my house, where in little over a month and a half he translated the lot, just as it is set out here.

Translators

It took me fifty minutes to draft that translation of 424 words from *Don Quixote*. Another ten minutes to change a few words, without keying them in, and there were two points I had to check with a Spaniard and a better dictionary. Let's say 400 words per hour for a 400-year-old text in my fourth-best foreign language. Even assuming I gathered speed as I got the hang of the text it would still take me six months to the Moor's six weeks. And while my version might just about pass muster, his is one of the finest bits of Spanish ever written. If that were all, I might still sleep at nights. But look at his rates! Since he actually asked for goods rather than cash, we know that the retail value of his two *arrobas* (22.5kg) of raisins is 100 Swiss francs. The quantity of wheat was just over 0.1 cubic metres in modern units. I don't know how much that costs, but I suspect that whereas the United Nations offers the (rather mean) rate of 220 Swiss francs per thousand words, that translator traitor took no more than 220 francs for half a million words. It is true that he got office space and expenses in spite of himself, but the idea of a man with so much talent and so little sense makes Don Quixote himself look like a boring civil servant.

'La traduction est un travail de con qu'un con ne peut pas faire.' Be careful how you translate that maxim into English. And do not infer from it that inability to translate is a sign of stupidity. But to assume that, because you can speak two languages indifferently (as the French say) you can translate between them, is like saying 'I think therefore I am a brain-surgeon'.

A nameless Egyptian in the fifteenth century BC advised 'Put writing in your heart that you may protect yourself from hard labour of any kind'. Those scribes kept the writing system complicated: it was not in their interest to develop a simple alphabet.[1] In the fifteenth century AD, Confucian scholars in Korea fought a furious rearguard action to defend the even more complex Sino-Korean system against Han'gul, which must be the most simple, accurate and elegant writing system there is. After ruling the roost since Gutenberg, the print workers were replaced in the 1980s with the word processor. Surely it is only a matter of time till translators go the way of the scribe and the typesetter?

I have another admission to make: my average speed over the year is nothing like 400 words per hour. You see, I translated the Cervantes on a Saturday afternoon when I was rested, I had read the text several times in the past, and above all it made sense. At work it isn't always like that. Besides which, whereas the narrator seems to have found the best and cheapest translator in history in a few minutes and without any trouble, I spend much of my time and ingenuity finding and keeping track of translators I can trust.

Translation has been described as the second oldest profession. I didn't choose to become one, but once when I was down on my luck someone offered me a few pounds for a quick job and one thing led to another. It wasn't the sort of work I thought I had any emotional attachment to, until they spoke of replacing me, or some of my functions, with a machine. 'The Good Ship Venus' sprang to mind: 'The first mate's name was MacQueen, who invented a (certain) machine'. I don't recall all the words, but I remember it ended badly. And it served him right.

---

[1] Florian Coulmas, *The Writing Systems of the World* (Oxford, 1989), p. 70.

The forgotten history of automatic translation

Machine translation is seen as a new discipline, something that began in the aftermath of the Second World War. Many failures are forgiven a science in its infancy - though a fifty-year infancy would stretch the patience of most parents. But the theoretical basis of such schemes goes back not five decades but three-and-a-half centuries.

I haven't finished reading Don Quixote, though this at least I have understood: the author is debunking the impossible quest of the knight-errant. The 17th century saw the final debunking of another impossible quest that had been going on even longer – a millenium or two – not for the Holy Grail, but for the philosopher's stone, the alcahest, the universal solvent, that which could transmute lead into gold. One quip that catches the victory of chemistry over alchemy is the one attributed to Robert Boyle, author of *The Sceptical Chymist* (1661). He pointed out that if the fabled universal solvent were to be discovered, there wouldn't be a container for it. (There is a solution to that, but this isn't the place for it.) The mystical was out, the practical was in. Of greater relevance to translation, the word was being ousted by the number. And surely number is something of a universal language? From this point onward when people looked for the universal solution to linguistic problems and differences, they turned not to real or imagined links with Hebrew (as the language everyone spoke before the collapse of the tower of Babel), but to numbers. The likes of Athanasius Kircher pursued the quest for the Holy Grail in terms of a procedure for turning one language into another without understanding it. His system (published in 1663) is described by Umberto Eco[1] Here is part of a table for translation between Latin, Italian, Spanish, French and German:

---

[1] *La ricerca della lingua perfetta nella cultura europea* (Roma 1993), pp. 211-215.

Latin	Italian	Spanish	French	German
abalienare I.1	Astenere I.4	Abstenir I.4	Abstenir I.4	Abhalten I.4
Abdere I.2	Abbracciare II.10	Abbraçar II.10	Abayer XII.35	abschneiden I.5

An enthusiast sent Kircher a message of congratulation using the method, but Kircher couldn't decipher it.

It is here, perhaps for the first time, that we see that combination of translation and code-breaking in mathematical operations or attempts at such that re-emerged in an egregious memorandum on machine translation three centuries later (more on this anon). And notice that with this emphasis on codes and secrecy, we are talking of language as power first, communication second.

While the intellectual argument against the impossible quest of alchemy was won, the urge, or one debased form of it, persisted. For the dream of turning base metal into gold was so seductive to those who needed gold for whatever reason that a certain category of alchemists realised that, in the theory itself, they *had* a way of turning base metal into gold. They used it to talk money out of their patrons. There is a painting by Rembrandt in the Louvre entitled 'The Philosopher in Meditation' - wrongly, I think, since it follows the iconography of the alchemist: the little man at the bellows over the furnace in the foreground is the 'puffer', the alchemist's assistant who did all the dirty work with mercury, sulphur etcetera. The irony is that the puffer and the financier were often the same person.[1]

In the course of the 17th century, the product on offer changed. Marin Mersenne was a priest who took an interest in prime numbers, especially the ones that can be expressed as 2^p-1, where p is a prime number; this made him a fore-runner of modern cryptography. In 1629, Mersenne told Descartes that a lawyer called des Vallées had discovered the matrix language whereby all

[1] See J. Holmyard, *Alchemy* (Harmondsworth, 1957), for the sociology of the business.

others could be understood. Descartes smelled a rat: '... et si-tost que ie voy seulement le mot d'*arcanum* en quelque proposition, ie commence à en avoir mauvaise opinion'.[1] Richelieu asked des Vallées to print his project; des Vallées stalled and asked for a state pension. Richelieu, who didn't win his cardinal's hat in a raffle, let the matter drop. Cave Beck, author of *The Universal Character* (1657) claimed that a universal language would benefit mankind in terms of trade and would make great savings on interpreters' fees;[2] de Maimieux (*Pasigraphie*, 1797), claimed that his written-only language would permit communication between Europe and Africa, serve to check translations, and expedite diplomatic, civil and military operations.[3]

While Descartes had dreamed of a language whose units would be the building bricks of thought, one that would do what de Maimieux claimed his *Pasigraphie* had achieved, he did realize it was a dream. The attempts of Leibniz to bring it to fruition failed, basically because he found that there is no objective, non-arbitrary classification of concepts. The encyclopaedia retreated to the pragmatic practice of mapping out existing areas of knowledge. As d'Alembert put it in the 'Discours Préliminaire' to the *Encyclopédie* (Paris, 1751), the order of the encyclopaedia '...is a kind of map intended to show the main countries, their positions and mutual relations, and the shortest path from one to the next – a path that is often blocked by a thousand obstacles ... which can be depicted only in highly detailed individual maps. These individual maps are the various articles of the Encyclopedia...'[4] I have to insist on the importance of this failure, because it crippled automatic translation from the outset. It was not a total rout – as we shall see. Perhaps just as important as the failure itself is that many proponents of automatic and later machine translation have remained blissfully unaware of it. As late as 1889 Frederick

---

[1] 'As soon as I see the word arcanum in a proposition I begin to take a dim view of it.' See Roberto Pellerey, *Le lingue perfette nel secolo dell'utopia* (Roma, Laterza, 1992), p. 27.
[2] Eco, *op. cit.*, p. 226.
[3] Eco, p. 317.
[4] Translated from R. Pellerey, *op.cit.*, p. 89.

William Dyer published his 'Lingualumina', which is reviewed in the *Histoire de la langue universelle*:[1]

M:	quantity	L:	space
S:	existence	B:	state
Z:	personality	K:	relation
V:	species or class	J:	'interchange' etc.

Li:	space	eil:	limit
lee:	line	eela:	point
lai:	angle	aila:	side etc.

The radicals are formed by joining various vowels to those consonants, whether before or after them... The *verbs* consist of 3 significant letters: the first shows whether the subject is a person or a thing (remember that **z** = *personality*: the second indicates number (les short vowels **i, a, o**, for the singular, the long vowels **ee, ah, au** for the plural); the 3rd indicates the tense: **b**, past; **d**, present; **g**, future. Thus the present tense of the verb *to be* is: **zinda, zanda, zonda; zeeda, zahda, zauda:** *I am, you are*, etc. Past tense: **zimba, zamba, zomba**, etc. Future: **zinga, zanga, zonga**, etc. There is also a *perfect* tense, produced by devoicing the past tense: **zimpa, zampa, zompa; zeepa, zarpa, zorpa**.

The author further complicates his conjugation with other 'subtleties'. Obviously, this so-called logical system could not be more arbitrary, fantastic and irregular. It has another drawback that derives from its author's nationality: an Englishman will never be able to conceive of a correct, international phonetic system, because of the execrable pronunciation his language accustoms him to. For what could be more absurd than to pronounce the simple letter *I* as though it were two vowels (*aï*), while rendering the simple *I* sound with two letters (*ea, ee*)?[2]

---

[1] Louis Couturat & Léopold Leau, *Histoire de la langue universelle* (Paris, 1903).
[2] Couturat & Leau, *op. cit.*, pp. 78-79.

Incidentally, the anglophobia that comes out in this passage seems to me to undermine the basic project of the authors, that of introducing an auxiliary language for international communication. If you can't stand your neighbours you are unlikely to agree with them on a new language to adopt.

The same authors point out that the attempt at pasigraphy, a written-only language that would be understood by all, did produce some systems that, though arbitrary, did win acceptance. The Dewey decimal bibliographical classification is one, and they show how it could tend towards language:

> Here is how the classifying numbers are formed: the corpus of human knowledge is divided into ten major classes, designated by the ten digits, 0 to 9:
>
> 000 Generalities
> 100 Philosophy and psychology
> 200 Religion
> 300 Social sciences
> 400 Language
> 500 Natural sciences and mathematics
> 600 Technology (applied science)
> 700 The arts
> 800 Literature and rhetoric
> 900 Geography and history.
>
>
> It is easy to see how this process of subdivision could be continued until a given idea or subject were set in a class of its own; it would be designated unambiguously by the series of figures that showed all the successive divisions. Here is an example of such progressive determination or specification:
>
> | 61 | Medicine |
> | 612 | Physiology |
> | 612.3 | Digestion |
> | 612.31 | Mouth |
> | 612.313 | Salivary glands |
> | 612.313.6 | Disorders of the salivary glands |
> | 612.313.63 | Salivary microbes. |

Thus, as the authors point out,

31   = statistics,
331.2   = wages,
677   = textile industry,
31:331.2:667 would thus mean: statistics on wages in the textile industry.'[1]

Of course, however refined, it would be of no help at all in most sentences: this one, for example. (It's also dated rather quickly, as librarians will know; who would give ten per cent to theology etc. these days?)

Wittgenstein's fresh attempt in the *Tractatus* (1921) to give rational order to the world led to what seems an even greater failure, in that, by the time of the *Philosophical Investigations* (1945, published 1953) he had given up on a coherent scheme:

> The best that I could write would never be more than philosophical remarks; my thoughts were soon crippled if I tried to force them on in any single direction against their natural inclination. – And this was, of course, connected with the very nature of the investigation. For this compels us to travel over a wide field of thought criss-cross in every direction. – The philosophical remarks in this book are, as it were, a number of sketches of landscapes which were made in the course of these long and involved journeyings.
>
> The same or almost the same points were always being approached afresh from different directions.[2]

If it seemed impossible even for one man to give coherence to his thoughts, how could there be any interlinguistic system robust enough to bear the weight of meaning in translation? Could the answer have been lost with the 'Filene-Finlay speech translator'?

I have come across a little volume from the library of the J.J. Rousseau Institute in Geneva, called *International Communication: A Symposium on the Language Problem*, by

---

[1] Couturat & Leau, *op. cit.*, pp. 6-8.
[2] *Philosophical Investigations*, p. vii.

Herbert N. Shenton, Edward Sapir and Otto Jespersen (London, 1931).

Shenton, Professor of Sociology at Syracuse University, contributes an essay entitled 'A Social Problem', and asks 'Can social engineers improve the international language situation?' He writes:

> Various mechanical procedures have been devised such as ... the Filene-Finlay Speech Translator, now regularly used by the International Labour Office as a permanent feature of its conference machinery. This telephonic device for the simultaneous translation of a speech into several languages was conceived by Mr Edward A. Filene of Boston, and was developed by him in consultation with Thomas A. Edison, General J.J. Carty, and others. It was finally perfected by Professor Gordon Finlay, a British scientist.[1]

This wonderful machine had been backed by J.J. Carty, a vice-president of AT&T, and Thomas Edison of light-bulb fame. What had become of it? Who switched it off? ILO is just across the road from where I work, so I skipped across one lunch time. Filene was a prominent Rotarian and founder of the Credit Union Movement. He was given to printing his thoughts on 'Why Men Strike' and 'The European Problem: A Businessman's View'.

I could find no trace of the machine at ILO. Shenton does provide a footnote: 'Described in detail in *Commercial Standards Monthly*, November, 1930 (a US Government publication)'. I have not been able to obtain it. Not even the British Library has a copy.

Never mind, there's the IBM home page. It says:

> 1931... Accounting machines are introduced in Japan. New products: - 400-series alphabetical accounting machines. 600-series calculating machines, which handle multiplication and division. First permanent installation of the Filene-Finlay Translator is set up at League of Nations in Geneva. 5% stock dividend declared.

---

[1] Shenton, Sapir and Jespersen, *op. cit.* p. 29.

All in a year's work for Big Blue. But wait! What is this machine? The League of Nations archives provide the answer, in a letter of 9 November 1927 from the Marquis G. Paulucci de Calboli Barone, Under Secretary-General of the League of Nations, to Mr Ake W. Hj. Hammarskjoeld, Registrar, Permanent Court of International Justice, The Peace Palace, The Hague, Holland. His excellency explains that Filene's scheme for simultaneous telephonic interpretation was tried out on a small scale in 1926 at the International Labour Conference. He goes on:

> The method employed at this year's [1927 International Labour] Conference was roughly as follows. The interpreter sits in the hall itself at a short distance from the speaker and hears the speech of course in the ordinary way as it is pronounced. He then speaks his interpretation in a low voice into a microphone which is mounted on his table and with which all the headphones are connected. It has been found in practice that by using a microphone in this way an interpreter is able to dictate his translation in such a low voice that it is quite inaudible to the speaker and does not interfere with him in any way ...

> ... his system of interpreting is, of course, in many ways much more difficult than the ordinary method as the interpreter has to listen to one sentence while translating the preceding one. It was thought at first that this difficulty might prove insurmountable, but several of the interpreters at the Labour Conference achieved excellent results.

Which goes to show that you can't take everything you see on the IBM home page as gospel. Not only did the Filene-Finlay translator not translate, but IBM didn't invent it. However, I would like to pay tribute at this point to Edward A. Filene, that 'odd chap' as he was called in an internal memo of the League of Nations. He pursued for many years, and against the better judgment of the experts, a system without which international gatherings today could hardly function. At the League of Nations, the head of the French translation and interpreting section was given a report by one of his interpreters on 3 September 1930. Here is part of it:

> The interpretation is imperfect because the interpreters must speak at the same time as the orator. This compels them to miss

out sentences – those pronounced whilst they are speaking themselves. They do not have the opportunity to make an intelligent summary or to include the passages omitted. It may be that the sentence pronounced by the speaker while they are translating and which they do not hear is one of the most important. The general effect is incoherent, and it is completely impossible to follow an idea or a line of thought in its entirety ... then there is the obvious unhealthiness of working in those little booths ...

Who could deny his arguments? But we now know that simultaneous interpretation works; it's like riding a bicycle. He does, however, make a point that has come home to roost: 'One fears that the introduction of a telephonic system might open the door to the demand for recognition of one or more additional official languages, which would entail costs infinitely higher than those of the installations themselves.' Incidentally, it is generally believed that simultaneous interpreting was first used on a large scale at the Nuremberg War Tribunal; we can now see that it was used in major conferences more than twenty years earlier.

Now, after three centuries of re-inventing the language cracker we come to the document that is often quoted as the first step in machine translation: a memorandum sent in 1947 by Warren Weaver, one of the founders of the discipline: 'One naturally wonders if the problem of translation could conceivably be treated as a problem of cryptography. When I look at an article in Russian, I say "This is really written in English, but it has been coded in some strange symbols. I will now proceed to decode."'[1] Apparently this nincompoop worked for the Rockefeller Foundation. The addressee was a crystallographer.[2]

The foreword to a recent book on machine translation admits that 'it is an open question whether the great investment that has been made in the enterprise (of machine translation) since the first

---

[1] David Crystal, *The Cambridge Encyclopedia of Language,* 2nd edition, p. 352.
[2] W.J. Hutchins and H.L. Somers (editors), *An Introduction to Machine Translation* (London, Academic Press, 1992) p. 5.

systems were put to use in the 1960s has resulted in any real improvement'.[1] One begins to see why.

Of course, machine translation (MT) has produced results: a Catholic chaplain on a cruise ship headed for the Antarctic wrote to *Machine Translation Today: Translating and the Computer* to say he had used a translation machine to translate his sermon into French and that it had gone down well with his French congregation. We are not told whether he used it for confessions.[2] Seriously, the Canadian weather service has been using a machine to translate its weather reports for a long time now – it always requires some revision, but it works. Systran is available free on the Web, and I for one will use it rather than pay a translator for a version of an article from German that I might or might not really need. If I *do* really need it, *then* I'll see about a proper translation. This modest service seems to be the best that MT can offer customers today: 'The military has always been a great believer in MT, especially the Pentagon. The Forward Area Language Converter (FALCon) was developed by the American defense section and is currently used by US Forces in Bosnia to assess the military significance of documents and to determine whether they should be translated. Six prototype systems are currently used in Bosnia by the Army's V Corps Forces and Special Operations Forces to translate documents from Serbian and Croatian into English.'[3] If better were available, the Pentagon would have it, and someone would have told us about it.

Art or Science?

Consider what has happened in five fields since the publication of *Don Quixote* in 1600 (the year *Hamlet* was staged): literature, alchemy, chemistry, lexicography and automatic translation. There

---

[1] Hutchins and Somers, *op. cit.*, p. xiii.
[2] 'Forty Ways to Skin a Cat: Users Report on Machine Translation', in *Machine Translation Today: Translating and the Computer* 15, Nov. 1993 (ASLIB; Association for Information Management)pp. 127-8.
[3] Sharon Denness, 'MT Summit Looks Back to the Future', *Language International* volume 9.6 (1997), 12-13, p. 12.

has been no discernible progress in literature. Indeed, the sight of the Hale-Bopp comet in the morning sky reminded me that there has been no discernible progress in literature at all. The last time that comet was near the earth, 4,200 years ago, was shortly before The Epic of Gilgamesh was written, and considerably before the God of Abraham cleared his throat. Gilgamesh poses the big questions just as sharply as Cervantes and Shakespeare. No answer.

Alchemy has bitten the dust. Consider the following description of five illustrations in an early 17th century alchemical manuscript:

> First, there is depicted a leper hanged on a golden gibbet: this is the operation of calcination. Next, a leper with his hands tied behind his back is about to be decapitated by the executioner, also leprous: this is distillation. The leper attached to a gilded wheel represents coagulation, and the silver chalice and three dice, solution. The fifth miniature, of a half-woman half-serpent having a leprous bust and transfixing a leper with a golden lance, while a leprous woman stands beneath the lance, represents the extraction of philosophers' mercury from the prime matter by means of the philosophic fire. The whole ... represents the exaltation of the common base metals, which are throughout considered allegorically as in a state of sin.[1]

Shed the mystical, allegorical and moral aspects and you have simple chemical procedures (at least as regards the first four). Chemistry arises from the wreckage, with much more modest aims: not Truth, but classification of phenomena in formulae of clarity, concision and elegance. Its progress in three centuries is almost unbelievable.

Another discipline arose, or gained maturity, in the same period: lexicography. For this was the century of the dictionary, starting with the Accademia della Crusca, followed rather later by the Académie Française and Dr Johnson. Just as chemistry is a classification of material phenomena, lexicography defines words, ultimately in a circular or systematic way, in terms of each other. Like chemistry, its aims are modest, sceptical, and strictly non-

---

[1] E.J. Holmyard, *Alchemy* (Harmondsworth, 1957), pp. 158-159.

metaphysical. The dictionary satisfies itself with classification in mere alphabetical order, which is absurd but eminently usable.

While lexicography and the exact sciences progressed by leaps and bounds from then till now, automatic translation never kept its promises. As the *Scientific American* put it in November 1996, '"Few informed people still see the original goal of fully automatic high-quality translation of arbitrary texts as a realistic goal for the foreseeable future", writes Martin Kay, a longtime machine-translation researcher at the Xerox Palo Alto Research Laboratories'. (p.24)

Why is this?

Because translation often confronts us with conundrums like that little question which turn out to involve not one discipline but several. And whereas in chemistry and lexicography a question is either tackled or deemed out of bounds, nothing is beyond the bounds of translation: it is a constant to-ing and fro-ing among systems, in order to guard against the 'Chinese whispers' effect – which of course is the sort of thing language machines produce all the time, because they cannot tell which system or what situation a given utterance belongs to. There is no algorism for solving problems which, ostensibly verbal, are connected root and branch, sense and synapse, with what we do and with what we say about it.

Language is social and historical: it takes two to talk, and that takes time. The weird thing is that that gets forgotten. One old saw from Saussure recurs like a bad penny: Richard Dawkins's version of it is 'we can define a word how we like for our own purposes, provided we do so clearly and unambiguously'. Steven Pinker's version is 'Since a word is a pure symbol, the relation between its sound and its meaning is utterly arbitrary'.[1] Arbitrary in that there is no organic connection between the word 'dog' and the slavering quadruped. In social terms, though, it is not arbitrary but conventional; there is a world of difference. And in semantic terms, if words are arbitrary, there can be no etymology. No etymology means no history, no sense. Garbage in, garbage out.

---

[1] Steven Pinker, *The Language Instinct* (London, 1995), p. 155.

(Incidentally, I disagree not only with Pinker's deduction but also with Saussure's premise; but that's another story.)

Let's stay with Pinker: he's a revelation.

> But to get these languages of thought to subserve reasoning properly, they would have to look much more like each other than either one does to its spoken counterpart, and it is likely that they are the same: a universal mentalese. (p.82) But grouping words into phrases is also necessary to connect grammatical sentences with their proper meanings, chunks of mentalese. (p.101) Deep structure is the interface between the mental dictionary and phrase structure. (p.121) At the very least I hope you are impressed at how syntax is a Darwinian 'organ of extreme perfection and complication'. (p.124) ...children's minds seem to be designed with the logic of word structure built in. (p.146) When memory has been emptied of all its incomplete dangling branches, we experience the mental 'click' that signals that we have just heard a complete grammatical sentence. (p.200) His results corroborate the suggestion that this particular universal is caused by the way that morphological rules are computed in the brain... (p.236) ...grammars can hop among the grooves made available by the universal grammar in everyone's mind. (p.244)

Like the description of alchemical procedures quoted above, Pinker's book provides genuine science (phonological in this case). Also a coherent grammar – Chomsky's system, which is neither elegant as Panini's Sanskrit grammar nor manageable as Kennedy's *Latin Primer*, but more universally applicable. From the evidence provided, though, it is, like the other two, a descriptive / prescriptive grammar, which means that its place is in the arts, not the sciences. For one reason and another that isn't seen as good enough. So, as the above quotations indicate, there are constant rhetorical claims that Chomsky's grammar is part of the brain. Judging from the plaudits on the back of the book, many people are sold on the idea. Just as early attempts were being made to model the brain on computer, someone came along to say that the brain behaved like a computer. It was so good, it had to be true. If, as a wise man once said 'meaning is what essence becomes when it is divorced from the object of reference and wedded to the word'[1], there will always be those who want to have their cake and eat it, with meaning and essence as one thing, particle and wave at once. It's alchemy again: there is no end to it.

Wax Fruit

Automatic translation – the attempt to treat translation as a branch of cryptography – floundered along for over three centuries, and failed in its grander aims when it became clear that lack of processing power was not the central problem. What was the main problem? And what can be salvaged from the wreckage? For unless, like Robert Boyle and the early chemists, its practitioners set clear and achievable goals, it too will muddle on, promising clients what they want to hear, with predictable results.

The central problem, the intrinsic problem of machine translation, has been hidden by the extrinsic problems that must be referred to here, because of the damage they do. Where demand is desperate and supply unlikely, charlatans thrive. When in addition the discipline is one without a memory, those concerned are unlikely to notice that history is recycling itself as neurodisney, as in Weaver's memo, above, or as in the many schemes for synthetic languages that still appear (Eurolingua is one I saw recently on the internet, with its elegant coinages such as 'weekfini' for weekend).

In addition to farce and outright fraud there is sharp practice, as evinced in the following argument:

> Translators are naturally reluctant to be responsible for what they consider an inferior product. Their instinct is to revise MT output to a quality expected from human translators, and they are as concerned with 'stylistic' quality as with accuracy and intelligibility.

> In assessing MT they need to adopt a different attitude, to acknowledge that perfectionism is neither always desirable nor always appreciated, particularly if it results in higher charges.

---

[1] Quine on Aristotle, quoted from Roy Harris, *The Language Makers* (London, 1980), p. 148.

> An MT system gives them the option of adjusting 'stylistic'
> quality to users' needs without sacrificing accuracy and
> consistency.[1]

This seems to blame translators for doing their job well, and to make a spurious distinction of style from accuracy and intelligibility – which are the two main elements of style in translation. It is further stated that, without an MT system, a translator is unable to adjust the type of translation to the user's needs. This is pernicious nonsense.

The intrinsic problem of MT, the one that serious practitioners have to confront, is that language is not code. Three demonstrations:

1 An interlingua (whether a matrix for translation like that of des Vallées or an international language) depends, semantically, on the establishing of a non-arbitrary ordering of concepts and phenomena such as that attempted by Descartes and Leibnitz and relinquished by the encyclopaedists, and by Wittgenstein. It depends on such an ordering because otherwise, while anyone could use the codes to translate from it, only its inventor could translate into it, since only he or she would know where a particular concept was filed. As we have seen, natural language covers many incommensurable fields, some of which evolve while others apparently do not. To put it simply, people change, the world changes, and any scheme for representing them must change: it must either lose its consistency or lose its relevance. It must be a living language.

A living language will be full of inconsistencies. The most used constructions will be the least regular. One word will gather a wild concatenation of meanings: 'Durman' in Russian denotes different flowers, depending on the area. It also means a fool, a kind of tobacco, a type of Astrakhan grape, an impassably thick forest, a strong wind on a lake, and the ore that contains 'kamen' samosvet', some kind of shiny stone that I can't find in the

---

[1] W. J. Hutchins and H.L. Somers, *op. cit.*, chapter 9, 'Evaluation of MT systems'; section 9.6, 'Evaluation by translators', p. 173.

dictionary. Obviously I could have found similar examples in English. I chose Russian because it's from a dictionary that was begun in 1965 and whose 31st volume (part of the letter P) has just appeared.[1] The print run has fallen from 4,500 on volume one to 1,200 on the latest volume, the paper of volume one will have rotted before the last volume comes out, but it struggles on, and I wish it well. Now, one can envisage a set of procedures whereby a machine would more often than not distinguish an Astrakhan grape from a wind on the lake and put the correct solution in a fruit bowl. But it would still be wax fruit.

2 The cryptographic approach to translation is statistical and abhors ambiguity. The human approach is contextual and depends on ambiguity. When we don't know or don't want to say we leave it vague; as diplomats and poets know, the latitude of that vagueness can be very precisely determined. A translator has to know a lot, not just about languages. And the one thing he (or more often she) must know better than anything else is when he does not know. He has to go up to the edge of that vagueness and look in. When it cannot be resolved to something definite, it must be reproduced in translation.

3 A code (a cipher) is the transformation of a set of signs. A language is a transformation of existence. Both code and language take the form of sign systems – hence the confusion on which MT is based – but in transit from one language to another the signs must run to earth. This can be a frightening process (read Sartre's *Nausea* for symptoms), though even if, as usual, it entails nothing more dramatic than passage through a translator's head, the sense can travel a long way from the signs before reformulation, as the following excerpt from a humdrum procedural text does show: 'En effet, celles-ci seront en général amenées au P.M.A. par simple brancardage. Il est donc souhaitable de faire en sorte que la distance parcourue par les secouristes soit la plus courte possible, ce qui entraînera pour eux une fatigue moindre et leur donnera une plus grande disponibilité donc la possibilité de prendre en charge chacun plus de victimes.' Translation: 'In general, patients have to

---

[1] *Slovar' russkih narodnyh govorov* (Moskva-Leningrad, 1965 – Sankt-Peterburg, continuing)

be carried to the medical outpost on stretchers, so the closer it is, the better for the rescue workers, since it leaves them less tired and better able to cope with a larger number of casualties.'

The Cost

Let's return to Alcaná de Toledo and that miraculously cheap, accurate and elegant text. How do you cut the cost of writing and translation? There are four obvious ways. One is for everyone to use the same language. Perhaps impatient with the many attempts to devise and impose a universal language, one author pointed out that there already exists a perfect language. Why don't we just drop the others and use it? Antoine de Rivarol was writing in 1785, and he meant French (*De l'universalité de la langue française*), but today's candidate is English. It has swept the board in the sciences, on screen and on line, and in international air and sea traffic. Even the warheads of Soviet SS-20 missiles are to be replaced with American talking heads. Perhaps the most remarkable sign of the dominance of English was turned up recently by my daughter, who showed me a book *in French* on how to train dogs, which advises owners to issue the commands *in English* because English is more concise. On the other hand, maybe the subtext is that English is a language fit for dogs... I remember talking to one Cameroonian who saw this linguistic dominance as a straightforward matter of progress: in Africa there are hundreds of languages, in Europe dozens, and in the United States, one (or two).

Truth to tell, there are still over 100 languages in the United States. Linguistic diversity is another of those resources we can destroy but could not replace. English has hegemony and indeed monopoly in many areas, but remember the arrogance of M. de Rivarol, and how his view of the world was to be overturned a few short years after he put it in print. English threatens many other languages in the world today – even languages such as French, Spanish, Arabic and Russian. But English itself has broken up: the Germanic slant of American English will soon be hispanicized too, and more importantly the different purposes it is used for have produced powerful dialects of their own. It would seem prudent as well as politic, therefore, to maintain the other international

292

languages, against the day when English becomes finally incoherent, so another can take the strain. Those languages in their turn, should allow for the others – not by coining vocabulary in them for abstruse areas of science, but by allowing them to live. This age of number, which began in the 17th century, has now reached a pitch where whatever can't be digitized has no value. With the speed of digital transactions, value has left meaning far behind. But meaning will survive with any of the neglected languages that escapes destruction.

A second cost-cutting option is the automatic generation of documents, which is a much simpler procedure than automatic translation. Consider this:

> In principle, if the communicational purpose is sufficiently closely defined, systematisation of the kind the European tradition developed makes possible an entirely automatic generation of the discourses that may be required. In practice, rhetoricians usually did not go this far since, quite apart from the laborious analysis involved, they preferred to emphasise the creative aspects of their art rather than its mechanical character. None the less, it is worth pointing out that precisely this step, which is basic to modern theories of generative grammar, was already taken within the scope of the *ars dictaminis* at the beginning of the fourteenth century by Lawrence of Aquilegia. Lawrence reduced letter-writing to a system which could easily be formulated as a set of rewrite rules of the type employed in the phrase-structure part of a transformational grammar. His system of communicational roles postulates seven types of addressee, which cover a wide range from popes down to heretics. For each type of addressee he provides a tabulation of alternative phrases and clauses, arranged consecutively in groups, in such a way that one item from each group must be selected at each successive stage in the derivation of a letter... This has the advantage, from the scribe's point of view, that it is no longer necessary to invent any materials, or consider the order of parts, or choice of words. Provided one can find one's way through the epistolary chart provided, writing a letter, as

one commentator has pointed out, does not even require the writer to know the language.[1]

The relevance of this to international organizations needs no elaboration.

The third way to cut the translation budget is simply to translate less: control the traffic. As it is, the user of information is almost drowned in a mass of junk. Automatic translation both increases the quantity of such rubbish and reduces its residual cogency. It becomes increasingly difficult to find any text of value. By contrast, there is no closer reading of a text than that done by a translator; the only practice approaching it is that of advocates arguing over the niceties of a contract in a court case, and for all the egregious expense of translation, it is much cheaper than the law.

Before I go on to option number 4, which will bring us back to the Good Ship Venus, I should explain where my conclusions come from, because this little essay has been an attempt to put into perspective 18 years' experience as a professional translator and 20-odd years' awareness that machine translation was somewhere out there – the ultimate in vapourware or the ultimate solution.

I have not focussed on recent (machine) translation theory – partly I admit because of the traditional hostility (to be found in many fields) between those who do it and those who talk about it, and partly because the principles of a discipline are most clearly seen in its initial phases; later they get submerged in detail.

Option 4 is computerization, and the three different approaches it entails have 17th-century ancestors: linguistic databases derive from lexicography, machine translation from cryptography, and computer-assisted translation from a compromise between the two.

Computers are perfect for lexicography, which manipulates unambiguously defined units in conventionally arranged

---

[1] Roy Harris, *op.cit.*, p. 100.

(alphabetical) fields. Computer databases are of immense and increasing help to translators.

In 350 years the automation of the translation process itself has not succeeded in crossing the divide from code to language. It may take as long again to do so, in might never succeed, or it might, through being used in any case, twist human language towards itself. (I believe the third scenario is the most likely: machine pidgin will be the vector of trade and the bane of my life.)

Computer-assisted translation – the compromise – will work better at the pole of lexicography than at that of translation. When, in other words, the text in hand approximates to a list, computer-assisted translation will be useful; when it is a highly articulate text, CAT can be a liability: it's misleading to be told that the version proposed by the computer is a 95% accurate rendering of the text when the 5% that is different completely reverses or subtly qualifies the meaning. It also slows you down when you are presented with six variously defective proposals for a phrase instead of being given the space to think.

So all of you who are still looking for the anonymous Moor from Alcaná de Toledo, stop wasting your time. If you want a text that talks to you, use a human being, and pay him (or her) like one. If you want a quick and very rough approximation use a machine translation programme. Remember that more and more texts are composed more or less automatically and more or less carelessly by cut and paste; nobody writes them and nobody reads them. It's perfectly apt to use a machine: that way nobody translates them either.

To expedite both processes in the long run, put 95% of your info investment into developing or buying the relevant databases and 5% into buying inexpensive machine translation systems off the shelf. Give them to your translators and watch what happens.

The Future

I sent a draft of this article to the poet Edwin Morgan, one of the great translators, and in a far more difficult field than mine. Part of his comment was 'I must admit I am divided in my mind about the whole business. I like the Shelleyan, evolutionary, all-things-are-possible viewpoint, and I suppose I engage in the "impossibilities" of translation for that reason, in other words we, everyone, even machines, can get better at it, and all avenues should be kept open. On the other hand, the creative juxtapositions of language can be simultaneously so unexpected and so powerful, especially in poetry, that one is tempted to want to say, Keep it, keep off! – this is it, nothing else will do!'[1]

What can I say? You may have noticed by this stage the frightened undertone of the threatened scribe in my words. I don't deny it's there. But I have tried my best to see the matter clearly. The central question seems to be this: is the dream of machine translation to be assimilated to that of perpetual motion or to that of manned flight?

My answer is that the current approach – which uses the cryptographic metaphor for language – falls into the former category. To demonstrate the point, I'd like to conclude by considering the mirror of this argument: we've been asking if numbers can cope with natural language. Can natural language cope with numbers? Take Richard Feynman who, in addition to being a genius of a physicist was an astounding teacher. His *QED: The Strange Theory of Light and Matter* (1985) is the best attempt I have ever seen by a scientist to put a difficult subject across to the innumerate public. But even there, though I understood the lectures step by step, I was never able to paraphrase what I thought I had understood. You can only go so far without maths. Perhaps it would be more precise to say that you can go only so far without realizing that, if you want to go further without wasting all your time translating every formula into words, you had better learn some maths. I venture to suggest that the moral applies equally and conversely to those who would use maths to render language: it

---

[1] Letter to P. McC., 27 October 1997.

works up to a point, beyond which the game is not worth the candle.

Fifteen Years Later

In the late 1990s, as I was working towards that conclusion, some papers by Ferdinand de Saussure were discovered (by Vincent Barras, I believe) in the conservatory of the family mansion in Geneva. I came across them the other day. One statement is bolder than Fermat's last theorem:

> We should be under no illusion. The day will come, and we are fully aware of the significance of (…), when it will be realized that the quantities of language and their relations can be expressed clearly, *in their basic essence,* in mathematical formulae.[1]

And yet, in the same book, we find:

> Should we declare our intimate thought on the matter? We fear that a clear perception of the nature of language will lead us to doubt that linguistics has a future. There is a disproportion, in this science, between the sum of operations needed to gain a rational grasp of the object, and the significance of that object: in a similar way there would be a mismatch between scientific study of what occurs during a game and the (…)[2]

And so, a generation later, amateurs are still inventing languages, the salesmen are still promising miracles that managers desperately want to believe, and the technicians are still telling us that instant translation will be with us in just a few years: ambulancemen will be able to use hand-held devices to translate the groans of patients as they race towards casualty.[3] The public uses machine translation

---

[1] *Ecrits de linguistique générale* (Paris, Gallimard, 2002), p. 206, tr. PMcC. The ellipses denote gaps in the original text.
[2] ibid., p. 87.
[3] http://uscnews.usc.edu/science_technology/the_doctor_can_understand_you_now.html
In medical facilities around the country, care is delayed, complicated and even jeopardized because doctors and patients do not speak the same

(MT) to get the gist of articles on the net; professional translators use whatever works in the way of IT – indexing programs and translation memory first and foremost, then machine translation to provide a draft of certain types of text. Chinese dictionaries have been revolutionized, which makes the recognition of characters and phrases ten or twenty times faster than it had been for thousands of years. In terms of language and politics, that is perhaps the most promising advance since the millennium.

Processing power has continued to double regularly, and my axiom that an increase in processing power will not solve the problem of quality machine translation still holds good. What I did not foresee in 1998 was a retreat from rule-based machine translation, to attack an area where processing power, and computer memory, can indeed make appreciable inroads. The inroads are major, but it's a road that ends in a swamp. I'll explain the problem and sketch a solution.

The area I'm referring to is statistical machine translation (SMT), and its biggest ever exponent is Google.

> In a meeting at Google in 2004, the discussion turned to an e-mail message the company had received from a fan in South Korea. Sergey Brin, a Google founder, ran the message through an automatic translation service that the company had licensed. The message said Google was a favorite search engine, but the result read: 'The sliced raw fish shoes it wishes. Google green

language – a situation particularly dire in diverse megacities such as Los Angeles and New York.
Now, USC computer scientists, communication specialists and health professionals hope to create a cheap, robust and effective speech-to-speech translation system for clinics, emergency rooms and ambulances. ... success on the project will require a system that can perceive and interpret not just words, but a wide range of human communications. 'We want to let people communicate,' he said. 'We need to go beyond literal translation to rich expressions in speech and non-verbal cues. We want to enhance human communication capabilities.' ... McLaughlin also emphasized that in addition to linguistic information, the effort will incorporate cultural cues and information. 'Our system will not only be bilingual, but bicultural,' she said.

onion thing!' Mr. Brin said Google ought to be able to do better.[1]

It's a reprise of the topos in the Rockefeller memorandum of 1947. How history repeats itself. But unlike Rockefeller, Google has come up with the goods: six years after that mistranslation, the Google Translate service 'handles 52 languages, more than any similar system, and people use it hundreds of millions of times a week to translate Web pages and other text.'

Google is ubiquitous, intrusive and secretive; its translation experts can be intelligent and clear in their appreciation of what a machine can and cannot do; they are also capable of making the most outrageous claims in the long history of the business. Franz Och, for example, who leads the company's machine translation team, told the New York Times: 'This technology can make the language barrier go away'. The only way to make the language barrier go away is to drop dead. Better live with it. Let's set aside the sales talk and consider the situation in 2010, when Google estimated that 99% of information produced in the world was not translated. 4%-6% of Africa had access to the internet. Forty languages covered 99% of internet traffic; Google therefore decided to translate its products into those languages.

As part of its aggressive appropriation of existing information, Google accumulated vast amounts of text on line, and those form the largest translation memory in existence. The Google corpus in English is immense; corpora of parallel texts in other languages include the document databases of the United Nations (in six languages), the European Union institutions (up to 23 languages), and Canadian Hansard (English and French). These are some of the human translations that constitute the Google translation repository. That top-quality product has been paid for by UN Member States, and by the citizens of the European Union and Canada. Google has taken that work as an immense windfall for its advertising business. That body of work is supplemented by translations commissioned by Google itself. Forty per cent of Google's own texts are translated by professionals, the rest by

---
[1] http://www.nytimes.com/2010/03/09/technology/09translate.html

volunteers. The volunteers get T-shirts and plaques for their efforts. In terms of volume, Google's own production would appear to be very small.

The mission of Google is to make information freely available to the public – but not information about itself. When asked how many translators they employ, they refused to indicate even an order of magnitude: 10, 100 or 1000. Judging from their own claim to have translated 5 million words into Arabic in the first 8 months of their Arabic program, and claiming a rate of 2000-5000 words per day, they had somewhere between seven and seventeen Arabic translators working for them at that time. Remember that the European Union employs thousands of translators full time. At one point, the Turkish translation operation of Google seems to have faltered because the student volunteer was doing his exams. Google is big business, but its translation operation seems to run on a number of shoestrings.

The repository covers 25 languages, but only a dozen in any depth. Google itself aims to cover 40 languages; it won't provide the 1560 possible combinations of those languages, so automatic translation from Portuguese to Turkish will have to transit through another language – probably English, thus compounding the damage done by automatic translation. In order to correct the result, the human reviser should really know all three languages, in addition to the subject area.

The wealth of material in English means that Google translations into English are far superior to translations from English (which is unfortunate, since international organizations require mostly translations from English).

Users of the Google Translator Toolkit can make their translation memories public or 'private'. The latter are not pooled with the general Google translation memory, and can be withdrawn from Google at any time; all the same, they are physically held on Google servers, which means that no political or highly confidential texts could be translated or transited through them.

Google Sites are translated by means of Google Translate and post-edited with Google Translator Toolkit. Google Sites will not publish translations where less than 50% is human translation; if 90% or less is human translation, clients are warned that they should not publish without human revision.

Google can be engagingly frank about the limits of machine translation: they themselves would never have legal or publicity material translated by machine, nor would they translate web sites automatically. Google made the sound distinction between machine translation for reading or 'gisting' (useful) and machine translation for publication (dangerous).

Machine translation can be used by companies to test whether people read the material in given languages. If there are readers, then the text will be re-translated by humans.

Google claimed that the Google Translation Toolkit could increase translator productivity from two thousand to five or even ten thousand words per day. Let's examine that claim. By way of comparison: an interpreter can be expected to convey 125 words per minute; interpreters work two, three-hour shifts per day, and are actually interpreting for perhaps half of that time. That means that they might interpret as many as twenty-five thousand words in a day. Interpretation, unlike translation, is not a permanent record. No one expects it to be consistently accurate. Revision of a machine-translated text entails reading and comparing both texts; someone who translates 10,000 words in a day therefore has to read 20,000, and read them carefully. Once the reading is done, they must do the repair work. The result must be clear and coherent; when the original text is neither, then ad hoc compromises must be made. That takes time; if it doesn't take time, an essential stage is being omitted. In short: for an experienced translator to produce two thousand words per day is commendable; to produce ten thousand is sheer carelessness.

So how are we heading into a swamp? When you run a text through Google Translate, what comes out could be close to perfection if it were in a language combination and subject area for which Google had rich holdings (the translation doesn't just happen when you press the button). If Google has no recollection of a similar text, it has to work it out from scratch.

It's as though you had a music archive on computer that consisted partly of studio recordings and partly (when no recordings were available) of musical notation that was scanned by machine and played through an inbuilt synthesizer. But while any fool can tell the difference between the Berlin Symphony Orchestra and a kazoo, the difference between a professional and an automatic translation doesn't always meet the eye. It doesn't always matter, but sometimes it really does.

Google depends on ever-increasing corpora of parallel translations in order to improve its output. It has famously appropriated the translations of the UN, the European Commission and the Canadian Parliament – holdings that took decades to produce and cost the taxpayer tens of billions of dollars. What is it going to do for the other languages? Where will it find comparable riches to plunder?

The answer is that Google wants *you* to do it. It will provide you with its Translator Toolkit; if you are a manager you will beat down the price you pay to translators; if you are a translator, you will revise the raw output from Google Translate and give it to Google to increase its store of human translation. Of course, most contributors won't actually be translators, while translators paid to do 10 000 words per day will cut the quality to match. What we can expect, then, is a translation repository that becomes more vague as it increases in size: a swamp. Some hope that Google Translate will, like Wikipedia, eventually provide a level of approximation that will enable a rough grasp of most subjects. Perhaps, but the more likely eventuality is that multiple crossing of language barriers would make it a great deal less reliable than Wiki: garbage in, fermented garbage out. Unless Google employs thousands of professional revisers, this isn't the way forward to high quality automatic translation.

I'm no expert on business models, but it's likely that the real aim isn't anything so lofty as a quantum leap in automatic translation. Google leverages its product on the good results that come out of extant human translation. Aside from that, its system is cheaper and bigger but not really better than what others in the language industry purvey. But if Google can take their business, it gets so much more advertising revenue. If it can use your work in the process, all the better. Itunes profits from apps in a similar way.

I pointed all of that out to Google at the time and got no response, but a year later they pulled – or 'deprecated', to use their own odd term – the facility for automatic translation of web sites, because people were doing what Google had told them not to: publishing unrevised machine translation on the web, that was sucked into the Google translation memory, corrupting it.[1]

Another year later the European Union, Google's greatest source of quality translation by humans, is running its own statistical translation system, but with stern gatekeepers on the translation memory. That should work. And given the repetitive nature of bureaucracies, the system should save a great deal of time and tax money.

Hats off to those who have automated what can be automated, thus expediting a colossal traffic among languages – particularly by providing the gist of texts but also, when systems retrieve good quality translation of similar messages, in obviating costly retranslation. So long as the corpora of parallel translations in a given machine translation system are carefully curated, this benefit will continue to grow not exponentially but incrementally. The core problem of translation quality therefore remains where it was before. As new fields of endeavour are opened up, new texts are written and new translations will be needed. Not everyone will accept a bushel of wheat or a T-shirt as payment.

Is there any hope of exponential improvement in machine translation? Just supposing that, at long last I could see where the paradigm shift might be, would my invention benefit humanity in the long run? It would of course benefit the bean-counters and bureaucrats, but that observation begs the question of whether

---

[1] http://kv-emptypages.blogspot.ch/2011/06/analysis-of-shutdown-announcements-of.html.

they/we benefit humanity in the long run, and that was answered by a T'ang poet who said that the law and social structures exist so that poetry can be written. (There has to be a subterranean link between that dictum and St Paul's, that law exists to foster crime.)

In the realms of translation and poetry, to which we finally return, what are the risks and hopes? It might be said that the risks are in translation and the hopes in poetry – as though translation was the goalkeeper and poetry the striker. Most dangers in translation are insidious, and few mistakes are traced back to the culprit, though people die and values are destroyed by blunders. Towards the end of World War II the German army prepared to defend a position on Monte Cassino. Part of the monastic library survived because some officer had manuscripts buried as a precaution. But a message was intercepted and mistranslated. It indicated that the 'abt' was in the monastery. The translator took that as an abbreviation for 'abteil', regiment, but it was the word 'abt', abbot. By the time the reviser had had a look at it the bombers were in the air and nothing could prevent the monastery that had guarded Latinity through the dark ages from obliteration. The defending army then took up position in the ruins and was not easily dislodged.

In September 2001 it seems that US intelligence was in possession of information that could have prevented destruction of the World Trade Centre, but did not have enough Arabists to translate it. That particular gap has been filled, if we can judge from the sardonic US response to recent tweets by the Muslim Brotherhood in Egypt,[1] but there is a screaming dearth of English mother-tongue linguists in the world, and that, I would submit, has three main causes: the flight from difficult university subjects; the assumption that it's up to others to learn English; and the notion – promoted by the press, like their scare stories on measles vaccination – that machines will soon solve the problem. The risk of further catastrophe, if things continue along this road, increases with every approximate translation.

---

[1] http://www.theatlantic.com/international/archive/2012/09/the-us-embassy-to-egypts-oddly-informal-twitter-feed/262331/.

And there is a still greater risk: the statistical manipulation of messages that have been stripped of their personal collateral (by machine translation systems based on perfected translation memory), while greatly increasing and accelerating the communication of messages, will dehumanize language. This won't always be a bad thing. It might turn out like the transition from herbarium to pharmacopoeia, allowing for the production of precisely calibrated effects (linguistic in this case), while unleashing elements that our senses aren't designed to manage: the ominous smell of bromine, the glottal rasp of carbon monoxide, the rage of pure lithium, and then certain radioactive isotopes that are completely off the sensory dial but inhumanly powerful. If language is reduced to operations where careful ambiguity is replaced with statistical approximation – however precise – and if we were to lose the knack of constructive ambiguity, it's not something we could recover in a hurry or recognize in our ancestors.

What are the hopes? At the Edinburgh Festival in 2012 I got the last ticket for a Bharatanatyam performance by the Mythili Prakash ensemble: great poetry embodied by a wonderful dancer, a singer, a violinist and a percussionist each of whom would have been worth travelling to see and hear. The combined effect took me into one of the high moments of art, something like the cloister of St Trophime just after the sculptors left, or a kirk in Leipzig where Bach was improvizing on the organ. Rather like the Kingdom of Heaven, such goods cannot be planned and built at will, but they can be prepared for. Some can then be preserved and transmitted through millennia against obliteration. Some can even be resurrected: archaeologists have unearthed from the last ice age in Europe a flute made from the wing bone of a griffon vulture about 40,000 years ago.[1] The diatonic scale that was played on it has survived or perhaps, like certain prime numbers, has been rediscovered, while average temperatures have risen by five degrees and humans have colonized the globe. It is likely, even as temperatures rise by another five degrees and humans lose their grip, that music and dance will survive for as long again. I'm not

---

[1] Jill Cook, *Ice Age Art* (London, British Museum, 2013), pp. 45-47.

sure that verbal language will make a decipherable mark on geological time, unless something can be done to bring out the essentials from the rising tide of useless information.

TM . IT = TMI

There is a final, sly hope to be cheated out of automatic translation itself. Consider these idle thoughts on 'contrepèterie', which dictionaries gloss, inaccurately, as 'spoonerism'. A spoonerism is an automatic inversion of the initial letters of words – 'a well-boiled icicle' instead of 'a well oiled bicycle'; 'beery wenches' instead of 'weary benches'. The French language does entertain spoonerisms – 'je vais pisser dans la glycine' for 'je vais glisser dans la piscine', but it glories in contrepèteries: 'ça me brouille l'écoute' becomes 'ça me broute les couilles' (I should note at this point that the spelling checker demurely suggested 'coquilles' for 'couilles' – which shows the vast creative potential still dormant in machines). Indeed, there are entire volumes of contrepèteries, graded by complexity if not obscenity, to such heights as 'l'aspirant habite Javel' (the cadet lives in the Javel district of Paris), which becomes 'j'avais la bite en spirale' (I had a spiral prick). This is no simple inversion. I can think of only three contrepèteries in English: 'I'd rather have a bottle in front of me than a frontal lobotomy', which is fair enough. Another, a hand-written sign in the window of a camping shop at the January sales in Glasgow: 'now is the discount of our winter tents'; and then, inspired by TS Eliot, 'this is how the world ends: not with a whim but a banker'. All of which prompts the thought that, if a text *can* be properly translated by machine, it's almost certainly been said already. If it's been said already, you don't need to read it. Thus the translation machine can give you the gist of a text or, by implication, a rather more accurate appraisal of its originality. While the language industry sees automatic translation as a means of increasing the availability of information, the T'ang poets among us will use it to divine scraps of new music in the machine's increasing noise.

306

Poetry and the Practice of Translation

Poetry is an ancient art that, like alchemy, has been handed on from one generation to the next long after its purpose has expired. It is an old poet who does not know when to stop writing and whose admirers will not tell him. The right wing is foundering in gravitas, the left in glossolalia, and a civil or cynical middle of the road recycles old conceits and sequences. It recycles cycles. As Denis Roche put it, in concluding his poetic œuvre (1962-1972), 'La poésie est inadmissible; d'ailleurs elle n'existe pas'.[1] Jacques Roubaud explained that, in terms of prosody, Roche had demolished the vain liberties of free verse. 'The calling into question of verse form, if conducted *radically*, very quickly leads to the rejection of *every form called verse*, with which poetry is identified; after which – silence (in poetry, that is)'.[2] There is a paradox in this endorsement from Roubaud, the grand old man of OULIPO who has published cataracts of poetry since he wrote those words twenty years ago – perhaps the paradox in every 'x is dead' argument: if x is dead, is there any need to labour the point? No, but it is worth considering now and then, and checking our options. In this essay, it is considered in conjunction with the practice of translation, which has suffered a lot of abuse since T.S. Eliot discovered Dante.

Roubaud was, to an extent, fighting the gradual bubble-gumming of French prosody. This was the death not of poetry, but of its

---

[1] Denis Roche, *La Poésie est inadmissible* (Paris, Seuil, 1995).

[2] '...le parcours de la mise en question d'une forme vers, s'il est mené *radicalement*, débouche très vite sur le refus de *toute forme appelée vers*, à laquelle est identifiée la poésie; après quoi le silence (en poésie s'entend).' - Jacques Roubaud, *La vieillesse d'Alexandre: essai sur quelques états récents du vers français* (Paris, Ramsay, 1988).

alexandrine branch. However, Laura (Riding) Jackson had taken the matter rather further. She had entitled her book of essays *The Failure of Poetry*[1]; its editor couldn't help subtitling it 'The Promise of Language'. Her argument, in its many iterations, runs as follows: I have taken poetry as far as it can go, and that's not far. It cannot speak the truth, so it should not speak. I trust her poetry, and am tempted to trust her judgement. My only get-out is that often I do not understand her clinching arguments; two examples from the introduction to *The Poems of Laura Riding*[2]:

> That there was, in the *difference* of poetic expression from 'ordinary' expression, the key to the *natural* in language, the use of words according to a principle of truth inspiring the relationship of understanding existing between human minds and language as their common instrument of self-corroboration, no poet of honorable linguistic sensitivity cannot have felt.

> There has been no recognition at all of the unchallengeable logic of my linguistic position, in the time of my working linguistically as a poet, and in my later working without affiliation with any categorically literary position. This is, that the objective of the linguistic best must eventually comprise a practical realization of the objective that transcends the division of the human linguistic possibilities into a mode of verbal practice at a general human level of linguistic expression and a mode at an absolute remove of difference from it in excellence-distance.

But this is not the place for confessions. The point is that, unlike the perhaps fortuitous accord between Roche and Roubaud, there is a strong bond between Riding and the post-moderns: one said poetry could not speak the truth, the other – that it has nothing to do with truth. So what *does* it have to do with?

The Language Poets tried to coin a medium that could not be exploited by the market (this is explained in *In The American*

---

[1] Edited by John Nolan (Ann Arbor, The University of Michigan Press, 2007).
[2] *The Poems of Laura Riding*, a new edition of the 1938 Collection (Manchester, Carcanet, 1980), pp. 4, 10.

Tree[1], though I don't recall precisely where). Avoiding the enemy's purchase is a sensible tactic, but not a viable strategy. For that, they would have to enlist something more powerful than the market – which is difficult to do when truth and other heavies are out of bounds. It is hardly surprising, then, that the market has caught up with them. In the two excerpts below I have corrected the spelling mistakes (at least I think that's what they were; it's hard to tell with pcoets). One is a language poem[2], the other – a machine-generated decoy for commercial spam.[3]

> Two-class agriculture: ouvrierist: deem hidden about glasses, forest as all their voice.
> Harlow's body in a row: traum reap: Montauk miles quiet, flesh by advance: answer where in the milk company houses over, doubled as wolf literature: etch time: 'Passos fixity':
>
> Error, constant within tried, force declaring static. Priority fox processed rooting processes.

...

> He account register site my please change.
> Every has that defines attributes such?
> Switchcase block inspects passed runs.
> Start mighty, keeper book knowledge contact. One step tutorial, showing layout.
> Mighty keeper book, knowledge contact, copy?
> Book color quoi everyone thank trace anonymous turbo, check. Turbo, check, object hooking.
> Nutshell whenever looks passing prototyped result callback, window. First queue if there. Active someone link score expression. Complex cant, were type id let.
> Make fine situation also both? Forward, your message kill application body regard urge. Its up, classes procedures define class not?

Computers have become pretty good at making poems, for two reasons: great new opportunities afforded by IT (There are only 10

---

[1] Ron Silliman, ed. (Orono, 1986).

[2] Peter Inman, from 'Dust Bowl', *Verse* vol.7 No.1, p. 36).

[3] Impersonal communication to the author, Spring 2008.

types of programmer: those who do binary code and those who don't), and a strong tendency to see the poem as a construct pure and simple. Machines come up with more surprising epithets, more daring syntax and more disconcerting semantic shifts; various randomization routines relieve the author of the (surely inappropriate) god-like responsibility for deciding which characters should prosper and which perish.

Poetry now is like painting at the advent of photography, with the twist that, this time around, the machine is better at cubism than at Constable. We will not return to the 19th century, but, outflanked by the market and the machine, where can the poets go? We do what painters did: find our comparative advantage and regain a modest market share. Too mercantile? Then here is the high-level argument: meaning is a function of mortality; we cleave to that – or would do, if the higher conventions of meaning hadn't broken down to bare grammar. Even the philosophers have binned their common ground rules; the austere epic they built up from Socrates until the Great War is acquiring a Homeric patina.

By this stage in the argument a few things should be clear: poetry as a pure construct should be delegated to machines; as a pure commodity, it should be left to the market. But we are tool-makers and traders; we have to learn again to manipulate rather than be run by what we make. The poetic avant garde is a remedial learning process. I want to look briefly at three of its experiments – talk poems, sound poetry and voice-over video, before moving on to examine a method of meaning that is ages with poetry itself. None of the three provides what I am after: in the first (talk poems) content is irrelevant to form; in the second (sound poetry), semantic content is avoided; in the third the text is a tool rather than a finished product. The talk poem was perpetrated by David Antin, at MAMCO, the Geneva Museum of Modern and Contemporary Art.[1] Here are two accounts of it.

First account:

---

[1] *Voix Off*, lectures en collaboration avec la Haute école d'art et de design, Genève, atelier d'écriture et l'Association Roaratorio.

Above all, what I see or rather hear in Antin is a vast culture and a knowledge of poetic tradition, not only Anglo-Saxon, but also continental European and particularly French; a sense of composition that I had the opportunity to hear as it was deployed in the experience/experiment of the 'talk poem', an attempt at a prosody of meaning, or snatches of meaning – marked in Antin's performances by the banal, everyday phenomenon of digression, which in this context becomes a motive force, an essential dynamic – the type of prosody that for me is the essence (or one of the essences, let's not be dogmatic) of the practice of poetry. In short, I try to hear, and I believe I do hear, some provisional solutions to things which I find really exciting as activities, things such as the formal tension that every act of language – speech in this case – imposes on thought, of which one would like to know: did it exist prior to, or does it exist outside of language, or in the floating state between the written and the spoken – an inexhaustible theme which, when tackled head-on as Antin does, becomes vital once more.[1]

Second account:

David Antin has a stick-shift Wrangler Jeep and his wife has a Cherokee Jeep with automatic transmission.

They own a beautiful, architect-designed home in several acres of woodland in California.

Some of the people nearby live in large and ugly houses that all look the same.

The Getty Foundation is negotiating the purchase of his archive, which includes 150 notebooks. His wife is a reasonably famous artist whose sculptures are displayed at the Whitney Museum in New York.

As a young man working on the Mexican border, he sent most of his wages home, and did not waste money on gambling or on prostitutes, which most of his colleagues did.

He believed that K. A., one of his graduate students, made money for her writing course by doing blow jobs in local massage parlours.

---

[1] Vincent Barras, translated from an e-mail exchange with the author.

He once hitched a lift to New York with a good-natured little Italian with a bad character – bad because he siphoned petrol out of someone else's car; the poet left him at that point.

(Hold property sacred, but not the body, which can be used ad lib for the production of property. The body as seed capital.)

As a professor, he got a generous golden handshake from the university, which set him up like Henry James – a writer on a private income. His wife kept her chair, since it is more difficult for women to become professors.

There was a forest fire around their home recently, and he and his wife dithered for a long time over whether to leave their property or escape to safer ground. Eventually, they loaded his archive into the Jeep and drove out.

They stayed with Jerome Rothenberg, and spent the time waiting for the fires to abate telling each other stories, and gossiping. He said it was like Boccaccio (buh Kaar-tcho) and his friends telling each other stories in the hills around Florence, evacuated during the plague.

Four times he quoted Mallarmé's most famous line, never getting it right.

The first account is by Vincent Barras, the second is my own. What disturbed me was the radically different way we understood the same performance, particularly since we have a lot in common: same age, same city; both poets, translators, day job in public health/medicine, fans of John Cage. With Jacques Demierre, Barras has written and recorded the epic sound poem of the City and State of Geneva, *gad gad vazo gadati voicing through saussure*.[1] This means that either Antin's discourse has a Shakespearian fecundity, a West-Coast koanity that allows every shopper to go home happy or disgruntled with their own set of goods, or there is some bigger and less obvious obstacle than the French/English language barrier in this. Barras was interested in the form, I was bored with the content; let's leave it at that for the moment, as I try to bridge the gap.

---

[1] Editions héros-limite www.madam.ch.

Barras mentioned 'a prosody of meaning' in Antin's use of digression, which could be an interesting notion: prosody as a metaphor for the organization of semantic rather than phonetic material. The trouble is that hammering phonetic repetition does work; hammering on at the same old themes (my house my car my archive me me me) is tedious; it has less to do with prosody than with the psychology of obsession, whether morose or that self-congratulation common to some of the Beats at their next to worst.

Barras had recently improvised a piece called 'Speech' (several times in French, and recently in German). It consisted of a series of connectives and quasi-logical suasions, leading to an almost musical conclusion – music understood as rhetoric with no specified object. It seemed to be as near abstract as you can get with words, aiming for a prosody not of sense but of syntax and rhetorical trope – very difficult, and unlikely to be mistaken for Antin's ancient mariner with no albatross, and no voyage to speak of. If Barras succeeds in that aim and in sound poems, then poetry could accede to the unfalsifiable state we associate with music: it really would have nothing to do with truth.

The third avant garde phenomenon was another performance at MAMCO. Sinister background sound and a mean voice complaining of pain and violence and suffering. A few minutes in, I was put in mind of one of Ellroy's comically over-the-top crime scenes, and the children's suicide note in *Jude the Obscure*. But then it got worse: the narrator was a hermaphrodite rape victim with brittle bone syndrome, whose only consolation was some grim species of masturbation. He rolled on stage and read a text in similar vein, which was followed by a film with the same text as voice-over. It involved extreme close-ups of body parts, an octopus with and without a Japanese woman, stitched-up lips, plastic sheeting and a grating sound track. Mid-way through, I knew that whoever did this intended to reduce the audience to not much. A grenade would have done it.

It was followed by an interview of the author (Philippe Mehry) by someone described to me as 'Miss Literature, Geneva'. She asked some literary questions and Mehry turned out to be an intelligent, good-humoured man in hat and wheelchair. What he was doing to us, it transpired, was a one-man 'good cop, bad cop' routine. First smack 'em in the face, then in the guts, and then come on like the human being he is. One chap asked him how other people with that syndrome reacted to his work, and he said he didn't know, but anyway he was not part of a sect. One young woman in the audience said I don't know much about literature, maybe what you wrote was poetry, and so I didn't understand it; there was clearly a great deal of hurt and anger, but it was only when you spoke to the interviewer that I could glimpse, even for a second, what your pain might be like; the film, I have to say, seemed simply pornographic.

Now here's the thing: the author came forward, smiling encouragement as she spoke, and answered her carefully. One member of the audience tried to suggest that the woman was simply a Calvinist prude, and the publisher leapt to the author's defence. But the author didn't need or want protection: there had been a moment of truth in the event – not in the reading or in the film, but in a courageous and honest response and acknowledgment. Is this a way out of the impasse? It is possible that L(R)J was wrongly trying to encapsulate truth in poetry, while truth is not in the pudding but in the speaking. Mehry does not see his work as poetry. 'Une rage folle tournée contre une rage folle', as he put it. But let's get out of the frying pan.

Today, as it happens, is Pentecost, where the Gospel of John trowels on the special effects: a loud wind in the house, tongues of fire on the heads of the cowering disciples and – this one would have defeated Spielberg – the converse of glossolalia: not speaking in tongues that no one understands, but understanding whatever is spoken. The disciples spoke and people of all nations understood them (so they were all speaking English, right? Where's the problem?) Can I be the only one to detect a hint of humour in St Paul when he tells the Corinthians – to each his talents: some have the gift of speaking in tongues, others have the gift of understanding what they mean.

When I trained as a translator and interpreter our teachers did point out that there was a high rate of mental illness in the latter profession. It was assumed, back then, that this was because the first generation of simultaneous interpreters, in the decades after the Second World War, came from the ranks of refugees. Their languages might have been all that survived of their family and home. But it is now clear that that instability can result from the pressures of a job where you do not know what, ten seconds from now, you will be presenting as your most deeply held and cherished belief; you do not know what sudden reference to Winnie the Pooh will be made by a tired chairman who is trying to ease the animosity in a debate on intellectual property. On occasion you do not know what you are saying. At once conference in sub-Saharan Africa, I was in the interpreters' booth, listening to one English-speaking delegate recount the terrible things that were happening in the long civil war in his country. Gradually, the audience started smiling, then laughing; the speaker was smirking as he spoke. One of the interpreters switched off the microphone for a second and said 'Pourquoi ils se marrent?' (What are they laughing at?); the other shrugged uneasily. All the sentences were translated correctly, but none of the three people in that booth had the faintest idea of what was passing between speaker and audience in the hall below. Worst of all for a poet – and the reason I went for written translation in spite of the longer hours – is the way simultaneous interpreting strengthens the links between languages in a way that can only fuddle associations within them. Still, impossible wishes, but I'd have waived the fee if I had got to interpret at the first, unrecorded meeting between Saints Peter and Paul. Because the rest is history.

In the interpreters' booth that day, and in the talk poem at MAMCO, there was a language barrier, but also an insidious gap in communication – one which, I am convinced, can be mended by focused utterance. A poem could do it. But if the breakdown in conventions and in the community of allusion has gone too far, we will have to learn again how to mean what we say. Trial and error will produce results; and there are resources in the practice of translation which contribute – though not directly. Let's turn to them now.

I've never been convinced that modern English literature on its own is an adequate subject for study: too much scope for opinion, no obligation to come to terms with something that won't make concessions to you, such as the periodic table, an unfamiliar grammar, musical theory, a forensic procedure. Not that college is the main vector of culture in any case. I went to university to study French and Russian; I assumed they'd teach me the languages and they rather assumed I knew them. Much of the staff had, like the pump attendant in *No Country for Old Men*[1] 'married into the job', so they may not have been the best teachers available. I certainly wasn't the best student. Still, a couple of tolerant lecturers, and a handful of brilliant fellow students, meant that not all the time was wasted. Tradition will always be haphazard, but there must be ways of increasing the chances of its survival and integrity. Translation of poetry is one way – but translation as reading first, then writing.

The one thing every translator has to know is when they don't know; the rest can be learned from other people, one way or another. A poet need know nothing more than how to manage silence. If, as many claim, the translator of poetry should be a poet, then the everyday duality inherent in translation is here compounded by a paradox or a division of the personality. Not all translators of poetry are florid schizophrenics, so there must be a solution, for some.

It's said that there are no good translators under the age of forty: it takes time to accrue the general and scientific culture in the relevant languages. But for poets, at one stage, the opposite seemed to apply: Byron, Keats and Shelley among them wouldn't have triggered a telegram from the queen. And for those who don't die young, some kind of menopause is likely, which might be difficult to avow. The internal conflicts that give the poets subject matter and force are often resolved by the time they are forty; then there's all that technique and nothing left to use it on. You've had your bananas, as some say in Brazil. Might as well translate.

It isn't always so chronologically simple: poetry comes and goes, and verse translation might be one good way of honing your wits in waiting. Poets who have something of their own to write

---

[1] Cormac McCarthy – book or film, though the Coen brothers' film is better in that particular scene.

shouldn't waste time translating verse (I think Mandelshtam said that, but I can't locate the quote, and it doesn't really matter who said it). If poetry and verse translation alternate, as they often seem to do, then there's another thing for the bards to keep in mind: when you are translating verse you're not a poet; you're only a translator. And if you don't know the languages concerned, then you're not even that.

'Not even that'? Setting aside, for now, the caste aspersions, I would note the following: a human brain is the most complex litre of property in the known universe, and language is its most sophisticated abstract construct. The transfer of comprehension from one language to another (because, yes, this language thing comes in a few thousand ill-defined variants, each seen by some as Language itself) is perhaps the most complex operation in that universe. I say perhaps because recently two things have happened that might knock the procedure from its perch: some areas of philosophy may have outgrown the grammar that nurtured them, and computers might, at current rates, outstrip that complexity in a few years. But while prosody (like chess games) can be programmed, the rules of language will never be set out exhaustively.[1] Machines will imitate but not generate translations, producing likely matches by statistical methods from vast corpora of texts already existing in more than one language. They will bypass the business of understanding languages rather as you might step around a drunk who was sleeping on the pavement.[2] Meaning, once again, is a matter for mortals.

In translation of verse there are three broad options.

---

[1] See previous chapter.

[2] For example: machine translation systems for aircraft manufacturers require pre-editing of text to avoid words such as 'replace', because of the ambiguity, hardly noticeable for a human but undecidable for a machine, in a sentence such as 'remove and replace faulty machine parts'. An electronic testing system could be devised that located faulty parts and substituted them (rather than unscrewing them then screwing them back in again) without passing through language at all.

First option: Learn the language, learn the poems, bring whatever you can back into your own language. Simple, no? No. It often happens that you learn the language and love the poems, but cannot bring the goods back (ask Orpheus). Some such people find themselves sending back rather more than poems; more on them anon. Or you bring it back and it goes ugly or insipid, or absurd like this snatch of Mayakovsky:

> Come, you unforgiving!
> You will be the first
> To enter my kingdom of heaven

The poet is trying to turn the Beatitudes on their head, and the translator more or less reverses the meaning with the rhyme: either you pronounce heaven 'hivving' and keep the sense, or you pronounce it as normal, and unforgiving becomes 'unforgiven' – which is too close to the meek in the original Beatitudes. [1]

Second option: you know, perhaps, some local languages and you've seen translations from a more exotic language that you think you could improve on, or – as in Middleton's Andalusian poems – you translate from another translation. (His introduction to that collaborative effort shows just how double-elbowed that procedure is, even when done by such an experienced translator.)[2] The words of Christ come to us in the translation of a translation (which may be part of the problem). Simple arithmetic shows that such a procedure is often necessary: if there are four thousand distinguishable languages, there are 4000x3999 language combinations, and we cannot expect one in every three or four hundred people on the planet to engage in literary translation. Nevertheless, this relay translation is possible only if enough people do their neighbours the courtesy of learning how to talk to them. Fortunately, most people do, and an adequate minority is in the habit of translating. The 1955 edition of Emily Dickinson that I

---

[1] One of mine, I'm afraid: hastily translated for *Hugh MacDiarmid and the Russians* (Edinburgh, SAP, 1987), p. 143.
[2] *Andalusian Poems*, Translated by Christopher Middleton and Leticia Garza-Falcón from Spanish versions of the original Arabic (Boston, David R. Godine, 1992).

have just found in the Geneva flea market has some verse translations penciled in the margins. The slight surprise is that they are in Russian.

Third option: realizing that mastery of your own language is the most important skill in the process, you might decide to leave the donkey work to the mules and sell whatever they smuggle across the border. Those who engage in this pursuit are in a curious double minority: monoglot and hyper-literate. Some anthropologist ought to be told. Their offerings will be lambent at best, at worst a process of appropriation and re-packaging.

Ideally, you start out with mastery of your own language and culture and the art of translation, and the best grip you can get on the source language and culture. For your own language, that means good primary schooling, parsing and grammar. For the foreign language – secondary school tuition will do, plus a couple of years among those who speak it. That shouldn't be too much to ask, but in certain cultures it is. When you find yourself thinking in the other language (not composing a phrase for the shopkeeper) or dreaming in it, then you have achieved sufficient mastery of it, or it of you. But can a body serve two masters? That's a deeper question, of which more later.

What I want to do here, then, is to present translation of poetry as a 'practice', as defined by Alasdair MacIntyre in *After Virtue*.

> By a 'practice' I am going to mean any coherent and complex form of socially established cooperative human activity through which goods internal to that form of activity are realized in the course of trying to achieve those standards of excellence which are appropriate to, and partially definitive of, that form of activity, with the result that human powers to achieve excellence, and human conceptions of the ends and goods involved, are systematically extended. Tic-tac-toe is not an example of a practice in this sense, nor is throwing a football with skill; but the game of football is, and so is chess. Bricklaying is not a practice; architecture is. Planting turnips is not a practice; farming is. So are the enquiries of physics, chemistry and biology, and so is the work of the historian, and so are painting and music. In the ancient and medieval worlds

the creation and sustaining of human communities – of households, cities, nations – is generally taken to be a practice in the sense in which I have defined it.

> ... It belongs to the concept of a practice as I have outlined it ... that its goods can only be achieved by subordinating ourselves within the practice in our relationship to other practitioners. We have to learn to recognize what is due to whom; we have to be prepared to take whatever self-endangering risks are demanded along the way; and we have to listen carefully to what we are told about our own inadequacies and to reply with the same carefulness for the facts. In other words we have to accept as necessary components of any practice with internal goods and standards of excellence the virtues of justice, courage and honesty. For not to accept these, to be willing to cheat ..., so far bars us from achieving the standards of excellence or the goods internal to the practice that it renders the practice pointless except as a device for achieving external goods.[1]

In order to illustrate, as briefly as possible, the real difficulties in this practice, I want to concentrate not on how I translate what I can do, but on why I can't always translate what I'd like to: the second of the three options above. By focusing on translation of translation, I can amplify the risks inherent in any genuine translation. I will therefore return to an unsuccessful seminar I gave recently at Geneva University, on Chinese-to-French translation of T'ang dynasty poetry. I didn't know enough Chinese, the students didn't know much about translation of poetry, and we were all a bit too timid to bridge the gap as we might have done.

I introduced myself as someone who had been bottom of the Chinese class for seven years, and had translated about ten poems, written a thousand, and translated five million words, over the years, from a number of languages. I wanted to gauge how much they knew about verse, but chickened out. I'd have asked not 'how often have you read a poem for yourself in the last six months', but when is the last time you read a poem for yourself? (That's a UNAIDS survey trick: they reckon it elicits more credible answers

---

[1] Alasdair MacIntyre, *After Virtue: A Study in Moral Theory*, 2nd edition (London, Duckworth, 1987), 187, 191.

than 'how often do you...'.) My guess is that three or four out of twenty would have said a week or a month ago; the rest – a year.

A translation is a performance. No harm is done to the original text in translating it, though it is true that, like a crass screen adaptation, it might damage the reputation of the original. In a performance anything goes, though not everything passes muster, and performances are judged in different ways. If Gustav Leonhardt performs Bach's Musical Offering that's one thing: if Webern re-sets it that's another; people listening to Count Basie's 'Bach goes to Town' judge the performance by looser criteria, and as for Suzanne Vega or Paul Simon lifting a theme – we might not notice. Bach did that himself; every musician does.

A century ago, several new bridgeheads were made to the Middle Kingdom. I want to mention two, for their distinctive approaches to Chinese Poetry. My Swiss class didn't know much about Ezra Pound, so I presented him as the man who said 'make it new' (no, not King David). He came to Europe and did the troubadours, providing (for me at least) an introduction that was not bettered till I came across Jacques Roubaud's *La Fleur inverse: l'art des troubadours*,[1] Abdelaziz Kacem's *Culture arabe/Culture française: La Parenté Reniée*[2] and recordings such as Paul Hillier's *Proensa*.[3] Pound knew his Provençal, and though he knew no Chinese at the time, he quickly latched on to the poetry, publishing Cathay in 1915, 'for the most part from the Chinese of Rihaku, from the notes of the late Ernest Fenollosa, and the decipherings of the Professors Mori and Ariga'. So while he revitalised the roots of the modern lyric, he also looked for new grafts. The benefits of these strategic moves far ouweigh the following cavils.

---

[1] 2nd edition, (Paris, les belles lettres, 1994).
[2] (Paris, l'Harmattan, 2002).
[3] ECM Records GmbH, 1989.

Pound did learn the language, and forty years after 'Cathay', published *The Classic Anthology defined by Confucius*[1]. The following lyric gives a fair idea of the whole.

SANS EQUITY AND SANS POISE

'Dentes habet'
Catullus

A rat too has a skin (to tan)
A rat has a skin at least
But a man who is a mere beast
might as well die,
his death being end of no decency.

A rat also has teeth
but this fellow, for all his size, is beneath
the rat's level,
why delay his demise?

The rat also has feet
but a man without courtesy need not wait
to clutter hell's gate.

Why should a man of no moral worth
clutter the earth?
This fellow's beneath the rat's modus,
why delay his exodus?

A man without courtesy
might quite as well cease to be.

(no.52)

Read it out and you catch the musical sense that Pound is famous for. And while this translation does not bring a new theme into English letters (one of the great services that translation renders to the receiving cultures), there is a touch of novelty to the vituperation, I think. But what is Catullus doing there? That's the

---

[1] (London, Faber, 1955).

52nd poem; the 54th has an epigraph in Greek, and the translations are peppered with incongruous Italian, French and German also; Thomas Hardy, Vlaminck and François Villon make guest appearances. I don't know if 'make it new' was still his watchword at that stage, but I don't see much excuse for the register of

> Hep-Cat Chung 'ware my town,
> Don't break my willows down   (no.76)

especially when it cohabits with

> a man should not bring his olde (sic) wife pain   (no.35)

or

> Tis to lack seven robes
> lacking thine,
> which gift could a peace define   (no.122)

And as for entitling the English version of an ancient Chinese poem 'La madone des wagons-lits' (no.105), this is obviously a man who just has to get in the way of his own translation. If you are more interested in the translator than in the translation, that's fine.

At around the same time as 'Cathay', Victor Segalen published his *Stèles* (édition originale hors commerce imprimée à Pékin sur les presses des Lazaristes (1912)[1] Unlike Pound, Segalen knew Chinese by then, and indeed had seen more of China than most Chinese of the day. He had met the emperor and was much taken by the experience (an unfortunate chime with Pound, there). But he was fascinated by the stone steles he found all over the Chinese countryside. My first attempt at reading Segalen didn't get far, because I couldn't make out what was going on: each of the 65 prose pieces was prefaced by a few Chinese characters that were not translated and seemed to be obliquely connected to the French, an exception being the stele establishing a Nestorian Christian

---

[1] (Paris, Poésie/Gallimard, 1973, 2004).

Church in the T'ang capital – a stele that had been made famous in Europe by Athanasius Kircher, in the seventeenth century. Worse, the first couple of texts were anti-Catholic polemic in Chinese dress. I just didn't see the need for the Chinese garb.

But Jacket Magazine[1] drew my attention to a new edition[2], which answers many questions. The procedure is as follows. The 'stèles', as Segalen himself explains, are in five categories, because in China, steles facing south (like the emperor's throne) bore decrees; those facing north – messages of friendship; messages of love faced the dawn, and martial steles – the bloody sunset. Others, that simply faced the road they were set on, were addressed to travellers, and the last group – the middle – were some kind of relics from earlier empires. They are prose poems. Here is one example, from the 'south-facing' steles.

> Hommage à la Raison
>
> J'enviais la Raison des hommes, qu'ils proclament peu faillible, et pour en mesurer le bout, j'ai proposé: Le Dragon a tous les pouvoirs; en même temps il est long et court, deux et un, absent et ici, - et j'attendais un grand rire parmi les hommes - mais
>
> Ils ont cru.
>
> J'ai proclamé ensuite par Edit: que le Ciel inconnaissable avait crevé jadis comme une fleur étoilée, lançant au fond de Grand Vide ses pollens d'étés, de lunes, de soleils et de moments,
>
> Ils ont fait un calendrier.
>
> J'ai décidé que tous les hommes sont d'un prix équivalent et d'une ardeur égale, - inestimables, - et qu'il vaut mieux tuer le

---

[1] http://jacketmagazine.com/34/klein-segalen.shtml.

[2] *Stèles* / 古今碑錄, Volume 1, by Victor Segalen. Translated, edited, and annotated by Timothy Billings & Christopher Bush with a foreword by Haun Saussy (Wesleyan University Press) ISBN: 0-8195-6832-5

Stèles / 古今碑錄, Volume 2: *Chinese Sources and Contexts* Translated, edited, and annotated by Timothy Billings & Christopher Bush www.steles.org.

meilleur de ses chameaux de bât que le chamelier boîteux qui se traîne. J'espérais un dénégateur, - mais

Ils ont dit oui.

J'ai fait alors afficher par tout l'Empire que celui-ci n'existait plus, et que le peuple, désormais Souverain, avait à se paître lui-même, les marques de gloire, abolies, reprenant au chiffre un:

Ils sont repartis de zéro.

Alors, rendant grâces à leur confiance, et service à leur crédulité, j'ai promulgué: Honorez les hommes dans l'homme et le reste en sa diversité.

Et c'est alors qu'ils m'ont qualifié de rêveur, de traître, de régent dépossédé par le Ciel de sa vertu et de son trône.[1]

---

[1] Homage to Reason
I envied the Reason of men, which they deem most sound, and to measure it, I said: The Dragon is all-powerful; it is both long and short, two and one, absent and present, - and I expected them all to laugh, but They believed me.
I then decreed that the unknowable Heavens had burst like a flower, sending pollen of summers, moons, suns and moments to the ends of the Great Void
They made a calendar.
I decided that all men are of equal value and equal – inestimable – ardour, and that it is better to kill the best camel in the caravan than the lame camel driver who lags behind. I hoped for dissent, but
They said yes.
I then had proclamations posted throughout the Empire to the effect that it no longer existed and that the people, now Sovereign, had to fend for itself, signs of glory, abolished, reduced to the figure one:
They started again from nothing.
So then, giving thanks for their trust and grist to their credulity, I decreed: Honour men in man and the rest in its diversity.
It was then that they called me a dreamer, a traitor, a ruler divested by Heaven of his virtue and his throne.

'Hommage à la Raison', has an epigraph of ten characters which, as Billings and Bush tell us, mean 'In this country there is no leader; the people have neither desires nor covetousness'. That comes from a strangely anarchistic dream by the Yellow Emperor, recorded in a Chinese source book with parallel French translation.[1] The body of the text is Segalen's own. So the Stèles are not translations? Correct: we have to find another word for this kind of transformation of source text and source form (the notion of the steles) into the body of French prose poetry.

What do Pound and Segalen tell us about translation from Chinese? What do they lead to? Pound sanctioned the extravagant gesture in translation, Lowell's *Imitations* being a famous follower. But as Gustav Leonhardt once said (I return to the notion of translation as musical performance), there are certain flourishes which, in live performance, find their place, but which in a recording would quickly pall. Examples are the 'sugar daddies' in Lowell's Dora Markus[2], the 'hep cats' in Pound. All the same, Paulin's parodic translations from Mallarmé show that, while they are fresh, such gestures can enliven a reading.[3] For me, they also cast doubt on the notion that a translator of poetry ought to be a poet. Should the translator of cookery books be a cook? (Or is that an accountant?)

What did Segalen bring? People like him have gone a step beyond translation, into the land behind the text. Here Charles Doughty comes up, with his *Travels in Arabia Deserta*[4]; Charles de Foucauld in the Western Sahara[5] and – to return to China – perhaps the greatest of them all: Matteo Ricci. The by-products of this Jesuit's twenty-eight year mission to China were, for the Chinese, the Gregorian calendar (newly introduced in the West by Ricci's former teacher), the first Chinese map of the world,

---

[1] L. Wieger, *Pères du système taoiste* (1913).
[2] Robert Lowell, *Imitations* (London, Faber, 1958), p. 109.
[3] 'Paulin's (Con)versions', a review by Adam Watt of Tom Paulin, *The Road to Inver*, *PN Review* 181, 33-37.
[4] Cambridge UP, 1888; 2nd edition, in one volume (London, Cape, 1923).
[5] See René Bazin, *Charles de Foucauld: explorateur du Maroc, ermite au Sahara* (Paris, Plon, 1921).

Euclid's geometry, watch-making and (I think) chiaroscuro portraiture. For the West: a Chinese dictionary and grammar, and a careful analysis of Confucius, Lao Tzu and Buddha in terms of what was and was not compatible with Christianity.[1] Such people go beyond our scope, from translation into transmigration.

Can the translator learn from them? I believe so. A good example is the approach taken by Jean François Billeter, a former professor at Geneva University, in his *Leçons sur Tchouang Tseu*. Having studied Chinese and Western philosophy, he found that the existing Western versions of Zhuangzi seemed to leave too much in the dark. His approach, to summarise bluntly, was to look into himself for what the author might mean, and to look into Western philosophy for analogues of what the text might be saying. On the later work of Wittgenstein, he notes:

> ... his procedure is a patient description, constantly recommenced, of certain elementary phenomena.That is what makes his late writings so disconcerting. With extreme attention, he studies what might be termed *the infinitely close* or *the almost immediate*.

> I noticed that, in certain texts that I knew well, Zhuangzi, in his way, was doing the same thing. I had assumed he was a philosopher, in other words that he thought for himself and drew on his own experience first and foremost. I now discovered that he was *describing* it, and that his descriptions were very precise and equally interesting. They were descriptions of the infinitely close, of the almost immediate. On the basis of some of them, I could understand certain important elements of his thought. From there, I went on gradually to other parts that were still obscure to me.

> Wittgenstein said that one has to know how to stop at description. This means two things: we have to know how to suspend our habitual activities in order to examine attentively what is right in front of us, or even closer to us, and then describe exactly what we observe, taking the time to find the right words, resisting the discursive drive, by steadfastly

---

[1] Matteo Ricci, *Della entrata della Compagnia di Giesù e Christianità nella Cina* (Macerata, Quodlibet, 2000).

imposing on language our intention to say exactly what we perceive, and only that. This latter exercise requires a perfect command of language. It is no coincidence that Wittgenstein and Zhuangzi, though very different, both have such remarkable style.[1]

Billeter's method is controversial, and his refusal to render the word 'tao' with the same French word at each occurrence does not meet with general approval. In terms of performance, an analogy would be Webern's orchestration of the Bach Fuga (Ricercata) a 6 voci from the Musical Offering (BWV 1079) – which again is controversial. Instead of giving each voice of the fugue to a separate instrument, he has a relay of instruments take up each voice. Some hold that this wilfully obscures the argument; to me, it sounds like a hologram looks, where the outline of a shape changes colour constantly. It isn't Bach, but then what is?

There is always a risk in this possession by two cultures, a risk to the integrity of the message, and to that of the messenger. So why not just avoid the risk? Save yourself the bother of working at something that has been known to split a mind in two? This question had never occurred to me till I saw, in the review of Paulin mentioned above, a quote from 'Fourteen notes on the Version' by Don Paterson. The version at issue is 'a version of Rilke', but the notes are much more interesting. What caught my eye was this:

> Perhaps the truly great poems *all* contain just such a breathless record of their own composition, and are unthinkable without them.

> While these can be translated, they are not, however, something that can be honestly versioned. A translation tries to remain true to the original words and their relations, and its primary aim is usually one of stylistic elegance (meaning, essentially, the smooth elimination of syntactic and idiomatic artefacts from the original tongue: a far more subtle project than it sounds) – of which lyric unity is only one of several competing considerations. It glosses the original, but does not try to replace

---

[1] Translated from: *Leçons sur Tchouang Tseu* (Paris, Allia, 2004), p. 14.

it. Versions, however, are trying to be poems in their own right; while they have the original to serve as detailed ground-plan and elevation, they are trying to build themselves a robust home in a new country, in its vernacular architecture, with local words for its brick and local music for its mortar.[1]

The noun 'version' is used as a verb, as though ordinary grammar couldn't cope with the originality of the (spurious) distinction. I am not going to argue with it when a good text book can do the job for me; watch (3) below.

Although approaches to translation vary from culture to culture and from one period to another, worldwide there have been three basic stances. (1) The text in the original language is seen as all-controlling: form, prosody and lexicon in the host language must be as 'faithful' as possible. (2) Literary values are viewed as less important than content, and in any case unattainable in translation; consequently, full translation in sense (1) should not be attempted: all poetic texts should be rendered in plain prose. (3) The literary *effectiveness* of the translated text is considered primary: form, prosody, and lexicon must be adapted to the requirements of the new language and culture: the translation must be as much like an original work as possible. Most of those who have commented on translation do not distinguish between renderings of poetry and renderings of prose; until very recent times, the same standards tended to be applied to both. Approach (1) sees translation as the rendering of *words*, approach (2) as the rendering of *information* and *ideas*, approach (3) as the rendering of *spirit* and *style*.

A translator's relationship to current literary values in the language into which he is translating is frequently what determines the approach taken. Tradition-minded writers and some academis favor approach (1); most academics favor approach (2); and those friendly to current literary values favor approach (3). Although it remains true that over the centuries translation practice has varied enormously, approach (3) has deeper and more universal roots both in the West and in the East. This is usually understood as a matter of practicality rather than anything idealistic or romantic: as Feng Yuan-Chun

---

[1] Don Paterson, *Orpheus* A version of Rilke's *Die Sonette an Orpheus* (London, Faber, 2006), p. 73.

explains, 'good writing encourages us to advance, while bad writing drags us back.' Chinese, Italian, and other Eastern translators have felt that the texts they produced had to be primarily successful as literary equivalents of their distinguished originals. So too St Jerome, in the preface to his translation of Eusebius, declares forthrightly that 'I have at once translated and written a new work'. *Non verbum e verbo, sed sensum exprimere de sensu* was his rule: 'Not word for word, but sense for sense'. [1]

This shows, at the very least, that in order to 'version' poems you need know nothing about previous practice in the art of translation. The fourteen notes go on to claim that you don't need to know the language either. Indeed, it is better if you don't:

> At least the ignorant monoglots tend to triangulate their versions from multiple cribs for fear of missing anything, for fear of missing *everything*; whereas the fluent tend to work from one, their own - which might be no better (and is often worse) than those available from other sources. [2]

Can Paterson seriously believe that real translators pay no attention to each other's work? Or that they do not read critical editions in the language of the poet? Knowing nothing about the practice of translation, he might. But he crosses the line when he asserts that his ignorance of languages confers on him a humility that translators lack (his note 13).[3]

For my peace of mind, I'll leave his notes at this point to ask – does any of this matter? Paterson made a canny choice in Rilke, since there are many English translations to show the way but none except W.D. Jackson's that seem entirely satisfying. Also the work is out of copyright. Paterson's attempts are not bad at all: clunkily iambic in places, with a surprising amount of translatorese 'O happy Earth, O Earth on holiday'.[4] These exclamatory 'ohs' are all

---

[1] *The New Princeton Encyclopedia of Poetry and Poetics*, edited by Alex Preminger and T.V.F. Brogan (Princeton UP, 1993) from the entry on Translation, pp 1303-4.
[2] Paterson, p. 82.
[3] Paterson, p. 83.
[4] Paterson, p. 23.

over the place. A translator would have told him that the lyric 'oh' doesn't fly in English, because of unfortunate but ineluctable associations with no, damn, shit, fuck and bugger. There is also a strange nod to William McGonigall in 'O beautiful friend of the infinite cry'.[1] But once again – does it matter? Counterfeit money, if it passes into circulation, is still money. As Don Paterson puts it, in his note 8, 'There are no ghosts, no gods, nothing secretly lurking in the temple of the poem whose vengeful wrath we will incur through our failure to honour it'.[2] So it doesn't matter. I might therefore instruct a discreet Geneva law firm to take certain measures if, within a century of my death, anyone puts his name on the spine of a book where mine should be.

But peace! Though he is wrong about bilinguals (they do NOT tend to be the best translators)[3], and though he ought to have another go at Saussure, Don Paterson is dead right that command of the source language is no guarantee of a decent translation; this is particularly clear in Chinese to English or French. Translators in China are publishing English versions of T'ang and Song dynasty poems where the rhymes make you run for cover. They are trying to produce what sounds like English verse; many Europeans want to hear something that sounds Chinese – whatever that might mean. Here it's better to stick to classical Chinese, since contemporaries, such as the 'Misty Poets', are complicating things by drawing on Paul Celan and Wallace Stevens. T'ang Dynasty poems of 25 or 28 characters *look* beautiful in a way that Western poetry probably never will. The sound of them, like stone bells, is more imitable. The lack of conjunctions – something not natural to Chinese, but a deliberate paring down by the poets – passes more easily into English than into a highly articulate language like

---

[1] Paterson, p. 27; see also 'The Tay Bridge Disaster'.

[2] Paterson, p. 79.

[3] I taught translation for five years at the Geneva University School of Translation and Interpreting, and I have helped raise children who are as trilingual as it gets; even when the language streams flow perfectly in parallel, there is a hesitancy in bilingual students: the lateral switch from one language to another is not so sure as it is among those who, starting from one language, have learned the others later on. There are exceptions, but they are very rare.

French, but even there can cause untoward mirth – as Frank Kuppner, above all, has noted, when he takes on not only the bald style, but also the hackneyed themes of old Cathay:

> He stands stock still in the doorway of a village house:
> Seventeen years a soldier in a foreign land,
> Yet all in this room is exactly as he remembers it;
> Except for the family of Mongolians.[1]

How can a European translator avoid the pitfalls? One thing to bear in mind is that translating poems is a lot like translating jokes. Analyse, repack, cheat if you need to but don't over-explain. Imagine, for example, the poor translator confronted with the following three groaners, dropped in passing by Thomas Pynchon in his immense *Against the Day:*

> Canadian walks into a bar – goes, 'Ouch, eh?' Two Italians prospecting in the Yukon, one comes running into camp, 'I found gold!' – the other one says 'Eh, a fangool-a *you* and-a you mother, too.' What's the favorite pickup line in Alaska? 'Woof, woof.'[2]

I told the Geneva seminar that US Americans reckon Canadians are always saying 'eh?', that 'bar' can be 'iron bar' or 'café bar', and that I wasn't going to be drawn on woof woof. Five minutes later, one giggled at the two Italians. In this case, they could simply cheat by lifting a few cracks from 'blaguedébile.com' or similar. In the two poems I chose, and that we finally turn to, the translator does not have that option.

Pick a poem you love; if it says something to you, it is yours. Learn it by heart and leave it for a while. One advantage of learning it by heart is that the translation comes out of you in many respects like a poem of your own. You lose the temptation to go word by word, and you feel the shape emerge in various ways: visual, aural, iconic. If you are lucky, you can hit on the right

---

[1] *A Bad Day for the Sung Dynasty* (Manchester, Carcanet, 1984) stanza 300.
[2] (London, Vintage, 2007), p. 152.

approach very quickly; in other cases, it might be years before you suddenly realise you have the right route. Most often it just lies around, occupying valuable space. You need to know all you can about verse technique in both languages. In the Geneva case, Jacques Roubaud, *La vieillesse d'Alexandre* for French prosody, and François Cheng, *L'écriture poétique chinoise*[1] for Chinese poetics. I would recommend the Cheng for English speakers, also. It shows, in passing, the pitch of concision reached by T'ang poets, and the collapse that would probably have happened even without the fall of that dynasty. In English, there is Wai-Lim Yip, *Chinese Poetry: An Anthology of Major Modes and Genres*[2] but ask a sinologist. I also provided them with excellent notes by Jeremy Prynne on translation of poetry from Chinese; unfortunately, these have disappeared from the web site where I found them.

I suggested two T'ang poems – one (by Tu Mu) a universal theme of parting, though with an almost brutal directness to it; the other (by Chia Tao), a peculiarly Eastern theme, that could perfectly well be translated without the translator catching the second meaning - which is a different kind of problem.

Cheng's edition gives the Chinese, a transliteration (but without the tones), a character-by character translation, and a polished French translation. (Wai-Lim Yip's edition gives Chinese, literal and polished translations, but no transliteration.)

Poème d'adieu

Une grande passion ressemble à l'indifférence:
Devant la coupe, nous restons muets, sans sourire.
C'est la bougie qui brûle les affres de l'adieu:
Jusqu'au jour, pour nous, elle verse des larmes.[3]

---

[1] (Paris, Seuil, 1977).
[2] (Duke UP, London, 1997).
[3] Poem of Parting: Great passion resembles indifference: / When the axe falls we are mute, impassive. / It is the candle that burns our pangs of separation: / Till day, for us, it sheds tears.

I couldn't help them with the Chinese, but only point out that it takes a very fine poet to find anything striking to say about such a common situation, however poignant. And a fine translator to manage it.

A parallel is Hölderlin's '*Der Abschied*', where once again I depend on the translation. It begins:

> Trennen wollten wir uns?
> Wähnten es gut und klug?
> Da wirs thaten, warum schrokte, wie Mord, die That?

Michael Hamburger's translation runs:

> So we wanted to part?
> Thought it both good and wise?
> Why, then, did the act shock us as murder would?

To me, that somehow muffles the blow. But Christopher Middleton's account seems to hit the mark:

> Did we intend to part, thinking it good and wise?
> Why did the act once done shock us like murder?

The other poem, in Cheng's edition, is 'Visite à un ermite sans le trouver', by Chia Tao. The text itself seems quite clear:

> Sous le sapin, j'interroge le disciple:
> 'Le maître est parti chercher des simples,
> Par-là, au fond de cette montagne.
> Nuages épais: on ne sait plus où…'[1]

François Cheng's footnote is interesting:

> This is an important theme in Chinese poetry… The visit is often the occasion for a spiritual experience; the absence of the hermit

---

[1] Under the pine I question the disciple: / 'The master has gone to look for simples, / That way, at the end of that mountain. / Thick cloud: we don't know where…'

accentuates the spiritual divide between him and the visitor. In this poem, the four verses containing the information from the disciple (which become increasingly vague) mark in fact the four stages of the master's spiritual ascent: verse 1: an inhabited high place; verse 2: a path or a road; verse 3: deep communion with nature; verse 4: spirit completely detached.

It's an allegorical meaning, like the cow-herding pictures explained in Suzuki's work on Zen Buddhism.[1] Do we need to know?

By this stage in the seminar, I was empty handed – but oddly reminded of a poem by Mandelshtam that had been in my head for years and only emerged in English that same week:

> Come and we'll sit in the kitchen, us two,
> Where the white kerosene smells sweet;
> A sharp knife, and a loaf of bread.
> Go on: you can set the stove to roasting
> Or maybe gather up some twine
> To tie the case shut. Before dawn
> We could take a tram down to the station
> Where they'd not think to look.[2]

I have not respected the jaunty trochaic metre or the aabbccdd rhyme scheme.[3] For Aleksandr Blok, the trochee was the prosody

---

[1] D.T.Suzuki, *Essays in Zen Buddhism* (London, 1950), 3 vols, volume 1, essay 8, 'The ten cow-herding pictures'.

[2] 'My s toboi na kuhne posidim', O. Mandel'stam, *Collected Works in Three Volumes*, ed. Struve and Filippov, 2nd edition (Washington, Inter-Language Library Associates, 1967), p. 224.

[3] But it is possible, on occasion, to salvage the form with the poem in translation, as in this translation of Blok's 'The Kite' from my *Hugh MacDiarmid and the Russians*, p. 108:
Circling, ring on even ring
Above the drowsy huts it hovers
And watches the deserted green.
A cottage hearth; a harrowed mother
Says - eat your bread, son, take the breast,
Grow big, be good, take up your cross.

of death; I don't know whether Mandelshtam shared that view, but there is a clear contrast between the almost childish surface of this poem and its increasingly sinister movement. Readers of Nadezhda Mandelshtam will seize the context immediately: they are in Leningrad, in her sister's kitchen,[1] living on thin air. The cosy opening slides very quickly to panic and flight.

It is only thanks to the recalcitrance of much of his other work that Mandelshtam is not always read in this biographical mode – looking through the wrong end of binoculars. But the Chia Tao poem pulled me away from that kind of reading – not into mystical allegory, but into the middle ground where this could happen to anyone, and in one sense happens to all of us.

The last tip I had for translators of poetry was to wool-gather: rhymes, analogies, things that fit together from quite different places, especially if you don't understand how. Here's a simple case:

> A servant-girl is sweeping a palace pathway;
> Her mistress walks through the river on marble slabs;
> Every year, the wilderness encroaches further;
> Already, unknown fish live in the pool.[2]

The lake was moved by strange tides. Sometimes, as at the present moment, it sank to a single, opaque pool in a wilderness of mud and rushes; sometimes it rose and inundated five acres of pasture. There had once been an old man in one of the lodges who understood the workings of the water system; there were sluice gates hidden among the reeds, and manholes, dotted about

---

The years go by, the wars go on,
Rebellions flare, and burn the burghs.
You never change, my ancient land,
In all your beauty, in all your sorrow.
How long should the mother mourn?
How long will the black kite turn?

[1] See O. Mandel'shtam, *Stihotvorenija, proza* (Moscow, Biblioteka poeta, 2000), p. 647.

[2] Frank Kuppner, *A Bad Day for the Sung Dynasty*

in places known only to him, furnished with taps and cocks; that man had been able to control an ornamental cascade and draw a lofty jet of water from the mouth of the dolphin on the South terrace. But he had been in his grave fifteen years and the secret had died with him.[1]

... the key element in their irrigation management (millennial rice terraces in Bali) was the system of water temples. Every major weir has a temple, to which the groups of farmers downstream form the congregation. At temple meetings, farmers coordinate their plantings and the routing of the water, sharing their knowledge of local pest densities and laying out a series of traditional rituals which will accompany their agriculture. This ensures the right schedule of irrigation for every farmer. The computation involved in regulating the system is impressive; there may be dozens of sluices, hundreds of blocks of fields, and each block needs to receive an allotment of water appropriate for its crop and phase in the cycle, all within the available water supply. The agreed schedule is regulated by an indigenous calendar, the *tika*... (used) for tracking the concurrent cycles relevant to the management of many separate farms the period of the *tika* is 210 days...[2]

Which brings us back to Laura Riding Jackson, the possible demise of poetry, and how it might, in some form, return. When the major arts falter, the humbler ones are vital. If the vatic silence poets draw on is corrupt, we might find what we need for now in the unkempt space between me and you.

---

[1] Evelyn Waugh, *Scoop* (1938), chapter 2.
[2] D. Nettle and S. Romaine, *Vanishing Voices: The Extinction of the World's Languages* (Oxford UP, 2000), 168-9.

The Good of Art

Our first flat in Geneva was a mile from the main gates of CERN and our first friends here were CERN physicists and translators. I read a lot of 'physics for poets' and had a few individual tours of various experiments, understanding one thing at least: physics apart, CERN was the civil engineering project of the century, akin to Chartres in its combination of the massive and the minute, though two orders of magnitude more massive and several more minute. Very early on I was shown the world-wide web on a CERN workstation, slowly loading the welcome page of the Vatican Library. The same day I saw an engine on a ten-yard length of rail flanked by two walls of DAT cassettes; as requests for the recordings of various particle events were sent to it by researchers from around the world it moved back and forth along the track, raising its light/video camera head to the appropriate shelf, removing a cassette with its robotic arm and loading it into a DAT player. This was a massive machine, a small railway engine. The amazing thing about watching it for a few minutes was the way it would stop and return to rest position, as though pondering for a moment before scooting down the track to retrieve the next cassette. I'd have dubbed it Sepulchrave. Mischievous students tried to derail it by sending simultaneous requests for cassettes at opposite ends of the track. It was quickly made redundant as the web gathered speed.

My mathematical know-how came a cropper somewhere between Napier and Newton, and in the long run that was a greater handicap than my ignorance of physics. And while I can overcome my inability to programme computers by paying someone to do the clever stuff for me, I can't pay someone to understand maths. And

338

even had that been possible, I'd have needed very deep pockets. In his *Mathémathique: (récit),*[1] Jacques Roubaud writes that, when Andrew Wiles cracked Fermat's last theorem in the 1990s, Roubaud – by then a retired professor of mathematics – set himself the task of understanding how the proof had been made, but having progressed as far as Mordell's 'Three Lectures on Fermat's Last Theorem' of 1921, realized that, to progress further up that particular mountain, he would need a guide.[2]

Alasdair MacIntyre has some hard words to say about managerialism in *After Virtue*, but this does come down to a problem frequently faced by managers and negotiators. A manager has three options in dealing with staff: understand their work, trust that they understand it, or find someone else to do the job; when running a highly technical operation, the manager won't have that first option. Someone leading complex negotiations, even if they are thoroughly familiar with the field, will at times have to conclude that, though they don't understand what's going on at a given moment, participants x, y and z appear to get it and concur; the leader will then have to accept that their understanding trumps his or her ignorance, and move on. This does, of course, expose everyone to the risk that the decision-maker is misinformed or otherwise misguided. At a certain stage in every viable system, executive power will exceed executive awareness. But to our muttons.

Popular maths books play on the relation between maths and music, but overplay it when they claim that, as with music, the layman doesn't need to understand the theory in order to appreciate the elegance or beauty of the piece. The relevant analogy is not between a theorem and a piece of music but between a theorem and a musical score, both of which *do* require technical knowledge, and only one of which can be directly transmuted, for the public, into more or less bearable noises. The non-mathematician can only check the viability of analogies and seek to appreciate indirect ways in which the manipulation of signs

---

[1] (Paris, Seuil, 1997).
[2] pp. 214-6.

enhances our manipulation of things.

Roubaud again, same book: 'Mathematics is paraphrasable (it is perhaps the most and the most infinitely paraphrasable object), and in that respect it sits at the opposite pole from poetry'.[1]

He goes on to qualify this maxim; before we let him do that, note that Dante, in the *Convivio*, paraphrases his own poems thoroughly. In the process, and by default, he demonstrates the breath-taking progress (largely thanks to mathematics) that has been made in astronomy since he wrote. Roubaud *suite et fin*:

> ... part of mathematics is totally paraphrasable ... there must be a continuous effort to reduce the constantly expanding gap between those who propound theories and those who try to improve their understanding ... (In the course of the (20th) century this expansion of intergalactic space has indubitably accelerated.) The practice of paraphrase is equally indispensable to the progress of mathematics itself ... In this sense, mathematics too is a great art of language. The non-paraphrasable part of mathematics ... *terra incognita* of theorems to be demonstrated, territories to be re-mapped ... represented ... that which ... its visionaries, such as David Hilbert, sought to reduce. By contrast I see poetry as essentially not subject to paraphrase; the non-paraphrasable part is poetry itself. (The paraphrasable part is didactic, at best...)[2]

For Roubaud, the only bit of mathematics that can't be paraphrased is the bit that hasn't been written yet, while the only bit of poetry that *can* be paraphrased is the stuffing, which isn't really poetry. (The poem is a thing made of words; it often draws on simple mathematics for a stable structure. It's amusing that mathematics relies just as heavily on language in testing its own structures.)

The paraphrasing habit of mathematics is akin to the musical performance. When the signs can be consistently played or paraphrased then, as with the deciphering of cuneiform, we are in the presence of a real utterance. The proof of music is in the

---

[1] section 88, p. 194.
[2] pp. 194-5.

playing; the proof of mathematics is in its coherence and perhaps in application; where's the proof of poetry?

Helen Vendler refers to '… an axiom of Stevens' poetics: "The poem must resist the intelligence / Almost successfully"' (306). She continues:

> Why did Stevens wish his poem to resist the reader's intelligence 'almost' – but not entirely – successfully? He alerts us, by that qualifying adverb, that the package the poem offers is not unintelligible. Eventually our intelligence will unwrap it, he promises (it is a promise he always keeps), but we may at first find ourselves in a state of some bafflement…[1]

Vendler's laconic parenthesis says that there is one reader at least who has never been failed by the solemn ecdysis of Stevens's work, a consoler of those who no longer can believe in organized religion. There are functions of religion, important ones, that he does not cover, and there are quasi-religious areas – fortunately not central to his poetry – that won't win many converts: the 'major man' and other themes that hint at a supermanic striving. That's an arguable point; much clearer is what is not covered by his work: a social function, something that can bring different kinds and classes of people together on moral and spiritual matters, a narrative that has something for adults and children, labourers and intellectuals. This isn't a flaw in his work, it's a limit.

At the same time, there should be no doubt that major religions can and do continue to assimilate or co-opt such art for their congregations – by making it paraphrase scripture, which is kept, translated, interpreted and reinterpreted. In the arts we have the canon, which is a lot less rooted, particularly since so many are canonized while still alive. In science canonization is achieved through the virtues of concision, consistency, consonance with observation, practical effect – and being first to publish. These formal recognitions are retrospective activities that aspire to the

---

[1] Helen Vendler, 'Stevens and the Lyric Speaker', in *The Cambridge Companion to Wallace Stevens*, ed. John N. Serio (Cambridge UP, 2007) pp133-148; p. 135.

condition of axiomatics – objectively in the case of maths, dogmatic in religion; the literary canon has neither logic nor faith as a basis, since poetry regularly challenges anything it might be based on. Ultimately it takes nothing on trust. This isn't the impression you would get from reading through a large random sample of verse, but that's because most verse has nothing ultimate about it.

But axiomatics is housekeeping. What does it clear space for? Take a lift to the top of the ziggurat and consider the whole trivium and quadrivium. The more abstract the work, the more it cleaves to constraints (against vertigo): logical constraints in maths, dogmatic in religion, shifting in poetry. The more the work depends on evidence (hard science), the more backward-looking it becomes – of necessity: evidence doesn't come from the future. The prophetic work is in art and religion, possibly in maths, though in this last area the most-quoted example of a prophet (in the vulgar sense) is David Hilbert, because in 1900 he hazarded a very public guess as to what problems would preoccupy mathematicians for the next century or so. That isn't very long term; to be accurate, it sets no term or conclusion at all, in that solutions in maths lead on to further problems. More to the point, the famed ability of mathematicians and musicians throughout the world to overcome the language barrier is perhaps an indication that they're not actually saying anything. While music is rhetoric without content, maths appears to be logic without content. And none the worse for that.

There is a temptation that increases with the progress of science and technology, to let that vast machine do the listening for us, to allow it to scope the future. The result can be discouraging: entropy in physics, random development in biology, game theory in society. Yet, as suggested in the chapter on symmetry, science explains things away; it can't predict the next phase. Biology – an anti-entropic movement – couldn't have been deduced from the laws of physics. And though random interaction can account for the presence of life, it gives and can give no indication as to its purpose – which frequently leads to the logically unwarranted deduction that there is no purpose.

The only purveyors of meaning are politics, art and religion. As noted above, religion is structurally able to co-opt art; it can also provide a community of response to its own central narrative, from specialist to habitual believer. Oddly, the same is true of politics. Both are able to make use of individual works of art to forward the central goal, and feel justified in doing so because the practitioners in both fields have performed the same operation on themselves. (Remember that art includes philosophy, which gets suborned just as easily as anything else.)

At certain moments in history the synergy or collusion of art, religion and politics produces dazzling results: the gesture of coronation on the portal of Rheims cathedral; the cave sculptures at Da Tong, where the emperor figures as Buddha; Palestrina and the liturgy. It's win-win-win for everyone but the peasant.

The fact that, every day, cynical powers use belief to keep the poor in their place – you'll get your reward in heaven, you're indigent because of your karma, you're in the land of opportunity so you ought to succeed – does not invalidate the need to know that things can be better. Religion does defend a space for that, though perhaps an over-determined one.

Is there no way in which the arts can produce something that speaks to an attentive society without being hijacked by ideological bureaucracies? Is there really nothing in the intellectual arts that can touch the less articulate? No consolation?

At the funeral of a theologian, priest and political activist I was asked to read from the first epistle of St Paul to the Corinthians, and I did, and managed to mean it:

> Brothers and sisters, listen, I will tell you a mystery! We will not all die, but we will all be changed, in a moment, in the twinkling of an eye, at the last trumpet. For the trumpet will sound, and the dead will be raised imperishable, and we will be changed. For this perishable body must put on imperishability, and this mortal body must put on immortality. When this perishable body puts on imperishability, and this mortal body puts on immortality, then the saying that is written will be fulfilled: 'Death has been swallowed up in victory.' 'Where, O death, is your victory?

Where, O death, is your sting?' The sting of death is sin, and the power of sin is the law. But thanks be to God, who gives us the victory through our Lord Jesus Christ.[1]

Death hadn't stung him because he had died old, cogent, true and quickly. Once you're dead, there's nothing death can do to you. As to imperishability, I've no notion of it. I can't guarantee the existential commitment that such texts demand; my response can be merely aesthetic. I do wonder, at times, how alone I am in my hyena-like vacillation. Take a psalm such as 'By the rivers of Babylon'; it's almost as popular as 'The Lord is my shepherd' in times of grief, but few would sanction all of it: 'Daughter of Babylon … happy is the one who seizes your infants and dashes them against the rocks.'

Even Tarantino wouldn't get away with that. How many regulars simply take what they need and discard the rest, believing what eases their minds? It remains possible that the art co-opted by the spiritual and temporal bureaucracies is what people turn to in preference to dogma or the party line. If so, this is a relationship that misrepresents but does no real harm to art; and if that art can subsist, and doesn't sap or spurn the ones who need it most, it can do them only good.

---

[1] 1 Corinthians 15:51-57

Conclusion

Prison & exile writers are pushed into certain moulds or modes; court poets – partly in order to avoid such sanction – into sycophancy. In modernism a Jock the Rapper and Jack the Reader symbiosis between poet and academic was the dominant model. Towards the millennium it sheared into self-sufficient academic theory on the one hand, and on the other the poetry reading or performance, which encourages the production of thinner, more easily digested work that shades into stand-up comedy at the popular end. Meanwhile, performance poetry drew on theatre, music and video. The piper's paymaster thus was government, then academia, then the public. There were always outliers, and these included some of the great poets.

Depending on biographical situation, art for art's sake could function as anything from a refuge to – oddly enough – a radical form of political protest (the young Joseph Brodsky). While respecting the reticence of certain poets, and the refusal of many artists to join any kind of mainstream, I'd insist that poetry is big enough to mobilise every aspect of thought and feeling, including the substance of politics and religion. It won't die in the attempt. Though it is true that I have complained about the tendency of Tom Leonard's politics to shout down his poetry, it seems a waste for Mallarmé to focus on swans and alabaster when his letters contain in passing some striking aesthetic views of political events. The aestheticizing of the political sphere in Nazism and its converse in Bolshevism might – who knows? – have been tempered if Mallarmé had put the subject through the lens of his verse. It could hardly have made matters worse. I would therefore echo Christopher Middleton's radical call, from *Bolshevism in Art*, 'to recover the spontaneity of the individual self not only for art's sake but also for the sake of human survival'. How?

Let's review the systems available to poetry: language and number.

People ask how many languages there are in the world, as though they were integers waiting to be counted. The very question is a function of literacy and politics. Empires impose their language (France) their orthography (Soviet Russia), both (China) or more (Ameringlish), unifying the polity in distinction from its neighbours. Thus – to take a random example – the Azeris in Azerbaijan write their language in adapted Cyrillic while those across the frontier in Iran write in Arabic script (neither script, curiously enough, was devised for a language of that family); that, plus the Iron Curtain, effectively cut the Azeri community in two. How many languages are there? How many dialects? What's the difference between a language and a dialect? A dialect – as Max Weinreich reminds us – doesn't have an army. (As often, the generalization bears its own exception. Weinreich's aphorism was made in Yiddish, which doesn't have an army, but *is* a language.) The crassness of geopolitical distinctions can blind us to the gentle immensity of living language that subtends it. Let's take a step back.

There is a linguasphere. Distinctions between words are conventional; so are distinctions between languages. Until the advent of writing, nationality and mass migrations, differences between languages will have been no more than the sum of distinctions between words. One language gradually shaded into the next. The linguasphere consists of umpteen billion idiolects that are more or less widely and firmly grouped depending on literacy and other forms of power. Umpteen because each human being has more than one to play with.

The play of language comes down to two activities: self-identification of the speaker, and communication of messages. It uses distinctions of accent, register and attitude to show who the speaker is, and combines conventional signs to transmit sense to others. The two activities are fused in certain areas of silence, assumptions about what an audience will understand without further explanation or clearer articulation. It is odd that the entire project of automatic translation, from its origins in the 17th century, has operated as though the only function of language was the transfer of information. And yet this dual function is what distinguishes language from number, which really is impersonal.

Number. The frontier between word and number should be explored by someone who masters both realms. Failing that, here is a view from one side of the wall. Numbers cover only one of the two principal functions of verbal language: the combination of signs for communication. They do not express the identity of their user. This abstract quality has been used for as long as poetry, 'numbers', has existed. It has been the poet's taciturn, austere interlocutor, a help in managing the hilarious loquacity of language with the concision, elegance and symmetry proper to maths and classical forms of music. It has pulled poetic utterance out of the sphere of truth towards the sphere of beauty. Some of the resultant numerical patterns – the sonnet, or the alexandrine – ruled for centuries. Free verse seemed to knock that on the head, but the need for number reasserted itself, not necessarily in prosody.

Number does not express identity, and yet and yet: through geometry it encodes symmetry, which *does* express identity not symbolically but physically, in the animal, plant and mineral kingdoms. By incorporating symmetries into poems, poets can both state the identity of the poet linguistically and confer an identity on the shape of the poem that rhymes with the figures of nature.

This dual invocation by very different methods in one work is a sort of magic, not always well used. A book by William Empson has just been rediscovered and published, on dissymmetry in sculptural representations of the Buddha.[1] It analyses photographs of various busts, and concludes that the difference between right and left side of the head is of devotional significance. I don't doubt

---

[1] *The Face of the Buddha* See 'Spring Pictures', by Rupert Richard Arrowsmith, *TLS*, 2 December 2011, p. 18.

it, though I do doubt the general intentionality of this effect: Empson first got his idea in Nara, whose camphorwood sculptures are among the greatest sculptural portraits in existence; these were perhaps the summit of a tradition of Buddhist sculpture that began in Gandahar under Greek influence and ended in multiple copies of bloated dolls. As noted in part I, in the animal kingdom bilateral symmetry of coat and plumage sets specimens apart from their habitat. It is such a primordial statement of identity that even vital protective camouflage is subordinated to it. But in the human realm, chirality and other forces lever individuals out of that special symmetry. Busts of the Buddha are sculpted by people who are right or left handed, and this fact produces differences, however subtle, between one side and the other of the heads they fashion. This might be down to poor technique, it might be deliberately symbolic, and it might be done from observation, because artists know that human faces do develop asymmetries – some of them startlingly beautiful. Symmetry seems to be an axiom, or a milestone, a sign we are on a viable road – but it's not a final destination.

With all this in mind, how might we 'recover the spontaneity of the individual self not only for art's sake but also for the sake of human survival'?

First we have to reckon with the kinds of poet who would not share that, or any, ambition for the self, which they regard as nothing more than a spectre haunting language. There is language poetry that disengages from the market and conventional exchange, and from the self as a crier on that floor; in an ambiguous middle ground there is the poetry of Prynne, where the self presents as something of a bear market. In neither is there a persona that calls the shots. As a consequence, neither body of work sets up the definite areas of silence mentioned above, where the waves of identity and communication cancel out to create a tacit understanding with the reader: the one can be blithely senseless, the other undecidable.

For other poets, the self is the only guarantor of sense, meaning being a function of mortality, awareness of which is available only to individuals in social groups. This looks like the binary divide –

one and zero – between West and East. The Golden Rule itself is split by it: on the one hand 'do as you would be done by'; on the other 'don't do what you wouldn't want others to do to you'; proselytism, or the quietism of caste.

But beneath the theology of it there is the physiology: a vocal apparatus, managed by the brain and fuelled by the heart. All those lights and lungs mean presence rather than absence; surely somebody's there? And yet all meanings depend on distinctions and nothing anchors any distinctions to anything solid – which rather suggests zero. (This is the sex/gender debate again, but at the other end of the torso.)

John Cage to the rescue – and I mean Cage the mycologist as much as Cage the Buddhist. In a strong response to totalitarian 19th-century composers who killed improvisation by putting every last trill behind bars, he frees things up and tries to remove intentionality from his work. The paradox of deciding to erase decision from composition is one that he lived and worked with. The chance operations that he used in his poetry, music and painting are not different in spirit from traditional techniques of rhyme and prosody – which also welcome the work and words of others into the creative process; Cage simply renewed that function with different devices. Chance in composition is matched with improvisation in performance. It is this dialogue between a vanishingly small authority, and performers and public, which gives Cage's work its life. I'm thinking mostly of his music and graphic work; his writing is a festival fringe. While Cage's work is essentially musical, ostensibly an art for the sake of it, its means of production effectively implicate society. And the very effort at self-abnegation brings that weak force into pinpoint focus where it is needed.

First step towards an answer, then, to the Middleton question, since I am not adjudicating but taking sides: the individual self shall wield word and number with heart and mind. That's the first freedom. The next is individuation, remembering that no one is bound to one idiolect. There is always a choice, and that choice is not inherent in the language used; it precedes it. In this book – setting Dante apart – the clearest and most determined exemplar of that freedom to choose is Tom Leonard. But the very mention of Alighieri brings in Beckett, who really knew his Dante, and Eliot who really didn't, since both of them exercised this choice of language – one using the estrangement of a foreign tongue to voice an alienated world, the other with rather less clarity. Eliot's 'Tradition and the Individual Talent', as I recall, fails to point out that the individual is free to choose which tradition to espouse – an odd omission, in his case. This individuation, whether angrily asserted or spoken in bewilderment or not clearly grasped, is always enacted against a tradition. It's how the specimen stands out from the species and begins to speak for itself.

The next step in the recovery of spontaneity is surely self-expression. Well, actually, no it's not, not in this book, which regards unbridled self-expression as tedious. The next step is to get into conversation with the taciturn, austere interlocutor mentioned above: number. And then to figure out where the conversation is going, because number can offer a way out of intentionality, or a symbolic link to the forms of the world, or simply a pleasing symmetry. But one step at a time, and bearing in mind that Middleton's hoped-for spontaneity might turn out to be a cousin of Anderson's disinterest and Dawkins's altruism: something you need but can't have.

OULIPO should come with a free bag of toffees, it's such a clever bunch of schoolboys. It appears in these chapters not because of great art it has produced (though some members *have* produced wonderful books) but because of its systematic review of literary form. Hats off, once again, to Jacques Roubaud, their senior mathematician and a most enlightening student of Provençal and French prosody.

The editor's note to its first major anthology states that OULIPO '… is not random literature'[1]. The *Atlas de littérature potentielle* puts it rather more forcefully: 'The members of OULIPO have never concealed their horror of random writing, salon fortune-

---

[1] (Gallimard, 1973), p. 11.

tellers and haphazard junk: OULIPO is anti-random … potential is uncertain but it is not down to chance'.[1]

Cut to Jackson Mac Low. 'In the spring of 1960 I devised my first deterministic yet nonintentional system – that is, I didn't employ chance operations, but gathered words according to a variety of methods to find words that were already waiting there in the source.'[2] That system closely resembles the OULIPO S+7 method, whereby each noun in a given text is replaced by the nour seven positions past it in a given dictionary.

The question isn't how they hit upon a similar method (it was chance rather than design: OULIPO was aware of Cage, and though Cage knew Mac Low and had worked in France with Boulez, he had no dealings with the group). Nor is it why OULIPO was strongly opposed to chance operations – that sprang from Queneau's opposition to Surrealism. The question of relevance to this discussion is this: is there a real difference between uncertainty and chance when a mathematical formula is transferred to the realm of letters? It's obvious why S+7 has greater appeal to mathematicians than sticking a pin in the dictionary. In mathematical terms it is indeed a different operation. But in the realm of words there is no effective difference, because the alphabetical ordering of words, unlike the ordering of numbers, follows no logical sequence. This means that, though in mathematical terms the method is not a chance procedure, in semantic terms it is.

One type of numerical operation therefore loses its structure in transit from formula to verse; another type – the sestina form, for example – retains it.

This fact is another way in which poetic creation comes to resemble biological growth, where symmetry at simple molecular level is lost in large molecules, recovered as cells divide, lost again as the cells diversify, then relocated in the creature's physical shape and – like some kind of signature – in its fell or plumage.

---

[1] (Gallimard, 1981,1988), p.25.
[2] *Thing of Beauty* (UCal Press, 2008), p. 49.

In every poem, in every period there is an apt grade of symmetry and discord. And just as untrammelled self-expression plunges into tedium, the pursuit of symmetry can be taken much too far. Once again Morton Feldman warns us not to let the structure do the listening for us.

We have considered a series of attempts to leave the beaten path, several of which seem to run into the sudden, enigmatic silence that took Rimbaud – and perhaps Shakespeare. Particularly dramatic, in recent times, are the instances of Laura Riding and Denis Roche who declare that poetry is finished, and not just for themselves. I can't believe it, though I much prefer poets who stop writing to poets who stop writing anything of interest.

This book has put forward a way of reading that draws on the practice of translation, which begins in a certain silence, an attempt to infer the rules that govern the utterance. Whether things are hidden to be discovered (the Dantean subtext to Blok's *Twelve*), or structural devices not intended for discovery (as in late Prynne), or deliberate obfuscation (Peter Pathelin's barrage of nonsense, wonderfully translated by Edwin Morgan), or on the contrary exhibit a puzzling excess of information such as the emotional pornography of sentimental writing, the pragmatic reader has to assume that something is being transmitted. Think of all the languages you will never know, and of what each speaker says about herself in the very act of speech, quite apart from any explicit, transferable information. If that reader can't in the end discern who is saying (if anything) what, can't get to grips with any message, then the silence remains inert, not complicit. But the angel is the message.

Index

Lightning Source UK Ltd.
Milton Keynes UK
UKOW06f0201261013

219851UK00007B/16/P